Following

Jesus

There is still much to do!

The vital work of evangelism today

dy Banton

DayOne

©Day One Publications 2017

First printed 2017

ISBN 978-1-84625-593-9

Unless otherwise indicated, Scripture quotations are from The Holy Bible, English Standard Version (ESV), copyright © 2001 by Crossway Bibles, a division of Good News Publishers. Used by permission. All rights reserved.

A CIP record is held at the British Library

Published by Day One Publications, Ryelands Road, Leominster, HR6 8NZ

☎ 01568 613 740

FAX 01568 611 473

email—sales@dayone.co.uk

web site—www.dayone.co.uk

Cover design by Kathryn Chedgzoy

Printed by TJ International

THE OPEN-AIR MISSION

4 HARRIER COURT

WOODSIDE ROAD

SLIP END

LUTON

LU1 4DQ

tel: 01582 841141

oamission@btinternet.com

www.oamission.com

'Christ Jesus came into the world to save sinners.' (1 Timothy 1:15)

Registered as a Charity - No. 215409

To all evangelists of the Open-Air Mission,
both past and present

In a lively and very readable way, Andy Banton challenges Christians and churches concerning the necessity of evangelism, both personal and collective. He writes from twenty years' experience working with the Open-Air Mission and his own zeal for making Christ known to those without God and without hope is clearly evident throughout the book. His plea for open-air preaching should be studied by all, especially those sceptical of such an approach in twenty-first-century Britain. The author writes from sound biblical principles and has himself been influenced by the best evangelistic preaching and mission work of past generations. I warmly commend the book to every Christian and particularly those in leadership positions in local churches.

Philip H. Eveson, former Principal of the London Seminary

In this book Andy Banton of Open-Air Mission shows the great need for us to get involved in regular evangelism in our locality. He shows that biblically this is not something that we might leave to others but it is an integral part of every Christian's life. He then moves into practical help in planning evangelism. Of great interest are the two chapters on 'Getting the Knowledge', which include subheadings like 'Know Your Testimony'. We all need to be ready to give an answer for the hope that is within us (1 Peter 3:15), and sharing our testimony is one of the best ways of doing this. There is a very helpful chapter on creation and how to answer evolutionary error which so dominates the average person's mind, being indoctrinated by the latest natural history programme on the television. There are chapters on using visual aids, and on the dangers of using performing arts as a supposed means of sharing the gospel. Andy stresses the importance of preaching as God's ordained way to reach the many unchurched today, and also emphasizes the need to walk in a holy and blameless way before an increasingly hostile world. There is a passion in this book as Andy not only relates the many experiences of open-air preachers, but also stresses that this is the way Christ Himself preached and lived. I warmly recommend this book.

Prof. Andy McIntosh, speaker and author, Leeds

If you have doubts that open-air ministry is relevant for today, you need to read this book! There is nothing more encouraging for those who seek to work for the Lord than seeing that it is the Lord Himself who is at work. Today we stand in need of constant encouragement that Jesus is still in the business of seeking and saving the lost. This book is rooted soundly in Scripture and is theologically solid and packed with thrilling examples of lives touched by those seeking to make their Saviour known. Andy has been at the 'coal face' for years and knows only too well the particular blessings attached to being engaged in open-air ministry, as well as its relevance to every generation. However, the content of this book is wider than simply open-air evangelism; it is a real spur to us all to enter the joy of making Christ known in the strength, grace and power He promised to all who obey his command to 'Go!'

Mike Mellor, former Open-Air Mission evangelist and former pastor of Hope Church, Ferndown, Dorset

God wants heaven full. None should be content to go alone, but we should all long to take others with us. There Is Still Much to Do! *by respected evangelist Andy Banton will help you do exactly that. It grips, educates and inspires on every page. If you need help reaching others with the good news, read this book.*

Jeremy Brooks, Pastor, Welcome Hall Evangelical Church, Bromsgrove

CONTENTS

Preface

'Not another book about evangelism! Is it really necessary?'
Maybe you are asking this question.

Many years ago, my wife, Ruth, and I were helping on
our church young people's summer camp, which was based
in North Wales. One very wet afternoon we all went for a
ride on the Ffestiniog Railway. As the train trundled along
and we were enjoying the delightful Welsh countryside, I
suddenly noticed a small sign that had been put up a few feet
from the railway line in the middle of nowhere. This is what
it said: 'There is still much to do!' Since then I have often
thought about those words, which we could perhaps apply
to many aspects of our lives. But to what more serious aspect
do they bear relevance than to the work of evangelism, of
communicating the gospel with others? Yes, indeed, there is
still much to do, still much for all of us to do. The well-known
missionary hymn puts it like this in the first verse:

Facing a task unfinished
That drives us to our knees,
A need that, undiminished,
Rebukes our slothful ease,
We who rejoice to know You,
Renew before Your throne
The solemn pledge we owe You,
To go and make You known.
(Frank Houghton)

I hope and pray that this book will go at least some small
way to encourage you to see just how much there is still to do,
and also that you will be persuaded to be involved in the actual

doing as well. Maybe this book will help to stir some up to be involved in evangelism for the first time—how wonderful that would be! My hope is that we will all be encouraged to see sharing the gospel with others as a priority, both for our churches and for ourselves as individual Christians.

One comment before we get started. You may be wondering if this is going to be an academic type of book. That can easily be answered by my telling you that I have at least one thing in common with Winnie-the-Pooh, and it is not a love of honey: I am a bear of very little brain. All that is contained in this book is from twenty years of experience in all sorts of evangelist endeavours while working with the Open-Air Mission. Part of that experience has involved mistakes that I have made, but also hopefully learned from. A large part of that experience has been the privilege of working alongside very godly men, who have consistently displayed great zeal and wisdom in seeking to reach the lost for our dear Saviour and Lord.

1 Setting the scene

[Jesus] said to them, 'Follow me, and I will
make you fishers of men.' (Matt. 4:19)

By way of introduction, allow me to share with you something that was sent to me a number of years ago by a friend who has a great heart for evangelism. It is an anonymous modern-day parable called 'The Fishless Fishermen's Fellowship'. When I first read it I smiled, for two reasons: one, because it is funny, and two, because it is true—perhaps too true in places—about where we are in our attitudes towards the work of evangelism. See what you think.

The fishermen were surrounded by streams and lakes full of hungry fish. They met regularly to discuss the call to fish, the abundance of fish and the thrill of catching fish. They got excited about fishing!

Someone suggested that they needed a philosophy of fishing, so they carefully defined and redefined fishing, and the purpose of fishing. They developed fishing strategies and tactics. Then they realized that they had been going at it backwards. They had approached fishing from the point of view of the fisherman, and not from the point of view of the fish. How do fish view the world? How does the fisherman appear to the fish? What do fish eat, and when? These are all good things to know. So they began research studies and attended conferences on fishing. Some travelled to faraway

THERE IS STILL MUCH TO DO!

*places to study different kinds of fish with different habits.
Some got doctorates in fishology. But no one had yet gone
fishing. So a committee was formed to send out fishermen.
As prospective fishing places outnumbered fishermen, the
committee needed to determine priorities. A priority list
of fishing places was posted on bulletin boards in all of the
Fellowship halls. But still, no one was fishing. A survey was
launched to find out why. Most did not answer the survey,
but from those who did, it was discovered that some felt
called to study fish, a few to furnish fishing equipment and
several to go around encouraging the fishermen. What with
meetings, conferences and seminars, they just simply didn't
have time to fish.*

*Now, Jake was a newcomer to the Fishermen's Fellowship.
After one stirring meeting of the Fellowship, he went fishing
and caught a large fish. At the next meeting, he told his story
and was honoured for his catch. He was told that he had a
special 'gift of fishing'. He was then scheduled to speak at all
the Fellowship chapters and tell how he did it. With all the
speaking invitations and his election to the board of directors
of the Fisherman's Fellowship, Jake no longer had time to
go fishing. But soon he began to feel restless and empty. He
longed to feel the tug on the line once again. So he cancelled
the speaking, he resigned from the board and he said to a
friend, 'Let's go fishing.' They did, just the two of them, and
they caught fish.*

*The members of the Fishermen's Fellowship were many,
the fish were plentiful, but the fishers were few! (Anonymous)*

The person who came up with that parable certainly knew

THERE IS STILL MUCH TO DO!

what Christians can be like at times. Perhaps there are a number of things in the parable for us and our churches to chew over. It certainly isn't very commendable for us to be all talk and little or no action. Someone once said, 'When all's said and done, there is usually a lot more said than done.' May that not be true of us or of the churches to which we belong! In fact, may the opposite be true. There is often a good deal of talk about evangelism in our churches, and that can be a positive thing; but sometimes the talk needs to stop and the work needs to begin. I remember hearing a pastor once say that evangelism was at the top of the agenda at every church meeting in his fellowship. I wonder where on the agenda it is in your church?

The Lord seemed to have three favourite occupations that He frequently included in his teaching to help describe and illustrate the work of evangelism. They were fishing, farming and shepherding. In Matthew 4:18–22 we read about the great episode in the lives of Peter, Andrew, James and John when they were called to stop being fishers of fish and instead begin being fishers of men. The Lord called them to follow Him, and also to learn how to go and catch, or 'go after', people, for the purpose of establishing His heavenly kingdom. We may have no trouble in our minds with the concept of following Jesus, but whether we have been a disciple of Jesus for many years or for just a short while, we have to appreciate that part of that following, part of that discipleship, involves fishing. The Lord never divorced the following from the fishing, and neither should we.

Five key things in this passage in Matthew 4 introduce us to the work of evangelism.

THERE IS STILL MUCH TO DO!

1. THE GREAT FISHER-OF-MEN HIMSELF

The history of the church is littered with the ministry of 'evangelists'. What a mixture they have been down through the centuries! Quite literally, they have been made up of 'the good, the bad and the ugly'. Christians might disagree over which category particular evangelists fall into, but surely no one would dispute that the one great evangelist, the fisher-of-men *par excellence*, the one who eclipsed every other, was the Lord Jesus Christ. That being the case, He is the right place to start when we want to think about evangelism.

The Lord's very reason for coming here to Planet Earth was to bring glory to His Father in fulfilling the great mission, which was something He had volunteered to carry out. Never think of the Lord Jesus as some kind of reluctant hero who somehow felt compelled to enter the fray. Not at all! He came on the world's greatest rescue mission out of love for His Father and love for His people, and that love began way back in eternity past, long before the creation of the world. The mission He came on was aptly summed up by Jesus after He had brought about the conversion of a swindling tax collector named Zacchaeus: 'For the Son of Man came to seek and to save the lost' (Luke 19:10). What a gracious Saviour He is: that He, the very Lord of glory, the darling of heaven, was so willing to stoop so low for the likes of you and me!

During the first weekend of December there is a huge Christmas market in the city of Lincoln. The Open-Air Mission has held a witness there for quite a few years. It can be quite cold, as you would expect, but there are always many profitable conversations, and over the years there have been some who have trusted the Lord as their Saviour. One very encouraging encounter was with a young woman called Nicola. Having listened for ages to the gospel preaching, she started to walk away. One of the team went after her and asked Nicola what she thought of the message. She was very apologetic, saying that she didn't think the message could be for her. Upon being asked why not, Nicola answered, 'Because I'm such a sinner, it can't be for me.' She was then asked if she knew why Jesus came. She replied, 'No.' Her face lit up when she was told, 'Jesus said this: "I came not to call the righteous, but sinners to repentance." So you qualify.' Nicola listened with great interest as the gospel was shared again, and as she went away with helpful literature she said she would read it as soon as she got home and consider carefully what she needed to do.

When members of the Royal Family are invited to visit places in the UK, it is usually to open something, whether it be a new school, theatre or hospital. When the eternal Son of the living God entered our world, it was also to open something. It was to open something of the greatest magnitude, something that no man or woman could open; something that was closed off in the Garden of Eden and which had remained so ever since. It was the way of salvation for sinners.

Everything in the entire life of Jesus was focused on, and devoted to, achieving that end. The enemy of souls tried early on to divert the Lord away from His task, but he was forced to go away, with his evil ambition unrealized, because the Lord Jesus stood firm. And three years later, after much opposition from men and demons, the Lord Jesus would be able to testify, 'I have glorified you on earth, having accomplished the work that you gave me to do' (John 17:4).

THERE IS STILL MUCH TO DO!

2. THE GREAT FISHER-OF-MEN HAD PEOPLE TO SAVE

Upon calling the fishermen, Jesus immediately wanted them to understand something of this important truth. It reminds us that evangelism is actually based on the initiative of God: 'For *God* so loved the world, that *he* gave ...' (John 3:16); 'you shall call his name Jesus, for *he* will save his people from their sins' (Matt. 1:21); 'God shows *his* love for us in that while we were still sinners, *Christ* died for us' (Rom. 5:8, emphasis added).

That saving work would be completed upon the cross, but on the way there, Jesus would busy Himself in fishing for men and women. The pages of the Gospels are full of the Lord's encounters with groups and individuals who were drawn into the gospel net and rescued from their sins. There were all sorts of people: the immoral, like the woman at the well and the woman caught in adultery; the afflicted, like the man born blind, the man with the withered hand, the leper and the paralysed man; the tormented, like the Gadarene demoniac, Mary Magdalene and the epileptic boy; the greedy, like Zacchaeus and the rich young ruler; the criminal, like the dying thief, actually a dying murderer (Mark 15:7); the religious, like Jairus and Nicodemus; the beggar, like Bartimaeus; the wealthy, like Joseph of Arimathea; the broken-hearted, like the widow of Nain; the happy family, like Mary, Martha and Lazarus; and even the foreigner, like the centurion and the Syro-Phoenician woman. Yes, even the non-Jew was to be the recipient of divine grace and mercy! What a revelation that was to all!

One of the exciting aspects of open-air evangelism is that you never know what type of person you may meet next. One of the problems we have in the UK today is that our churches are, in the main, very middle class. On the streets of our towns and cities we can meet people of every class. Several years ago, a multi-millionaire, on holiday from Germany, was spoken to in Covent Garden. One of the young people who was on an outreach team there that day approached him after he had listened to the preaching for a few minutes. The multi-millionaire's name was Michael and he openly described how rich he was, even boasting that he had been given a jar containing moon dust by no less a person than Neil Armstrong. The young team member was completely unfazed by this and asked him, 'Yes, but do you know the one who put the moon dust on the moon?' This took the wind out of Michael's sails, and he listened as the gospel was explained to him.

At the other end of the spectrum are those who, humanly speaking, have next to nothing. Many thousands of people, even in 2017, still live on the streets of our cities. I remember speaking to a homeless man in the centre of Leicester. As I shared the gospel with him I became aware that the man was standing in a pool of water. I didn't comment on it, but I realized that it wasn't water at all. He had urinated as we were standing there talking. He was a tragic figure who had lost a good job, his home, his wife and his children. Life on the streets had left him incontinent and with a very hard shell. However, he heard something of the gospel message that day, and who knows what the Lord may have done in his life.

It is wonderful to notice that the Lord offered salvation to all sorts of needy sinners, and he did so even before He had put His team together: 'From that time Jesus began to preach, saying, "Repent, for the kingdom of heaven is at hand"' (Matt. 4:17). This was before He called the disciples. The Lord knew that all the people around Him were sitting in darkness, but, as He began to reveal Himself and to preach the gospel, the life-transforming light began to shine.

3. THE GREAT FISHER-OF-MEN CALLED OTHERS TO JOIN HIM IN HIS WORK

The Lord began to call to Himself those who would eventually be known as 'men who have turned the world upside down' (Acts 17:6). There they were, ordinary men, going about their business of fishing for fish, with nothing special about them at all, but then they received what would be a life-changing invitation.

Sadly, in many churches it seems that there is little or no appetite for evangelism. If that is the case in your church, you must pray for change, work for change and, if you're brave enough, ask for change. Sometimes we can be challenged even by the unbeliever where this lack of appetite is concerned. Take a day back in June 2007 at Epsom Races, where the Open-Air Mission has had a witness since 1854. On the Saturday of this world-famous event there is the horserace called The Derby. The Queen is always in attendance, along with around 120,000 others. We were heading back to our stall in the market area on Epsom Downs having preached in another part of the racecourse. Standing in the hot sunshine in the thoroughfare of the market was one of the traders. He began calling to people to turn into his stall and look at the great offers available. His calling soon turned to pleading, as he urged passers-by to check out his wares. The man showed such energy, such passion, and sweat was pouring off him, and yet all he was selling was ... shoes. Shoes! A commodity that would last people only six months, a year at the very most! I felt greatly challenged by the zeal of that man. I had just been seeking to preach the everlasting gospel, but had I shown the same measure of zeal as that man? Was I as concerned to see people give attention to the old, old story of Jesus and His love as that market trader was for his shoes?

A member of a respectable church congregation was once asked, 'How are things in your church?' The reply came back instantly, 'We are all united—frozen together!' It's one thing to be united—in fact, it's a very biblical thing—but we are not to be frozen as members of our churches. Rather than being cold in our hearts towards others, we are to be on fire— for the Lord Jesus Christ and His work in the world.

Not every believer can be a paid, full-time fisher of souls, but we are all called to be on the lookout for opportunities to throw out the gospel net and seek to win the lost. A famous American evangelist from the nineteenth century, D. L. Moody (1837–1899), had an apt turn of phrase: 'The gospel says to the sinner "come"; it says to the Christian "go".' We have received the blessing of salvation for ourselves; now we must go and offer it to others. We surely don't want to be 'armchair' evangelists—happy to watch others, happy to support others, but not to do any evangelism ourselves?

4. THE GREAT FISHER-OF-MEN WOULD TRAIN THEM TO GO AND DO THAT WORK

The twelve disciples would spend the next three years learning to minister like Jesus, and that is the supreme challenge for us

THERE IS STILL MUCH TO DO!

all: to *be* like Christ and to *do* like Christ! Notice that the Lord did not take these men away to a secluded venue for those three years. Their times in a secluded place were very limited indeed. They would learn to be fishers of men by watching and imitating, by going and doing.

So how are we to learn to catch men and women for the Saviour? Let us begin with three very simple things:

(a) We must rely on Him

Jesus promised, '*I* will make you fishers of men.' The disciples would not achieve it by themselves, and neither will we. Without Him, nothing can be achieved of any lasting value. Jesus said in the upper room, 'Apart from me you can do nothing' (John 15:5). How completely and utterly dependent we need to be on Him in the work of catching men and women.

If we ever go out of the door to serve the Lord in our own strength, we might as well step back in again. One of the things about outreach like door-to-door work and street evangelism is that it shows up how foolish it is to go in your own strength. We don't know who we will meet or what may take place, so we are thrown upon the Lord, both before and during the outreach, for His help, His wisdom and His strength.

We will come back to this later, but I sometimes tell Bible-college students that there is a world of difference between preaching in a church and preaching in a pedestrianized shopping precinct. A church service is fairly predictable (not that there is anything wrong with that). I have only ever been heckled twice in thirty years of indoor preaching. On the streets, heckling can happen at any time. Not only that, but missiles can come towards you at any time, comments can come at any time, and indifference will certainly fly at you a lot of the time. The point is, we won't deal well with these things on our own. We always need the Lord's help.

In the tremendous book *Pilgrim's Progress* there is a character called Evangelist. Listen to how John Bunyan describes him: 'A man who had his eyes up to heaven, the best of books was in his hand, the law of truth was written upon his lips and he stood as if he pleaded with men.' Oh, to be more like that; to look to heaven first and foremost—in other words, to be looking to the Lord, and relying on the Lord, to bless us and to use us in all we do!

(b) We must copy Him

The Lord's zeal for His Father's honour and His love for the lost were evident. The disciples struggled to keep up with Him because of it. In the night Jesus was often up praying; during the day He was either out preaching or in conversation with individuals, showing them their sin, answering their questions, inviting them to trust in Him for salvation, not to mention performing amazing miracles. And the disciples saw in the Lord the 'how' of evangelism not only in terms of what He did, but also in terms of the attitudes He showed.

Some Christians are put off open-air preaching because they have seen it done badly. Maybe the preacher they saw was harsh, cold and condemning. The Lord Jesus reserved his strongest words for hardened religious hypocrites. However, with everyone else He emanated the love of God. Yes, He spoke with authority, He was firm with people at times, but the Lord never, ever broke the bruised reed or quenched the smoking flax. You see, it is not enough to do the right thing in terms of evangelism; it is also about doing the right thing in the right way. People are condemned already by their unbelief; it is not our job to heap further condemnation on them. George Whitefield (1714–1770), one of the greatest evangelists of the eighteenth century in both Britain and North America, when he prayed for himself said, 'God, give me a deep humility, a well-guided zeal, a burning love and a single eye.' Do we ask for such things when we are praying for ourselves?

(c) We must study others
Understanding 'where people are at' will help us to be able to reach them with the gospel—where they are at in their priorities, their ambitions, their worries, their fears, their hopes and their dreams.

For that reason it is good to have spent time in the workplace. It is good to have or have had a secular job. In the early 1990s I worked as a postman in Loughborough for six years and I learnt much during that time. Working in a sorting office where the air was often blue wasn't easy, but it was a good education.

Someone once said, 'When you take your rifle, aim low.' Why? Because you are more likely to hit the target! So, for example, we need to use simple, uncomplicated, everyday language when we are witnessing to people—unless, perhaps, you are speaking to a university professor! In the workplace you get to know what people think and believe, including the wrong things they think and believe. Then you are able to scratch where they itch.

THERE IS STILL MUCH TO DO!

In the service of the Lord Jesus the disciples would encounter all sorts of people. This is one of many reasons why I believe open-air evangelism is so valuable: it gets us out among people. It gets us talking to them, hearing them ask their questions, raise their objections and share their views. It helps us to keep our ears to the ground. There's a danger for pastors, in particular, of losing touch with unconverted people if they spend all their days in the study. One preacher said, 'Most of my best friends are dead'—referring to the authors whose books adorned his study bookshelves. We need to spend time with the living. We must study people so we understand where they are spiritually.

5. THE GREAT FISHER-OF-MEN PROMISED A CATCH

The Lord did not leave Peter, Andrew, James and John in any doubt about their catch, and so we needn't be left in any doubt either. Jesus said, 'I *will* make you fishers of men' (Matt. 4:19, emphasis added). There is real certainty and assurance in these words, in this promise. Of course there is: this is none other than the Head of the church talking! This is the King of kings and Lord of lords.

We know that at times, when we have made our plans and perhaps confidently shared with others all that we are going to do, unforeseen events have ended up scuppering those plans so that they didn't come to fruition at all. Praise God, that cannot happen where the Lord Jesus is concerned! He knows the end from the beginning, and the end is that He has a people to save and a church to build. Jesus has promised that even the devil and all his hordes will not prevent Him bringing His people to Himself.

THERE IS STILL MUCH TO DO!

This is vividly illustrated in the conversion of a man called Alan. Alan was from Edinburgh. He couldn't find any work locally so he moved down to London for a few months. While he was there he decided to visit Covent Garden. Walking through James Street he came across someone preaching next to a display board. Alan listened for a while, and when the speaker offered a free John's Gospel at the end of his message, Alan went forward and accepted one. Over the next few weeks he began to read it. Alan wasn't able to find work in London so he returned to Edinburgh at the time of the Edinburgh Festival. One Thursday afternoon he was about to enter his local pub when he suddenly heard the sound of bagpipes. Liking them very much (there's no accounting for taste!), he turned on his heels and went to listen to the piper. As he did so, Alan noticed there was a preacher nearby like the one he had seen in London. Alan moved away from the piper and stood close to the preacher so he could hear what he was saying.

The Lord spoke powerfully to Alan through the preaching. An evangelist on the team was able to have a long conversation with him afterwards. Alan was under conviction of sin and said that he wanted to get right with God there and then. The evangelist took Alan to a quiet church nearby and went through the gospel message with him once more. When the evangelist had prayed for him, Alan bowed his head and sat in silence for quite some time. He then asked the Lord Jesus to be his Saviour.

Alan was saved that day and subsequently found a job as a postman and also joined a good local church where he was baptized. But note this detail: one of the festival stewards was

THERE IS STILL MUCH TO DO!

very much against the preaching taking place and so, that afternoon, had instructed a piper to stand as near as possible to the outreach team and play her bagpipes. In the Lord's providence, the very thing that was meant to disrupt the outreach was the thing that drew Alan to come near. At times the devil oversteps the mark and the Lord has His sovereign way in people's lives. And one more thing: after the piper had finished, she gladly accepted a copy of John's Gospel.

The Lord was saying in Matthew 4:19 what was definitely going to happen, and therefore it would happen, without a shadow of a doubt. Hopefully we can see that that promise is for us, too. The Lord hasn't done with saving people yet. There are more fish to be brought into the net, as well as more crops to be harvested and more sheep to be found. Which is exactly why there is plenty more evangelism to be done. We just need to make sure that the message we share and the methods we use are ones that are clearly based upon God's precious Word.

THERE IS STILL MUCH TO DO!

2 Embracing the message

*Jesus came into Galilee, proclaiming the
gospel of God. (Mark 1:14)*

Sometimes the subject of evangelism throws up lots
of questions, particularly because so many books
have been written about it. We need to ensure that
we find biblical answers to those questions. That is
of vital importance if we are going to keep on the right track
in serving the Lord. After all, we claim to be Bible-believing
Christians. That's what evangelicals are: we believe the Bible,
we believe that the Bible is the Word of God, from Genesis 1:1
all the way through to Revelation 22:21.

It is in the Bible that we find what is known as 'the gospel'.
The English word 'gospel' comes from the Anglo-Saxon
'god-spell', which means 'good story'. The noun in New
Testament Greek is *euangelion*, which means 'good news'
or 'good message'. The famous English Reformer and Bible
translator William Tyndale (1494–1536) said in his prologue
to the New Testament that *euangelion* signified 'good, merry,
glad, joyful tidings that make a man's heart glad, and make
him sing, dance and leap for joy'. Does the gospel have
anything like that effect upon us? As evangelicals, we're often
a little afraid of any displays of emotion; but if this really
is the good news it claims to be, and if we have been saved
through hearing it, then can there be anything wrong with

jumping for joy—at the very least, in our hearts—when we hear or read about it?

The New Testament Greek verb which is related to the noun is *euangelizo* and it has the sense of communicating that good news. It means to bring or to announce glad tidings, to declare or proclaim that good news to others. Yes, we believe this good news ourselves, but we should want others to believe it as well. If they are going to believe it, they need to hear it. So evangelism is all about sharing or communicating that good news with other people.

The text that heads up this chapter informs us that this gospel is the gospel *of God*. It originated with Him and it is about Him. Of course, it is our gospel as well, in the sense that we are saved through it. However, it certainly isn't ours in the sense that we should think we can tinker or tamper with it. It is important that we really know the gospel so we are able to share it correctly with those around us. In very forthright language in his letter to the church of the Galatians, Paul warns about other gospels that were being peddled, false gospels that were leading people away from God, away from His truth.

So to think about the true biblical gospel a little more will do us no harm. That gospel is the news of how sinful people (that's our problem—we are completely rotten to the core) can be reconciled to a holy God (that's His character—He is completely pure and holy). It is about what He has done to bring lost and fallen creatures like us to know our divine Creator.

The gospel is the glorious and gracious way which has been provided by that Creator through His only begotten

Son, the Lord Jesus Christ! It was provided through the unique, wonderful, perfect life that Jesus lived, keeping the law on our behalf in every jot and tittle; and then through the horrendous suffering and death that He endured on our behalf on the cross of Calvary!

Not only that, but we believe in the bodily resurrection of that same Lord Jesus, who conquered death and then made Himself known to His disciples—proving beyond doubt that the message they were to communicate to others was about Him: who He is, why He came and what He accomplished. Someone put it like this: 'The evangelistic message seeks to tell the story that God has already acted out.' If we are true Christians, that is the message that has saved us: the message of Jesus Christ and Him crucified. But here's the thing: does that message grip us? Have we embraced it as something that not only fills our hearts with thankfulness every day, but also compels us to take that same message to others? If it does not have that twofold effect upon us, we need seriously and humbly to examine our hearts before the Lord.

But even if that message is believed and there is a genuine desire to make it known to the world, the church in many quarters seems to have done something quite incredible, even strange. It has decided that, in order to best reach the world, it should use the ways of the world. In other words, the view is held that we can afford to go about the work of evangelism with our Bibles largely closed. Here is the root of the problem which exists in many churches today: they have decided to look elsewhere than the Bible for the best way of doing many things in the life of the church, including evangelism. As a result, the wisdom of the age has tended to replace Holy

Scripture. That should frighten us. Why? Because it sets us on very dangerous ground! If we ever planned to go ice skating on a lake in winter, it would be sensible to ensure that the ice was nice and thick; that will keep us safe from going through and going under. Thin ice will lead to disaster! Doing evangelism on a paper-thin foundation likewise risks disaster.

So where have many churches looked to find their models for evangelism? They seem to have turned to businessmen, of all people. After all, it is argued, businessmen know how to handle people; they know how to give people what they want for the right return. They have the expertise to 'get the job done'. But we need to ask, 'What is the job that needs to be done?' Is evangelism all about filling our churches? Is our game the numbers game? Is it the notion that we must 'get them in' at all costs, and as long as we can keep them in, that will be the measure of our success? In his little book *Hollywood Evangelism*, James A. Stewart (1910–1975), one-time evangelist with OAM and later founder of European Mission Fellowship, quoted Herbert Lockyer, who said, 'We cannot journey far with God unless we are saved from numbers. It is sadly possible to think more of numbers than Christ, who in the days of His earthly ministry went not only to the cities, but to inconspicuous places, proclaiming the Word.'[1] Stewart, by the way, was hugely successful himself as an evangelist all over Eastern Europe during the 1930s. He saw large crowds attend the meetings where he preached, and many, many conversions.

But when numbers are our main focus, we are actually placing ourselves in particular danger: the danger of being willing to change whatever may be necessary in order to bring more people into the church and to keep people in the church! I don't want to be negative in this book, but there are times when it is unavoidable. This is one of those times. In Illinois in the USA there is an organization called the Willow Creek Association. Their message has become popular in the UK as well as in the USA. Sadly, their main emphasis is to make the sinner feel comfortable. Their rationale is that that way, people will come to church, will stay and will decide to follow Jesus, so it is important to make them feel as comfortable as possible. To achieve this, it may be necessary to tone down preaching on subjects like sin, repentance, judgement and hell. Jesus is to be offered as providing fulfilment as much as forgiveness.

There could well be legitimate changes that are necessary for us to consider making in order to make our church services more attractive. For example, hard old wooden pews could be replaced by chairs that are far more comfortable. We could have a welcome team on the doors for people as they arrive. We could offer refreshments after our services, thereby providing a good and friendly opportunity to get to know visitors. There may be a number of other things as well. However, what we must never consider doing is changing the message that the Bible says people need to hear. We need to take on board the Lord's instructions to Jeremiah: 'Stand in the court of the LORD's house, and speak to all the cities of Judah that come to worship in the house of the LORD all the words that I command you to speak to them; do not hold back a word' (Jer. 26:2). If we water down the message, we must be prepared to risk the Lord's displeasure, not to mention

THERE IS STILL MUCH TO DO!

the risk of producing watered-down conversions. That is no doubt why D. L. Moody wisely declared, 'Conversions should be weighed as well as counted.'

The first bishop of Liverpool, J. C. Ryle (1816–1900), wrote the following words in his excellent book *Christian Leaders of the Eighteenth Century* of mighty men of God like John Berridge, William Grimshaw, John Wesley and George Whitefield, who saw enormous blessing under their gospel ministries:

They did His work in the old apostolic way, by becoming the evangelists of their day. They taught one set of truths. They taught them in the same way, with fire, reality, earnestness, as men fully convinced of what they taught. They taught in the same spirit, always loving, compassionate, and like Paul, even weeping, but always bold, unflinching and not fearing the face of man.[2]

What an example and challenge those men should be to us, all these years later!

Yes, the gospel most certainly is good news, but for it to appear good to the unbeliever, it must be preceded by the bad news of what is really wrong with us. The unconverted people who may come to our services, or perhaps to a lunch or supper, do not just have a minor injury on the skin that a little cream will heal away. No, they have a fatal disease. They have a spiritual cancer growing inside. They must therefore be cut open, have the tumour removed and must then be sewn up again. An American preacher called Samuel Davies (1723–1761), who saw great revival blessing in his ministry, spoke about preaching the needle of the law before applying the thread of the gospel. Sinners need to know that

that is exactly what they are: that they are those who have rebelled against their Maker, those who have not only gone their own way, but are determined to continue going their own way. They need to be made to realize that their lives offend God every single day and that, unless they turn right around by admitting their sin and trusting in Jesus, they risk being lost from God and His blessing for ever and ever.

When people hear that, they may at first be offended, and we should not be surprised if that is the response. After all, few people are going to be pleased to be told that their whole philosophy of life is a sham and will lead to disaster—but it is through that painful truth that the Spirit of God deals with sinners. Take eighteen-year-old Ingram, for example. He stood in Bournemouth town centre listening to a local evangelist, who was warmly commending his Saviour. Ingram remained there, not because he was interested in the message, but because he was going to 'set this preacher straight'. How differently it turned out! As soon as the preaching finished, Ingram began laying into the evangelist. Without responding to any of his comments, the evangelist asked Ingram, 'If you died today and met with God, what would you tell Him, and why should He let you into heaven?'

Ingram quickly responded, 'I'm a good person and more religious than many other people. I think I'd be let into heaven.'

'No,' the evangelist replied, 'you would go straight to hell.'

When Ingram was relaying this conversation in an email to the OAM office, here is how he described what happened next:

THERE IS STILL MUCH TO DO!

I nearly choked. I was so offended and became quite aggressive.
I felt hot and angry, and I could have punched him. He thrust
some literature into my hands and made a speedy getaway. I was
flummoxed and in absolute inner turmoil. I made my way back to
my car and started driving home. I didn't get very far. I couldn't
concentrate, so I pulled over. I just sat there trying to come to
terms with the warfare that had just broken out in my head. I'm a
rational person and I don't normally get that angry with people just
for saying something like 'I'm going to hell', but on this occasion
it really got my goat. I started reading some of the literature,
which emphasized the fact that my sin was separating me from
the love of God. Sitting there at the side of a road I came to
repentance and prayed to God from my heart. In an instant things
were transformed; a burden was lifted from me and I was free.

What an encouragement that Ingram made the effort to
share his testimony! It shows that an angry response can be
the Lord beginning to work in a person's soul. So, on that
basis, we shouldn't be discouraged if that is the response we
find in people at times. The bad news about sin leads to the
good news of redeeming love and forgiveness.

There can be a huge lack of understanding about the work of
God and about human nature. It goes back much further than
Willow Creek. The father of modern evangelistic methods
was an American named Charles G. Finney (1792–1875). He
was a very famous and hugely influential evangelist. Helpful
analysis of this man can be found in two books: *Pentecost—
Today?* by Iain Murray, and Appendix 3, 'Charles Finney
and American Evangelical Pragmatism', in *Ashamed of the
Gospel* by John MacArthur. Both of these reveal very clearly
that Finney's theology was faulty and, tragically, that led
to his evangelistic methodology being faulty. Basically, his

watchword was 'the end justifies the means'. Finney was a man who genuinely loved the Lord and loved the lost, but if only he had realized that it is God's Word, the Bible, that should be our manual for both the means and the end.

If we convince ourselves that the end does justify the means, we may even go as far as actually watering down the message to get the results we want. But if the undiluted gospel really is 'the power of God for salvation to everyone who believes' (Rom. 1:16), then that is the message men and women, boys and girls need to hear, and our confidence should be in making that known. We should definitely not be resorting to a toned-down version instead. Someone wisely said, 'You can't put the elect off.' In other words, if God has set His hand upon people, those people will definitely come to know the Lord, even if they have to listen to what they might consider to be hard truth. Jesus Himself said, 'All that the Father gives me will come to me, and whoever comes to me I will never cast out' (John 6:37). The Lord's chosen mechanism for bringing about that coming is the proclamation of the gospel message, and nothing less than that.

This doesn't mean, by the way, that we can preach in a hard, cold, aggressive way, as we declare to people their lost condition. Shame on us if we think that is acceptable! We must preach and speak as the Puritan Richard Baxter (1615–1691) famously sought to do: 'As a dying man to dying men, as never sure to preach again!' That means preaching with a love and a compassion for our hearers, for the friend we may be talking to, or the contact we may meet on the street or on the doors.

What is happening so frequently today is that love is being

THERE IS STILL MUCH TO DO!

preached at the expense of sin. In Reading a few years ago an elderly gentleman named Leonard stood listening with interest to the gospel being preached by an outreach team. Afterwards, the preacher, Keith Bullock, who is now with the Lord, asked Leonard if he was a Christian. Leonard instantly pulled four shopping lists out of his coat pocket and rather proudly stated, 'I'm doing the shopping for four ladies, so I don't need to say any more, do I?' It was very plain that Leonard believed that his good works made him right with God.

After hearing that that was the very opposite of what the Bible teaches, Leonard said that he had recently been listening to an American preacher on the radio. Leonard asked Keith to guess which word the preacher had mentioned at least fifty times. To Leonard's amazement Keith answered, 'Was it love?'

'Yes! How did you know?' Leonard responded.

Keith explained, 'Because love is a very important part of the Christian message.' Then he went on to say, 'There's another word that I could have guessed alongside love.'

'Which word is that?' Leonard asked.

'It's the word "sin",' Keith replied.

To which Leonard quickly came back, 'Oh no, the preacher didn't mention sin at all.'

Leonard then listened as Keith gently shared with him that we are all sinners, and if our sin is not dealt with we can never be true Christians. Leonard seemed to be quite sobered on hearing this and asked to be shown in the Bible where it says that we are sinners. Keith took him to the classic verse Romans 3:23 and continued sharing the way of salvation

THERE IS STILL MUCH TO DO!

with him. At the end of the conversation Leonard was very pleased to accept a copy of John's Gospel and promised that he would read it.

So yes, love is a hugely important part of the gospel, but so is helping people to realize that they are sinners who need that love which was so fully exhibited upon the cross. An evangelist in Northern Ireland used frequently to put the following acronym in large letters on his open-air board for passers-by to read: G—God, O—Offers, S—Sinful, P—People, E—Eternal, L—Life. That gracious offer has love and mercy at its source, but it will only be received by those who see themselves as God sees them: as sinners needing a Saviour.

We need not only to make sure that we mention sin in our gospel presentations, but also to explain exactly what it is and therefore just how serious it is. In my early days in the Open-Air Mission (the late 1990s), I would preach in the centre of Derby every Tuesday afternoon. I was usually blessed to have some local Christians there to support the witness. One Tuesday in June, while I was preaching the gospel, a young woman named Clare stood listening intently. As soon as I'd finished she marched up to me and, without any greeting, demanded to know, 'What is sin, then?' So began what turned out to be a very positive conversation. Clare had been along to a local church a few times, but hadn't really heard anything about sin. I gently explained that it was us choosing our own way instead of God's way. I also shared that it was something rooted deep in our hearts and that we needed God's forgiving power and grace to take it away, and that could only happen on the basis of Jesus' substitutionary death upon the cross.

THERE IS STILL MUCH TO DO!

Clare seemed to be weighing things up as she parted with the John's Gospel she had accepted.

It wasn't until September that Clare turned up again, asking lots of other questions. She shared something that at the time I felt was extremely encouraging: 'Some of my friends, who also go to this church, have been going to the front at some of the meetings to supposedly become Christians, but I stay put, because I want it to be real.' Clare saw through the danger of the invitation system, which we'll cover in more detail in a later chapter. I encouraged her to seek the Lord with all her heart—something she seemed very keen to do.

I didn't see Clare in Derby again, but let me take you to the pretty seaside town of Tenby on the Pembrokeshire coast eleven months later. We were in the middle of our afternoon children's meeting on the sands during our two weeks of beach mission there. As I was trying to retrieve something from my sports bag at the edge of the meeting site, someone suddenly called my name. I looked up and, lo and behold, it was Clare, walking along the beach with a couple of friends. I dashed over to see her, and it was such a joy to hear her say that about six months earlier she had come to know the Lord as her Saviour and that she was now involved in helping with the youth work in her church.

If in our gospel communication we dumb down the gospel, softening it to suit the sinner, we make a fatal mistake. Not only has God's book, the Bible, been sidelined, but in effect God Himself has been sidelined too! Surely that is a terrible thought! But, sadly, it is going on every day as Christians and evangelists witness to others! And it's not as if we can salve our consciences by saying that the Lord hasn't given us any clear direction in these things. He has actually given very clear instructions and guidelines about how we are to go about the work of gospel communication—as well, of course, as giving the very clear message that we are to preach to the world.

We could say that the modern evangelist is a bit like a man who wanted to take up, say, fishing (yes, we're back to that again!). To get help, he decided to visit a local bookshop. Eventually, he found the section on 'fishing'. He immediately saw a fishing book by the most brilliant and most successful fisherman of all time! As our would-be fisherman read the blurb on the back cover, he discovered that for many years the writer had been the world fishing champion. His book had become a kind of manual for fishing—one that was universally accepted as the final authority on fishing! It sold far more than any other book on fishing, ever! The man was impressed. But then he noticed that there were other books by some younger fishermen on the shelf. They had produced very glossy books and they seemed to offer more trendy and more modern approaches to fishing. They boasted great and immediate success that anyone reading their books, and following their principles, could have.

The would-be fisherman chose to buy all of their books, but he didn't bother with the first book he had looked at. Now wouldn't that be pretty foolish? Sadly, however, many genuine Christians, who sincerely want to serve the Lord, have made that same mistake. The best book to read, study and know as well as you can is the book written by the One who knows everything there is to know on this subject— whether fishing for fish or fishing for men! Back in 1873 a gospel song was written that has become very famous, even sung by the likes of Johnny Cash. The song begins like this: 'Gimme that old-time religion, it's good enough for me.' We must make sure that the old-time religion of God's Word is good enough for us.

If you were to ask me to recommend five books on evangelism, rather than just one, that stand head and shoulders above any other, I wonder how you would expect me to answer? The books I would recommend are called Matthew, Mark, Luke, John and Acts. Do you really want to learn about evangelism? Do you really want to know how to do evangelism in the best way, with the best results? Then read and study these books till the day you die. Please do not think I am saying that these five are more important than the other sixty-one in the canon of Scripture: not at all. But when it comes to this subject of evangelism, these have the most to teach us. Of course they do: the four Gospels show us the Master at work, and the book of Acts shows us the Holy Spirit at work through those whom the Master left behind—the apostles and the church. It's very much worth noting, by the way, that the recorded sermons of the apostles lay their emphasis on the need for repentance and the risk of judgement, rather than on God's love.

Perhaps we need to be reminded what an honour and privilege we have as Christians today. We are among those who are left behind to be involved in the work of the Lord. The gospel baton has fallen to us. Like it or not, we are here, living in this century! The giants of the faith, like Martin Luther and John Calvin, have long since left the field of battle. Other great servants of God, like Whitefield and Wesley, have gone home to heaven and are enjoying their rest in that city that has foundations. Our time for rest will come later. Here we are in this generation, and the work of the gospel is as urgent as ever. So we must take very seriously this tremendous business of evangelism, and how we go about sharing the message should never be divorced from the message itself. They are closely— inextricably—linked! The great missionary to China, Hudson Taylor (1832–1905), coined the lovely motto 'God's work, done in God's way, will yield God's results'. It should seem so obvious. Why is it not to so many in the evangelical church? Should it not be natural for us to want to be biblical in our approach to everything we do—so in evangelism as well? We should be those who are eager to submit ourselves to Scripture and in all things, therefore, be guided by Scripture. The Bible is our compass to keep us in the right way. It will never let us down.

Perhaps we need to ask this very important question: what is the main purpose of evangelism? You might come up with various answers to that, but they would no doubt all be pretty similar, along the lines of 'to see souls being saved', 'to win people for the Lord', 'to help see God's kingdom grow'. Yes, these certainly are great reasons for doing evangelism. However, they are surely not the main purpose. 'OK,' you may be asking, 'what is it, then?' It is to glorify God. That has to be the number one purpose of everything we do as Christians, which must therefore include how we reach out to others with the gospel. You see, winning souls for Christ is not an end in itself. When that happens, glory will come to the Lord—there is no doubt about that at all. But we should want Him to be glorified in the means as well as in the result.

Forgetting the main purpose is what has led even very

genuine believers to adopt inappropriate methods. If glorifying God is our chief aim in evangelism, we will be careful how we go about fishing for souls. So we must embrace the gospel: not just part of it, but all of it. It is 'all' of the message that sinners need to hear. It's the bad news that makes the good news so very, very good!

Notes

1   James A. Stewart, *Hollywood Evangelism: An Earnest Plea for True, Spiritual Revivial* (1940), p.9.

2   J. C. Ryle, *Great Christian Leaders of the Eighteenth Century* (London: Chas J Thyme, 1911), pp. 22–23.

THERE IS STILL MUCH TO DO!

3 Following the Governor

*All authority in heaven and on earth has
been given to me. (Matt. 28:18)*

During my time as a postman, my employers,
Royal Mail, came up with what they called
a 'mission statement'. It seems to be quite
the thing these days for businesses and large
organizations to have one. I suppose mission statements
are regarded as being very important. They set out why the
company exists, what their aims are and what their customers
can expect from them.

I used to start work at 4 a.m. It was terrible! With bleary
eyes I walked past the Royal Mail mission statement every
day, and sometimes I even read some of it. But I never really
took that much notice of what it was all about. I did my job
as best I could, but that was it. The big picture of what the
company stood for and sought to achieve didn't seem to have
much to do with me.

Did you know that the church of Jesus Christ has a mission
statement? It is there at the end of Matthew 28. And yes, it
is still there: it hasn't faded away with the passage of time.
If you are someone who reads through the Bible, you have
no doubt read what is found there—a final section that is
known as 'the Great Commission'. Perhaps you have read it
many times. You have probably heard the passage preached

THERE IS STILL MUCH TO DO!

on more than once as well. Some quite likely even know it by heart!

So you're familiar with it, but, perhaps like me with the Royal Mail mission statement, you've never really taken it that seriously. You know it's there, but it has never really gripped you. Perhaps you have accented in your mind the importance of it, but that is where it has stopped. It has never really affected you, stirred you, motivated you or moved you to get involved in seeing that it is actually accomplished. Maybe you have even asked, 'Is it really that great?' Whichever of these is true of you, if any, I simply ask you to think carefully about the 'Great Commission', and to think carefully about its implications for your life, both as a member of a local church and as an individual Christian.

So why are the words of Matthew 28:18–20 called 'the Great Commission'? If we were thinking about the Great Wall of China, we would probably know why that is called 'great'. It is reckoned to be at least five thousand miles long. Some even raise that to thirteen thousand miles long. The classic Second World War film *The Great Escape* is so called because the aim was to set free hundreds of POWs at one time, which was unheard of before. The Great Train Robbery of 1963 was so called because the robbers stole £2.6 million, which today is reckoned to be around £49 million. So what makes the words of Jesus at the end of His life on earth so 'great'?

There are at least four answers: it contains a great claim, a great call, a great work and a great promise. We're going to look at the first of these in this chapter. This commission is so great because of what we find in the preface to the Great Commission: 'All authority in heaven and on earth has been

THERE IS STILL MUCH TO DO!

given to me.' This really is the foundation stone upon which the commission is built. It is really important to spend time examining that foundation, so that we are secure in why we are to evangelize.

It's worth just noting that if this claim is true (which of course we believe it is), then Jesus Christ is without a doubt the most important person anyone could ever have dealings with. No wonder His message needs to be heard in every corner of the entire world! And we as His followers need to pay very careful attention to all He says. More than that: it's time to obey all He commands. Perhaps it's time to obey Him more fully than we have done before. So let's look at the details of the claim that is made here. It wasn't made about an angel, an apostle, a bishop, a pope, a pastor, a church or an organization. It was made about Himself! In order to examine the claim we will try to answer three questions:

1. WHAT IS THE LORD ACTUALLY CLAIMING?

There are four 'alls' in the Great Commission, and here is the first one: 'all authority'. 'Authority' is translated from a legal word, from the verb meaning 'to be lawful'. This is important because it demonstrates that the authority the Lord was invested with is a legal authority. Some translations use the word 'power'. This is true of the Lord Jesus as well. He has been given all power; but 'authority' is better. A person can have power and yet can use it unlawfully or can lack the legal authority to exercise that power. An example is the president of Zimbabwe, Robert Mugabe, who has encouraged looting and violence over many decades, as well as being well known for manipulating elections time and again. These things have been an unlawful use of power.

The Lord Jesus, on the other hand, has all power and He also has the legal right to exercise that power. So how much authority does Jesus have? We're told that He has 'all authority'. Simply put, Jesus is in charge. A Welsh evangelist named John Elias (1774–1841), who served the Lord mainly on the Isle of Anglesey in North Wales, would often refer to the Lord simply as 'the Governor'. The scope of His governorship is revealed for us. He has all authority 'in heaven and on earth'. There is no place where He is not in control. There is nowhere outside His rule and His dominion. Jesus Christ is Lord of this entire universe and He is ultimately in control of all things. The Bible says He is in control of life itself (Col. 1:16–17). Paul makes it clear that everything was made by, and is upheld by, His divine power. The Lord Jesus has all authority over death as well (Rev. 1:17–18). He is the conqueror of that worst and last enemy! He is also the Lord of salvation (Acts 4:12). I am told that in the film *The Matrix*, which I watched for about ten minutes and then switched off, the hero is repeatedly referred to as 'the one'—'He's the one'. That film was fictional, but here is reality: 'Jesus—He's the One', the only One, the only Saviour.

What a contrast there is between the Lord Jesus and most men who have had great power in history, even those who started off with legitimate power, again like Robert Mugabe. Time and again power has had a corrupting effect. Someone once rightly said, 'Absolute power corrupts absolutely.' In John 6, after the miracle of the feeding of the five thousand, do you remember what the crowds wanted to do with Jesus?

THERE IS STILL MUCH TO DO!

They were going to take Him and crown Him their king. Think of other religious leaders in history: they would all have jumped at the chance; but not Jesus. He knew that His time had not yet come!

Jesus Christ was no power-mad despot out for Himself. He was and is a loving Saviour and Shepherd. The chief end for which He uses His power is to bring His sheep safely into the fold, to protect them and keep them for time and for eternity. Yes, His power is at present largely hidden from the world's blind eyes, but a day is coming when His authority will be manifest for all to see. That was prophesied in the Old Testament:

I saw in the night visions,
and behold, with the clouds of heaven
    there came one like a son of man …
And to him was given dominion
    and glory and a kingdom,
that all peoples, nations, and languages
    should serve him;
his dominion is an everlasting dominion,
    which shall not pass away. (Dan. 7:13–14)

This prophecy shows us that there is an eschatological (end-times) aspect to fulfilling the Great Commission: it doesn't merely affect history, it drives history! This prophecy also substantiates the great claim the Lord made about Himself.

2. WHAT GAVE THE LORD THE RIGHT TO MAKE THIS GREAT CLAIM?

There are two answers to this question. Firstly, it is something that has been given to Him: 'All authority … has been *given to me*.' In John 17:2 the Lord is praying in the hearing of His disciples and He says something similar: ... 'since you *have given* him authority over all flesh'. It is also asserted by the forerunner John the Baptist in John 3:35: 'The Father loves the Son, and *has given* all things into his hand.' Some try to argue that this indicates inferiority on the part of the Son, but that is not at all the case.

In John 10:27–30 the Lord states that, just as no one can snatch any of His people from His hand, so no one can snatch His people from the Father's hand. In this magnificent promise Jesus is not just speaking of oneness of purpose, as the Jehovah's Witnesses claim, He is describing oneness of power, too! Aren't you glad, if you are in those strong and safe hands?

The Jews actually knew more than the Jehovah's Witnesses do, as the passage in John goes on to record the Jews stating 'you, being a man, make yourself God' (v. 33). That's right: He is God, and this authority was given to Him as a reward for His completed work, for His victory over sin, death and hell. The Lord was prepared to take the form of a servant; now He has been elevated to the status of King of kings.

Secondly, this authority was earned by Him. During those forty days in the wilderness, when the Lord was weak and tired, the devil offered Him the crown without the cross. He held out a far easier route for the Lord to take, but Jesus knew of only one route for Him and that was via Calvary.

In 1214 King Philippe Auguste of France prepared for battle against the Flemish and English at a place called Bouvines. It is said that he built an altar and then removed his crown and placed it upon the altar. He also placed an inscription next to the crown: '*Au plus digne*', which means 'To the worthiest'.

THERE IS STILL MUCH TO DO!

The king said to his lords and knights, 'He who fights bravest and best and wins the day, shall be king in my place.' After the battle, those knights who were left gathered round the king and began shouting together, 'Thou, oh king, art most worthy', and they gave him back his crown. The king had earned it. The song of those who are in heaven now with Jesus Christ, and only because of Jesus Christ, is similar: 'Worthy is the Lamb who was slain, to receive power and wealth and wisdom and might and honour and glory and blessing' (Rev. 5:12). He is the worthiest! The Saviour, then, has absolute right to be 'Lord of all' (Acts 10:36), but especially to be Lord of His people—of us! We may sometimes hear the strange idea being taught that Jesus can become a person's Saviour but only later that person's Lord. If we are Christians, we belong to Christ the moment we are converted. That means He becomes our Lord and our Saviour at the very same time.

3. WHY DID THE LORD MAKE THIS GREAT CLAIM?

This is a very important question to ask. Was Jesus perhaps taking the opportunity to boast, as we might have done? No, He wasn't boasting! That wasn't, and never could be, true of the Lord. Why, then? I suggest three reasons:

(a) The Lord's great claim of authority provides us with our authority

His authority provides us with our authority to go forth with the message of salvation, to reach others for Him! This is very important when we bear in mind that we live in a pluralistic, multi-faith society. Religions are, if you like, viewed like the fruit growing on the trees of an orchard. You can go along and pick the fruit from any tree you like. Or you can choose

THERE IS STILL MUCH TO DO!

not to eat any fruit at all. But the truth that we are humbly yet confidently to proclaim to all is that all the trees in the orchard are actually dead and all the fruit is therefore rotten—except for one tree. Only one is living, only one has real fruit—fruit which is of such a quality that forgiveness of sin is gained and eternal life is assured. Such an exclusive message with a unique Saviour is totally out of step today. It is out of step not only with militant atheists, not only with the multi-faith lobby, but even with many inside the church as well. We can be viewed as intolerant, unfeeling and divisive.

Our exclusive Saviour is now our exalted Saviour. He has been raised to the highest place of all. He has been given a name which is above every other name. He is at the right hand of the Father. He really is the Lord of Glory. There are many *lords*, but this is *the Lord*, and it is this Lord Jesus who is commissioning His people to go out with the gospel. As we seek to do so, we will undoubtedly face more opposition as society hardens itself against the truth. A pluralistic society will tolerate everything except a message which claims to be exclusively true. The suggestion that there is only one God, one Book, one Saviour and one Way is now repugnant to many. How ironic that the ones who claim to be so tolerant, because they say that all paths lead to God, are actually very intolerant of evangelical Christians.

The Lord Himself faced challenges from people about His right to teach as He did, just as we will. After the triumphal entry into Jerusalem the religious leaders demanded to know, 'Tell us by what authority you do these things, or who it is that gave you this authority' (Luke 20:2). If only they realized who they were talking to! The Lord chose not to answer them

THERE IS STILL MUCH TO DO!

on that occasion, but on many others He did so very clearly. Read John 6–8 in particular.

The evangelists of OAM are regularly challenged in many different places concerning their authority to preach and talk to people about the Lord. Many a time a council official has claimed, 'You need permission to preach there', but in every case to date, upon enquiry that claim has been proved to be untrue, so the men have been able to continue. A marvellous incident in OAM history took place at Epsom Races (another famous venue for horse racing) during the 1920s, when an official tried to stop one of the evangelists from preaching. King George V, simply dressed in a suit and tie, was going over to visit an enclosure nearby and he saw what was happening. Once he arrived at his destination, he sent a servant back over to the preacher to commend him, in a loud voice, on behalf of the king for the good work he was doing. That doesn't happen every day! The official, unsurprisingly, immediately backed down.

At present, the Mission enjoys the legal right to preach on most streets in the UK, so long as those streets are part of the public highway. However, the Lord's people have a greater authority than Parliament in London to go and proclaim the gospel—such that we must still go and find places to preach even if and when we are barred from doing so by earthly authorities. And that day may come soon enough in the UK and throughout Europe. Much wisdom, grace and courage will be needed in the coming years!

I do wonder if some Christians would even notice if all our rights were taken away, let alone be willing to keep on going anyway, even at the risk of breaking the law. The apostles did

THERE IS STILL MUCH TO DO!

notice, and yet they still fearlessly went! How did they justify
it when they were challenged? 'We must obey God rather than
men' (Acts 5:29). It was as though the consequences weren't
even on their minds. All they could think about was sharing
the good news. They just wanted people to hear the truth as it
is in Jesus. They knew the cost could be suffering and in many
cases death, but it didn't matter. What conviction they had!
The King they loved had given them orders and that was all
that really mattered. It cost them very dear to carry out those
orders, and it may well cost us dear to make that stand. But
then there are many right now who are willingly paying the
price for their Saviour. Let me give just two brief examples.

Joshua in Saudi Arabia was the son of a prominent Islamic
scholar and had been involved in persecuting believers. One
day, he came across and read a book about Jesus. It moved
him so much he decided to go to a church he knew of to
find out more, and soon after he was saved. Joshua then did
something incredibly brave. He went to the mosque the same
day and told the congregation he now believed that Jesus is
God. His father gave him twenty minutes to flee before he
sent men after Joshua to kill him. For over eighteen months
Joshua lived in hiding, but he struggled to get help from
Christians, who were scared he might be a spy (reminiscent of
when Saul of Tarsus was converted). Joshua is now involved
in ministering to other converts from Islam.

Nauman Masih, aged fourteen and from Pakistan, was
brutally attacked by fanatical Muslims who were on their
way to Friday prayers. They asked him if he was from their
religion, and when he said he was a Christian they started
beating him. When Nauman tried running away, two older

boys went after him, poured kerosene over him and then set him alight. Nauman sustained 55 per cent burns on his body and he died in hospital four days later. Accounts like these humble us.

Terrible persecution is going on in numerous countries of the world: Vietnam, Laos, China, Egypt, Indonesia, Iran, Iraq, Yemen, Saudi Arabia, Turkey, Pakistan, North Korea and many others. It has recently been estimated that one in nine Christians suffer persecution! Could it happen here in the West? Yes, it could. Increasingly we are seeing attempts being made to deny the right to witness publicly for Jesus Christ. If these succeed, they will be followed by a denial of the right to worship. Make no mistake: if the one goes, the other won't be far behind! Yes, the outdoor witness will go first, but it won't stop there.

An interesting statement was made by a man at Epsom Races a few years ago. As he saw the team of evangelists start to walk away from the course during the late afternoon, he stopped one of them and said, 'I don't believe what you preach, but I do believe that it will be a sad day for this country when you aren't allowed to come here any more!' Thankfully that day hasn't come yet.

Does persecution still seem a long way off for us? Humanists are now pushing very strongly for Christians to be silenced in all sorts of walks of life. There is a strong attempt to secularize society. They want God and His standards out, and as quickly as possible. Of course, the devil will tempt us when the going gets tough, 'Has God really said you must go to others with the gospel? After all, it's far easier not to go. Why not stay at home, stay in church, and just keep your

THERE IS STILL MUCH TO DO!

head down until better times come?' May we ever be able to reply, 'Yes, He has called me to go, and I willingly go now, while I can.'

(b) The Lord's great claim reminds us of our privilege of serving Him!

The Lord could save all whom He purposes to save without the help of any human instrument. Yet, mostly, He doesn't choose to do things that way. He wants to use His people, His church. Paul reminds the Corinthian Christians, 'For we are God's fellow workers' (1 Cor. 3:9). How amazing is that!

The ascended Lord Jesus has the legal right to delegate His authority to His church, and that is what He has chosen to do. In doing so, He has condescended to use the likes of you and me! It's incredible: He chooses to use what the world sees as a foolish message, 'the cross', to save sinners, a foolish method like 'preaching' to communicate that message, and a foolish lot of mouthpieces like us to do the preaching and witnessing! The Great Commission is His delegating His building work to His people. It is the invitation for us to be involved in that awesome work. It is incredible to think that, although Jesus has everything in the whole universe at His disposal, He has called the likes of you and me to speak His word to others! He even speaks of us in very elevated language: 'How beautiful upon the mountains are the feet of him who brings good news, who publishes peace, who brings good news of happiness, who publishes salvation' (Isa. 52:7). What a gracious Lord He is to speak of people like us in that way!

So what a tremendous privilege we have to serve this One who has been given 'all authority in heaven and on earth'.

THERE IS STILL MUCH TO DO!

Perhaps we should at times feel ashamed that so many Christians feel so little sense of that privilege and, as a result, so much less is being done to obey the Lord than it could be.

While ministering in the UK in 1874, D. L. Moody visited the city of Sheffield in Yorkshire. He was shocked by what he saw and commented with strong words of rebuke which are very challenging to us today:

What is to be done for the unsaved masses? Here, for instance, in this town of Sheffield, I am told that there are 150,000 people, who not only never go near a place of worship, but for whom there is actually no church accommodation provided, even if they were willing to take advantage of it. It seems to me, if there be upon God's earth one blacker sight than these thousands of Christless and graceless souls, it is the thousands of dead and slumbering Christians living in their very midst, rubbing shoulders with them every day upon the streets, and never so much as lifting up a little finger to warn them of death and eternity and judgment to come. Talk of being sickened at the sight of the world's degradation. Ah! Let those of us who are Christians hide our faces because of our own, and pray God to deliver us from the guilt of the world's blood. I believe that if there is one thing which pierces the Master's heart with unutterable grief, it is not the world's iniquity, but the Church's indifference. Every Christian man and woman should feel that the question was not one for ministers and elders and deacons alone, but for them as well. It is not enough to give alms; personal service is necessary. I may hire a man to do some work, but I can never hire a man to do my work. Alone before God I must answer for that, and so must we all.[1]

(c) The Lord's great claim is the guarantee of our success!
On three occasions I have been invited to lead a seminar at the Irish Baptist College in Moira in Northern Ireland on

the subject of open-air preaching. After the first visit a friend called Colin, who had kindly driven me to the college and with whom I was staying, suddenly said, as he turned out of the car park and onto the road, 'You've talked about evangelism—let's do some!' He had noticed a farmer in a nearby field climb down from his tractor, so we both got out of the car and made our way over to him. Colin chatted to pass the time of day and then asked what had been planted in the field; we were told that it was winter barley. Colin then asked the farmer what proved to be a very interesting question: 'Are you expecting a harvest?' The farmer, who by this time had been joined by his son, replied very confidently, 'Oh yes, there's always a harvest.' Something of the gospel was shared with both men and they each received literature before we turned to leave. As we continued on our journey we remarked that it is surely a great encouragement to know that, in spiritual farming terms, 'There's always a harvest'. It reminded us of the words in Ecclesiastes 11:6, 'In the morning sow your seed, and at evening withhold not your hand, for you do not know which will prosper, this or that, or whether both alike will be good.'

The harvest of our labours for the Lord may be large or it may be small, but a harvest will come. The One who described Himself as 'the Lord of the harvest' will make sure of that. He has a people to save, and that should spur us on. We should not allow our 'reformed theology', if that's what we hold to, to dampen our evangelistic fervour, as some do. Let us remember that the problem is not in the theology; it is in the application of it that the problem can arise. The motivation is there before us: the people whom the Lord plans to save.

THERE IS STILL MUCH TO DO!

The thing we must be utterly convinced about is that God wants His people to evangelize—not *even as* reformed Christians, but *especially as* reformed Christians! There is a danger in our practice of becoming the very thing we would claim to loathe in our doctrine. I'm referring to Hyper-Calvinism: the teaching that we don't need to evangelize, and even that it is actually wrong to evangelize! That is a bizarre way to understand the heart of God, and I hope we recoil completely from this false doctrine. But what about our practice? Yes, we believe that the Lord will save His people, but surely that should be a spur to evangelism, not the opposite. It is because the Lord has an elect people to save that we should be driven out, and driven on, to keep sharing the gospel with others.

The Hyper-Calvinist has also wrongly become convinced that, because we don't know who the elect are, and because only the Lord can save the elect, we should not offer the gospel to all. Actually, the biblical approach says that, because we don't know who the elect are, and because only the Lord can save the elect, we *must* offer the gospel to all. If you think about it, most of the best evangelists in the history of the church were of a reformed persuasion. The doctrines of grace were loved by men like George Whitefield and Charles Spurgeon. It was those doctrines that warmed their hearts and stirred them into action.

Have you ever thought that the only reason why this world is still going around and around, and the only reason why clocks keep ticking, is because not all of Jesus' sheep have been brought into the fold yet? The gospel is going out

THERE IS STILL MUCH TO DO!

gradually into the entire world so that God's people from every tongue and tribe and nation will be saved!

The Lord Jesus will build His church! He is doing so today! The work cannot fail. It may look otherwise at times, especially in the UK, as it can seem so hard. But the gospel light is still shining. So may the Lord encourage us to be involved in fulfilling the Great Commission, which has been given to us by a Saviour so great that all authority has been given to Him in heaven and on earth!

Note

1 W. R. Moody, *The Life of Dwight L. Moody* (London: Morgan & Scott, 1937), p. 195.

THERE IS STILL MUCH TO DO!

4 Obeying the call

Go therefore … (Matt. 28:19a)

We have looked at the tremendous fact that all authority in heaven and on earth has been given to the Lord Jesus. As it says in Ephesians 1:21, He is 'far above all rule and authority and power and dominion, and above every name that is named, not only in this age but also in the one to come'. We saw that the Lord of glory has given His church the delegated authority to carry out His work on the earth. And that authority may at times have to override the authority of men. The gospel must be preached, whether the world likes it or not. So with the full weight of the Captain of our salvation behind her, the church is then given her orders. Matthew 28:19 begins with two simple and yet massive words: 'Go therefore'. This is a command—but not just any old command: it is a royal command, a divine royal command.

If you are still wondering why the commission is worthy of being known as 'great', it is because what we have here is a great call to obey. What was immediately brought before the disciples was the fact that Jesus Christ was calling them to active service. We most definitely need a reminder of that today!

We're regularly warned loudly and clearly about the dangers of overeating and of not taking enough exercise. There is a spiritual equivalent we need to be aware of: it is the danger of taking in good teaching over and over again, but rarely, if ever, giving out to others. In the summer we may go to conferences to enjoy great ministry and great singing, but what about opportunities for service at outreach events, like camps and beach missions?

Eight summers ago, a student from Cameroon, who had just finished studying at what is now London Seminary, stayed in the UK an extra two months just so he could take part in a beach mission. It was a joy to have him with us on the team in Sandown on the Isle of Wight. Here was a man willing to spend more time away from his wife and children, whom he hadn't seen for a whole year! I was deeply moved by that, as the longest I have ever been away from my own family is a fortnight.

Roger Ellsworth, a writer from the USA, says of the Israelites in his book *Moses: God's Man for Challenging Times,* 'They were more interested in being God's comfortable people than God's called people.'[1] Our natural tendency is towards comfort, isn't it? A manifestation of this rather inward-looking attitude, which can almost be a feeling of self-satisfaction, is seen in what we understand evangelism to be. We've convinced ourselves that the commission is merely to say to unbelievers, 'Come.'

Do fishermen expect the fish to come to them? Will lost sheep find their own way home? Do farmers sow their seed from an open window of their houses? The answer is 'no' in each case—but for many churches, evangelism is all about invitations. 'Come to this, come to that and come to the other.' Yes, that can be part of our evangelism, but we must put first things first. And what should be first? We must 'Go'. It's why we talk of doing *outreach*. We're to be reaching out to

THERE IS STILL MUCH TO DO!

others with the message of salvation. Whether we're thinking of the fisherman, the farmer or the shepherd, the emphasis is the same: they go. That's where true missionary work, true evangelism, has to start: with disciples of Jesus *going out* to find the unbelievers and share the gospel with them. That's exactly why the evangelists of OAM visit schools and retirement homes, why they hold open-air meetings and take part in beach missions, and, yes, for those who do come in, they speak at coffee mornings, suppers and lunches, and they preach in churches.

C. T. Studd (1860–1931), who was a missionary on three continents and the founder of the Worldwide Evangelization Crusade, once said this: 'Some like to stay within the sound of the church or chapel bell. I'd rather run a rescue shop upon the brink of hell.' The church building is safe; it is warm (usually!); but what about the lost who are not coming in? A retired pastor was once asked by a recently ordained preacher if he would give advice to sum up all he had learnt during his fifty-year ministry. He instantly replied, 'My advice is simply this: hurry up, my brother, and go and preach the gospel.' He was basically saying: 'You've got a message, a life-changing message, you've got a means of communicating that message, so go and do it!'

Let's try to answer two simple questions about that call to go with the gospel—questions which are fundamental to the subject of evangelism:

1. WHO IS THE COMMISSION GIVEN TO?
This might seem too obvious to mention, but it isn't! We know the commission was initially given to the apostles, but

some have suggested that this commission was *only* given to the apostles. If those people are right, we can all be at ease in Zion with a good conscience! Let's sit back and take it easy until the Lord calls us home.

But let's look at this carefully. If the Great Commission was just for the apostles, wouldn't we have to say that they failed? After all, they were never able to get to 'all the nations' in their lifetimes. Yes, there's the story of Thomas going to India, of Andrew going to Russia, but was the whole planet being covered? Not at all! So, that being the case, did they not fail their commission? Didn't the apostles let the Lord down?

Well, no. That is not the impression the book of Acts gives at all. Most of those godly men were faithful unto death—literally so. Actually, the apostles were greatly successful! The gospel spread like wildfire in those early years after the Holy Spirit was given to the church. But that wasn't to be the end of it: it was just the beginning! There's a sense in which Acts is still being written, and on every page of history until now! What a humbling thought: that our ministry, whatever it is, will be on one of the pages—not the pages of Scripture, but the pages of the history of the church of Jesus Christ! So no, the Great Commission was not just for the apostles. We cannot get out of it that easily!

Another point we must make in connection with this is that the role of evangelist is one that continues to be valid and vital. In Ephesians 4:11 we are told that God gave certain roles for the establishing and maintenance of the church: 'And he gave the apostles, the prophets, the evangelists, the shepherds and teachers to equip the saints for the work of ministry.' The only two offices which were restricted to the first century

THERE IS STILL MUCH TO DO!

were apostles and prophets. Ephesians 2:19–20 makes that quite clear: 'the household of God, built on the foundation of the apostles and prophets'.

Some Bible commentators have downplayed the role of evangelists and argued that they were mainly apostolic representatives, but actually their main function was gospel preaching. Philip is a fine example (Acts 8). I suggest that this coolness towards the role of evangelist is because often evangelists have operated outside the sphere of the church, which leaves us feeling uncomfortable; but that does not negate the biblical validity of the ministry of this role of 'evangelist'.

It is quite noticeable that open-air work seems to attract men who like to be their own boss in all they seek to do for the Lord. We might describe them as lone rangers. They like to work alone! Often they are those who wouldn't be given a pulpit to preach in, so a town centre is the next best thing. However, it's very, very important that evangelists are sent out by their churches and are under the authority of those churches. Every evangelist should be. We need the accountability, as well as the security, this brings!

One clinching proof, to leave you in no doubt if you're still not sure as to whether this Great Commission still stands today and therefore who is to go with the gospel, are the Lord's marvellous words at the very end of the commission: 'And behold, I am with you always, to the end of the age' (Matt. 28:20b). What is in view here? The whole gospel age! The Lord is making it very clear that the 'going' is to continue till the 'coming'—His coming again in great power and glory. So the conclusion we must come to is that Jesus Christ wants us to go for others, and to keep going for others until He comes for us! In Mark 13:10 Jesus says, 'And the gospel must first be proclaimed to all nations.' 'First' before what happens? Verse 7 records the Lord's answer: 'the end'. Just as we are to proclaim the gospel at the communion service with the bread and the wine 'until He comes', so too we must continue with preaching and witnessing until He comes.

The question that needs to challenge our hearts is this: we can see that we are commanded to go, but are we willing to go? This is a good moment to remember the prophet Isaiah. He saw the glory of God. Jehovah's holy and awesome majesty was on display in the vision recorded in chapter 6 of Isaiah's prophecy. The Lord is seated upon His throne and angelic beings are gathered around worshipping Him. After Isaiah's sin had been cleansed, the call to service immediately came. It is important to notice that Isaiah's willingness to go for the Lord was expressed before he was given the content of His message, and not afterwards. In other words, he didn't first wait to see whether he would be given an easy assignment or not. As he would discover, it was going to be a very tough assignment. Isaiah's call was to a large extent to preach judgement to a hard-hearted nation. Even so, he went and did that faithfully for many years!

What is so impressive about Isaiah is that, when the call to service as a mouthpiece for God came, he was willing to obey and to go. Haven't we too seen something of the glory of the Lord Jesus? Didn't we see it in Matthew 28:18? Don't we see it throughout the book of Revelation? And haven't we been cleansed from our sin? If so, when He calls us, will we obey? Will we say with Isaiah, 'Here I am, send me'? Or are we

THERE IS STILL MUCH TO DO!

more likely to respond with, 'Here I am, Lord—please send someone else'?

The world-famous preacher C. H. Spurgeon (1834–1892) wrote the following challenging words:

Oh, what a vast amount of sleeping we have in all our churches and chapels; for truly if our churches were once awake, so far as 'materials' are concerned, there are enough converted men and women, and there is enough talent with them, and enough money with them, and enough time with them, God granting the abundance of His Holy Spirit, which He would be sure to do if they were all zealous—there is enough to preach the gospel in every corner of the earth. The church does not need to stop for lack of instruments, or for lack of agencies; we have everything now except the will; we have all that we may expect to give for the conversion of the world, except just a heart for the work, and the Spirit of God poured out into our midst. Oh! brethren, let us not sleep as do others.[2]

A quick aside before we move on: if one day you become a leader in your church, or if you are already such, it will be part of your responsibility to teach your people to go, and to make sure you lead them by example! Some wise advice was given in the First World War by Rev. Studdart Kennedy to a younger colleague: 'Live with the men. Go everywhere they go … share all their risks … Your place is in the front … work in the front, they will listen to you.'

2. WHERE ARE WE TO GO?

'Go therefore and make disciples of all nations' (Matt. 28:19). Look at the two comparable passages in the other Gospels: Jesus said, 'Go into all the world and proclaim the gospel to the whole creation' (Mark 16:15), and that 'repentance

THERE IS STILL MUCH TO DO!

and forgiveness of sins should be proclaimed in his name
to all nations' (Luke 24:47). The Lord had a very important
point to press home to the apostles. Perhaps that is why He
summoned them to Galilee (see Matt. 28:10), which Isaiah
9:1 called 'Galilee of the Gentiles [or 'nations']'. Isaiah 9 is
that great chapter concerning the coming of Messiah. These
Jewish disciples had grown up with the mindset that God was
only for the Jews. In fact, the missionary work they had been
given to do thus far might have confirmed them in this view.
After all, Jesus once said, 'Go nowhere among the Gentiles
and enter no town of the Samaritans, but go rather to the lost
sheep of the house of Israel' (Matt. 10:5–6).

So was the Lord changing His mind in Matthew 28? No,
He was not. If I were to ask my son Luke to go to the corner
shop to buy something, it wouldn't mean that I would never
ask him to go to the centre of town to buy the same thing. It
is also very clear in other places that the Lord always had a
long-term plan of reaching Gentiles with the gospel as well
as the Jews. For example, in Matthew 8:11–12, before the
Lord sent out the disciples to serve Him, Jesus said, 'I tell
you, many will come from east and west and recline at table
with Abraham, Isaac, and Jacob in the kingdom of heaven',
and the most famous words in the whole Bible are 'For God
so loved the world ...' (John 3:16). If we were to look at the
full sweep of Scripture we would soon see that from eternity
God purposed to save people, not just from one nation, but
from every nation. Remember the promise to Abram, 'in
you *all* the families of the earth shall be blessed' (Gen. 12:3,
emphasis added). The rest of the Old Testament is peppered
with verses which show that Gentiles, as well as Jews, would

be among God's elect people. For example, in the shortest psalm we read the exhortation, 'Praise the LORD, all nations! Extol him, all peoples!' (Ps. 117:1). How blessed we are to be a part of God's worldwide church!

So how should we understand Matthew 10:5, then? We need to do what we should always do if we are a bit baffled by one verse. We should compare Scripture with Scripture, which is a sound hermeneutical principle. Acts 1:8 is very helpful here: 'and you will be my witnesses in Jerusalem and in all Judea and Samaria, and to the end of the earth.' This statement by the Lord Jesus provides a clear principle for evangelism, which helps to answer our question 'Where are we to go?' The answer is to start at home and move outwards! The Lord was laying down something that was both practical and spiritual. This would be true for the early church and for us today. A person may have big hopes and big plans for what he or she is going to do for the Lord. But where that person is now is already his or her mission field—perhaps even at home!

If a person cannot live a consistent, God-honouring life at home, where will he or she be able to do so? Yes, home, if it contains unbelievers, is probably the hardest place in which to witness (it's the place where others know you the best!). So home can be a person's Jerusalem. Or maybe 'Jerusalem' is somewhere else, like university, the workplace or the locality. As such, it may well be a place of learning, maturing, testing and growing. All these aspects should be seen as part of the preparation the Lord has for us for other types of going. Nothing is wasted as far as the Lord is concerned! He may

THERE IS STILL MUCH TO DO!

be preparing us to go on to the next phase of service, onward and outward.

A young girl called Mary Slessor (1848–1915) once heard a missionary give a talk at her church in Dundee of an evil place called Kalabar in Nigeria. From that day on she yearned to go as a missionary to Kalabar. However, she had to start her service for the Lord helping with a youth club in a tough area of Dundee. It was several years before Mary finally went to Kalabar to share the gospel, where she served the Lord faithfully for many years until her death in 1915. The Lord prepared her one step at a time!

Like Mary, the disciples had much to learn after their early gospel labours. Yes, they were very successful after their first outreach work. Sadly, though, the early success seemed to go straight to their heads. They announced on their return, 'Even the demons are subject to us in your name' (Luke 10:17). They needed a gentle rebuke from the Lord: 'Do not rejoice in this … but rejoice that your names are written in heaven' (Luke 10:20). Temptations can come to us in all sorts of ways and at all sorts of times, even when we're serving the Lord, which we have to admit to our shame. Had pride crept in? How easily it does so! Perhaps you hanker to go to darkest South Africa and do some great work for the Lord there, like Mary Slessor or world-famous pioneering missionary David Livingstone (1813–1873). Remember, you already live in darkest Europe and the needs here are even greater! Missionaries are now even coming here from Africa and Asia. I once met a Nigerian evangelist in Leicester. He told me that he had heard how dark the UK now was and he felt the Lord's call to come here and preach. It was sobering to hear that, since the UK was

THERE IS STILL MUCH TO DO!

once the place from which many missionaries were sent; now the tide has turned.

Perhaps your calling will be to stay in your homeland. After all, that is a mission field, isn't it? The population of the UK has now reached 65 million people. It is estimated that around 6.5 per cent go to church, but that is only once a month. We might be encouraged by that figure on the surface, but we mustn't forget that many churchgoers never hear the gospel. OAM evangelists regularly meet people on the street who comment, 'I go to church, but I've never heard this stuff about being born again before.' What a terrible indictment that is upon so many churches!

Yes, most people have heard of God—but it's a God who, if He's actually there, used evolution to make the world. This God doesn't make many demands on us, but then He doesn't seem to care about us very much, because He allows so many bad things to keep happening. People have heard of Jesus— that teacher, a holy man, who was supposed to have done miracles, but most scientists say miracles can't happen. And if He did die on the cross, it was only to give us an example of how to suffer. People have heard of the Bible—that dusty old religious book which we don't need now because science has all the answers. And anyway, it is full of contradictions. It's ironic that we like to believe we are a well-educated nation, when actually we are so ignorant!

So where are we to go? In a word, 'everywhere', 'into all the world'. But we must pause there for a moment. It's not just a matter of going. That might seem obvious, but it's not.

About nine years ago I was helping on an outreach team in the centre of Belfast in Northern Ireland. I was invited to

THERE IS STILL MUCH TO DO!

preach at an open-air meeting in a park a few miles away. It was a beautiful afternoon, but there was a problem—the park was virtually empty! Oh yes, there were the thirty or so Christians, who seemed to have a great time singing praises to God. But I wondered what on earth I was doing there evangelizing one man and his dog! It was a very frustrating occasion, and also quite sad that the church leaders hadn't thought about trying to find a location for outreach where the people actually were.

We need to draw upon the sanctified common sense that the Lord gives to His people. There's nothing unspiritual about thinking through very carefully where to evangelize and how. Strategy is not a dirty word. Surely it is wise to consider the place and the time. Let me illustrate why this is actually very important. All four of my children enjoyed a series of children's books called *The Garden Gang*. Each story would home in on one fruit or vegetable. A favourite was the story of Patrick Pear. Patrick loved to go fishing (yes, we're back to fishing yet again!). One day, he went fishing in the watering can that had been left outside the garden shed, but Patrick was disappointed that he didn't catch any fish. The next day, he tried fishing in a large puddle on the pathway after a heavy shower of rain. Again, he didn't catch any fish. On another day, he even tried fishing in the gardener's cup of tea, which he had left on a low wall, but poor Patrick still didn't catch any fish. Then one day, the Garden Gang all went on a trip to the seaside. Patrick decided to take his rod with him, and guess what happened? Patrick went fishing in the sea and, for the first time, he caught a fish!

The Lord Jesus employed a strategy during his ministry.

THERE IS STILL MUCH TO DO!

Mark 6:6 says, 'He went about among the villages teaching.' Put another way, He went where the fish were to be found. The apostle Paul also had a strategy: in all his travels he always went to the cities, the great centres of population. These were where he threw out the gospel net, and as souls were saved, he established churches in those places.

Six years ago, three of us were invited to go to Slovakia to help two Baptist churches begin doing open-air work. We tried different places in the capital, Bratislava, where we spent four days, and then we spent three days in a city called Zilina. In both places the church pastors had researched where would be the most suitable places for open-air preaching. Encouragingly, what we found was that, everywhere we went, there were people who were prepared to stand and listen. Not all, by any means, but there were some, sometimes a lot. Most listened very respectfully to the preaching, and lots of conversations took place afterwards with members of the churches who were there supporting. It was such a joy to see believers confidently sharing their faith on the streets. They are still going out on a regular basis.

To come back to Acts 1:8, as this is an important verse: we're often quite good about the two places at either end of the list of regions to reach with the gospel. We can see 'Jerusalem' as being the people who are living around our church, and 'the end of the earth' as being missionary work overseas, but it's the middle section that often seems to get neglected—'Judea and Samaria'. We can omit this region in between, which is made up of those who live elsewhere in our own country or those who live even just a short distance away.

I have known of churches on the edges of towns who will

refuse to go and do any outreach in the town centres, even though those centres may be full of people. The reason? 'We might meet people who wouldn't come to our church.' In other words, they are guilty of a kind of parochialism. The first mistake is that they are forgetting that actually the people of their estate go into the centre of town to do their shopping. The second mistake is that they have made up their minds that if the evangelism isn't going to specifically benefit their church, they don't want to be involved in it. Dear friends, if you have thought like that, may I humbly ask you: isn't there something bigger in evangelism than your own church? Isn't filling the kingdom more important than filling your building? Of course we want to see our own churches grow—there would be something strange if we didn't; but if you were to meet a seeking soul in the town centre who expressed an interest in going to church, wouldn't you feel it best to direct that person to his or her nearest evangelical church, rather than just think about getting him or her over to one of your services?

I know of a number of places where members of several evangelical churches work together in the open air and they do so very happily on the basis of sending an enquirer to the church closest to where the person lives. An example of that is Manchester. OAM has a week of outreach there every September. Three years ago, a man named Andy drew up in a motorized scooter and listened to one of the preachers all the way through his message. Afterwards the preacher had a lengthy conversation with him, during which time Andy expressed his desire to attend church and asked if a local one could be recommended to him. Andy was given a card with

THERE IS STILL MUCH TO DO!

the service details of a good church only about half a mile from his home.

He attended a luncheon club several times, followed by a Christmas Eve service. A few weeks later Andy was in his pyjamas one Sunday morning watching TV. At about 10 a.m. he suddenly felt an overwhelming compulsion to go to church that morning. He rushed to get dressed and just made it in time for the beginning of the family service. As the gospel was being preached Andy came under conviction of sin and cried out to the Lord to save him. We later heard that after a few months Andy was baptized in the same church and is going on well.

Your church may be in a suburb, but why not venture into the town centre? Find the places that are busy. Find the places where the people are to be found. Put up a board to identify who you are. Preach, give out literature and talk to people about the Lord.

More and more towns, as well as cities, are becoming cosmopolitan. Whatever we think about the politics of immigration, as Christians we should see the influx of more people as an opportunity for more gospel outreach. The world is coming to us. Our Jerusalem may well now contain people from the uttermost parts of the world. Listen to these words about London: 'Scarcely can you preach the truth in the streets of London without being encouraged to do so again … To preach in London is to preach to all nations and to all religions. There is scarcely a creed or a non-creed that is not represented in this metropolis.' Would you believe that that was written in an OAM report way back in 1854? How

THERE IS STILL MUCH TO DO!

much more true is it now! Shouldn't we be lifting up our eyes to see the harvest that is within our reach?

Notes

1 Roger Ellsworth, *Moses: God's Man for Challenging Times* (Darlington: EP Books, 2005), p. 164.

2 *Spurgeon: New Park Street Pulpit: 347 Sermons from the Prince of Preachers*, OSNOVA edn.

THERE IS STILL MUCH TO DO!

5 Doing the work

*... make disciples of all nations, baptizing them
... teaching them ... (Matt. 28:19–20)*

American theologian James M. Boice once wrote, 'The greatest thing going on in the world at any one time is the preaching of the gospel.' It's a blessed thought, and he was almost right. There's just one thing even greater than that. Can you guess what it is? It's people being converted through the preaching of the gospel!

The compelling reason why the church of Jesus Christ must go and preach the good news is the Great Commission He left us. We've seen that it has the backing of heaven and of the God who sits upon the throne there. We said that the great claim the Lord made about Himself was given to Him, on the one hand, and was earned by Him, on the other. We looked at the great call the Lord gave to 'Go' and saw some of the details of the going: the who, the where and the why. Now the Lord brings before us the 'what' of the going. This is the third aspect of the commission's greatness: it's a *great work to do*. 'Go therefore and make disciples of all nations, baptizing them in the name of the Father and of the Son and of the Holy Spirit, teaching them to observe all that I have commanded you' (Matt. 28:19–20).

These words contain three key verbs. When I learnt English at primary school back in the 1970s I don't remember being taught much grammar. However, one of the few things I do remember is that a verb is 'a doing word'. Here in the Great Commission there are three key 'doing' words. They are commands that have been given. They are things that must be done! The crew of a battleship must obey their commanding officer, and so must we!

The Great Commission is not optional for the church of Jesus Christ. In the commission we have our orders! Seth Joshua (1858–1925), a Welsh evangelist greatly used by the Lord, said in 1924, 'It is those who lose faith in the gospel as the power of God who fly to new experiments. "Go ye into all the world and preach the gospel" is still the standing orders for the church.' Standing orders are those that are current for the soldier or sailor. They still need to be carried out. These three verbs that the church has been given are orders that cover the whole range of gospel proclamation and service. The completion is in view, as well as all the parts. Military leaders have their ultimate aims and objectives in mind. The aims and objectives of the Lord Jesus are to glorify His name in establishing and building His church.

1. THE FIRST VERB: 'MAKE DISCIPLES'

'Go therefore and make disciples' (v. 19) can be literally translated, 'Having gone, therefore, make disciples'. Other Gospel writers record slightly different aspects of the work that the Lord wants His people to do. Mark emphasizes the going: 'Go into all the world and proclaim the gospel' (Mark 16:15); Luke focuses on the message to take in the going: 'and that repentance and forgiveness of sins should be proclaimed' (Luke 24:47); and both Mark and Luke refer to how it should

THERE IS STILL MUCH TO DO!

be communicated as they both emphasize public preaching. All of these things are indeed very important.

Here in Matthew, the emphasis is placed not so much on the declaration of the message, as in Mark and Luke, but on the positive response to the message from some of those who have heard it. In other words, it's about people becoming Christians—but it doesn't stop there. It also includes how those who become Christians should be helped in their spiritual lives. A term we often use to describe this is 'follow-up'. It can apply to those who have expressed an interest in spiritual things or to those who have made a profession of faith in the Lord Jesus. Either way, follow-up is an extremely important aspect of the work of evangelism. I would go so far as to say that if we fail to follow people up, we fail those people.

Some years ago, during OAM's week-long London outreach event in June, the team were in Covent Garden one day working alongside a small local evangelical church. Covent Garden apparently has the highest footfall (the number of people going through) in the whole of the UK, so it is a strategic place for gospel preaching. There are tourists from all over the world, as well as local people either shopping or on their break from work. One of the team spoke to a man named David, who had listened intently to the preaching. The Lord seemed to be dealing with him. He was under conviction and, after hearing the gospel and its implications clearly explained, David expressed the desire to call to the Lord for forgiveness right there and then, which he did. (As an aside, this is not something that should ever be done lightly. In fact, OAM's usual policy is to urge people to go away and prayerfully seek God, so as not to pressurize them, as will be explained further in a later chapter.)

The following day, I came to hear about David and I asked what follow-up had been put in place. I was extremely upset to hear that the team member who had spoken with David had allowed him, potentially a new convert to Jesus Christ, to slip back into the crowd without either giving or receiving any contact details. Most disappointingly of all, this meant that David was not given any church details. Now, you may say, 'Well, if David was saved, that is the main thing.' Yes, that is the main thing, but it is not the only thing. The Lord has called us to make disciples, not just to get professions of faith, and not even just to get converts. We are therefore not doing our job properly if we do not follow people up and do nothing towards their being discipled. Discipleship, by the way, should always take place in the context of the local church.

A little aside at this point: some Christians are cool at best towards missions like OAM and other home missions, because they don't like the whole concept of parachurch organizations. Well, in a way, neither do I. The Great Commission should ideally be carried out through the vehicle of the church. However, we need to be honest and make two points about that.

The first is that some churches are not willing to do what they should be doing in terms of outreach. There may be outreach opportunities around them, but they are failing to take them. If every church in a town with a pedestrianized shopping centre was out there preaching on a regular basis, there would be no need for OAM to exist.

THERE IS STILL MUCH TO DO!

Secondly, some churches are very limited in what they are able to do. They may have small and perhaps quite elderly congregations. In the term 'parachurch organizations', 'para' means 'alongside', not 'against', and certainly not 'in competition with'—in other words, 'in partnership with'. And that is how we ought to operate: not just doing our own thing, but working with local churches in every way possible to be whatever mutual help and encouragement we can be.

We may never know if David in Covent Garden was really saved that day. For me, it's a bit like the situation in the book of James: 'If a brother or sister is poorly clothed and lacking in daily food, and one of you says to them, "Go in peace, be warmed and filled", without giving them the things needed for the body, what good is that?' (James 2:15–16). The context there is clearly the need to meet a needy person's physical needs, but the application to meeting a person's spiritual needs is a reasonable one. In all good conscience we should not be content to let the newly professing Christian just go off and fend for him- or herself. Yes, we know that the Lord can and will keep His own, but we need to remember that the Lord uses means in every part of His work. He makes that very clear here in this commission. So we must be very concerned to disciple new converts. If we don't, we have no way of ensuring that they are in fact converts and not those who have made false professions.

The word 'disciple' lays emphasis on the mind. A disciple is 'a learner' or 'a pupil'. The new Christian must be instructed. He or she must be instructed in the ways of righteousness. Baby Christians need to be fed on pure spiritual milk. They must be nurtured and cared for. Of course, unbelievers must

THERE IS STILL MUCH TO DO!

first learn a certain amount in order to be saved. They must learn about themselves—what they are in the sight of God, lost and hopeless lawbreakers; and they must learn about God—that His justice demands that sin be punished, but that His mercy has provided a substitute to take the place of sinners, and that they must 'come as sinners to Jesus'! Then they must learn of their need to turn from their sin and receive the Lord Jesus as their Saviour. And finally they must be taught to follow the One who died for sinners and rose again.

The Lord Jesus wants to see the genuine article. A decision card is completely worthless in God's eyes, but a true follower is absolutely priceless. He wants lives, not just autographs! Too many today lay great stress on getting decisions out of people. But shallow methods will only lead to shallow results. Again, on the London outreach, an American Christian boasted to one of the ladies on the team, 'I've led five people to the Lord today.'

'Were they all genuine?' she wisely asked him.

'Well, I'm sure three were,' he replied. In reality, though, he couldn't be sure that any were! What a mockery it risks making of this great work, just to get someone to make a commitment to Jesus. 'Just say a prayer after me and you're now a Christian.' This shallowness and superficiality is far too common these days. When we remember that we are looking at the orders from above for gathering and directing His church, to the ends of the world, we dare not play fast and loose with such momentous things. Someone once rightly said that 'False conversion is no more than a religious milestone on the way to hell'. That's very sobering to think about from the point of view of the evangelist. We will have to answer

THERE IS STILL MUCH TO DO!

to God if we are responsible for persuading unbelievers they are the Lord's if they are not. In 1 Corinthians 3 the apostle Paul similarly had some very sobering words to say about this: 'Now if anyone builds on the foundation with gold, silver, precious stones, wood, hay, straw—each one's work will become manifest, for the Day will disclose it' (vv. 12–13).

A very famous American preacher in Chicago named A. W. Tozer (1897–1963) was regularly asked to preach in other parts of the USA. He was once preaching at a large rally in Long Beach, California. At the end of his message he said to an electrified congregation, who no doubt were expecting to hear him invite people up to the front for the altar call, 'Don't come down here to the front and cry about it. Go home and live it.' I don't think for one moment he was seeking to be unkind to his congregation; rather, he wanted to see real disciples, real followers of Jesus. Of course, it goes without saying that that is what the Lord wants too, and so should the rest of us!

A disciple is someone who is on a lifelong journey, so this learning is a process that ends only in heaven. That's why in the life of Christians church has such a vitally important place. We meet too many on the streets who profess to be believers, but who either have no affiliation with a local church or spend their time drifting around different churches and never settling anywhere for any length of time. There seems to be a low view of the doctrine of the church these days. In his extremely helpful book *Disciplines of a Godly Man* US writer Kent Hughes says, 'We now have a phenomenon unthinkable in previous centuries—a vast herd of professed Christians who exist as nomadic hitchhikers without accountability, without discipline, without discipleship, living apart from the regular benefits of the ordinances. As a result they are incomplete and stunted.'[1] Getting new Christians to see the importance of joining a good church is definitely an integral part of the Great Commission. To that end, churches should be geared up to providing some kind of discipleship course that can specifically help new converts. Encouraging converts to come to the meetings on Sundays and mid-week for Bible teaching, prayer and fellowship is also vitally important, as these will be of great benefit to them, as indeed they are for every Christian.

There is a real joy in seeing a young Christian grasp some precious Bible truth for the first time. I well remember Mike, a young Christian though around fifty years of age, very excitedly coming to me after a service in our church when the preacher had spoken about the Lord's second coming. Mike said, 'I've realized something amazing! Jesus really is coming back, isn't He!' Here was a well-educated man exemplifying a childlike faith. It was lovely to see spiritual life and spiritual growth exhibited like this.

Jesus said His disciples are to 'learn from me' (Matt. 11:29). The best way for new disciples to do that learning is to be doing it with other disciples. It's not much use our being in our own little boat alongside the battleship. We are to be part of the crew of the battleship; we have been saved to serve together! Hebrews 10:24–25 says, 'And let us consider how to stir up one another to love and good works, not neglecting to meet together, as is the habit of some, but encouraging one another, and all the more as you see the Day drawing near.' How important it is to take these exhortations to heart!

THERE IS STILL MUCH TO DO!

2. THE SECOND VERB: 'BAPTIZING THEM'

Baptism is something that Jesus Himself submitted to and it is one of the things He calls His followers to submit to as well. Going through the waters of baptism is an important part of being a disciple. The book of Acts illustrates this pattern time and time again, most famously of all on the Day of Pentecost (Acts 2:38–41). If we can say that conversion is a personal event between an individual and Almighty God, baptism is a public event, designed to show everyone that this person has been converted. It is public testimony to the fruit of the work of evangelism. That's why it is always such an exciting occasion in the life of the church.

Baptism is also a declaration that someone has broken away from the ranks of the world and gone over to God. Charles Spurgeon spoke of it as 'publicly burning your bridges with the world'. The radical nature of what it is to become a Christian, a disciple of Jesus, is in view: the convert is finished with the old life; now, instead, that person is following Jesus Christ. Baptism pictures the great truths that we as Christians have experienced: the washing away of sin through the blood of Christ, the dying and burial of the old life, and the rising again to the new life. And these are things we want others to know about. In some countries, necessity demands that baptisms be carried out in secret, but on the whole they are public events—and quite right too, for they are brilliant evangelistic opportunities.

There are a couple of vital points to note about who should be baptized. The first is closely linked to evangelism: baptism is for those who have come to Christ for salvation and who are seeking to live their lives for Him. Does that seem far too obvious to mention? In Newport, South Wales, an OAM evangelist met a young woman called Sharon, who approached him during an open-air outreach, wanting to share with him the good news that she was soon to be baptized. As the evangelist talked with Sharon about her faith and her understanding of the gospel, it soon became clear that she was not a Christian. It was a shallow-evangelism alert! This young woman was not ready to be baptized; more than that, she was actually not qualified to be baptized. It does make you wonder about the discernment of the leaders of the church she was attending. Sadly, we have to recognize that this is not an isolated case. I only wish it were.

The second vital point about baptism is that all those who really are trusting in Jesus alone for salvation should be baptized. Baptism is not the domain of a special group of Christians. It is not just for those who have received some special light, as one or two denominations wrongly teach. The only special light we need is Jesus Christ and what He has taught us in His Word.

I don't want to sound hard here, but how can a person really claim to be a wholehearted follower of Jesus if in one important area that person is disobeying Him? Refusing to be baptized as a Christian is wilfully saying 'no' to the Lord's express command. Towards the start of this book we said that the Lord's authority is very much at the heart of the Great Commission, but authority is an issue generally, isn't it? So many have the following kind of attitude: 'Who has the right to tell me what to do? Who has the right to have jurisdiction over me?' If we are believers we know the answer: we are under the jurisdiction of Jesus Christ, before anyone or anything else, including ourselves. He has the absolute right to tell His disciples what to do. Remember, He didn't say, 'Do what I say, not what I do.' No, He went through baptism Himself. So He says to us, 'Do what I say and do what I do.'

Many wonder how quickly new disciples should be baptized. That isn't the remit of this book, but I'll take a risk and say a couple of brief things, although I don't want to fall out with anyone. There is no time scale given to guide us in Scripture. Yes, the three thousand converted on the Day of Pentecost were baptized the same day. The Ethiopian eunuch, Cornelius, Lydia and the Philippian jailor were all baptized straight away, but it is undoubtedly the case that they lived in a day when the Holy Spirit was working in great power and the apostles had a level of discernment few of us would claim to have today. It therefore seems wise for there to be a period of assessment, to give time to see if there really is any genuine fruit.

What we know for sure is that we live in a day when there is so much that is false. It would seem irresponsible not to be as careful as possible in screening candidates for baptism. This pattern is very far from being new! As far back as the second century, those who professed faith were examined by church leaders before baptism. Evidence for this is to be found in the writings of a man called Justin Martyr, who was born about AD 100. His book *First Apology* makes this clear.

A while ago I was contacted by a group doing evangelism in South Wales who wanted OAM to be involved with them. An integral part of their orthodoxy was to baptize people as soon as they professed faith on the street. I didn't feel we could work with them. I sensed that the instant-results mentality,

THERE IS STILL MUCH TO DO!

as well as instant baptism, was very much to the fore in their thinking.

There is one more important aspect about baptism that we are given here—a particular name into which a disciple is to be baptized. Verse 19 tells us that baptism should be 'in the name of the Father and of the Son and of the Holy Spirit'. One name, not three! That is very important. We have and we serve a triune God: one God, one Saviour, one Lord, yet three divine persons in the one Godhead; equal and perfectly united in their essence, their will, their power and their glory, yet revealed as Father, Son and Holy Spirit. They have distinct operations that they perform and distinct roles in the great work of redemption. The Father formulated the plan of salvation and then sent His Son into the world. The Son voluntarily came to this earth in order to wash away our sin in His precious blood. The Holy Spirit lives in believers to make us better disciples than we are. How blessed we are that this one glorious God, who has revealed Himself in three gracious persons, is willing to have personal dealings with sinners like us!

3. THE THIRD VERB: 'TEACHING THEM TO OBSERVE ALL THAT I HAVE COMMANDED YOU'

It is of great importance to teach new disciples to obey the Lord. He has given commands and we are to obey them. If Jesus is our Lord, obeying Him will not be a heavy burden for us; it will actually be our heart's desire. King David wrote in Psalm 40:8, 'I delight to do your will, O my God; your law is within my heart.' How vital it is, then, to teach new disciples the Word of God and, in so doing, to show them how the Lord wants us to live out our new lives. The famous Olympic

THERE IS STILL MUCH TO DO!

runner and gold medal winner Eric Liddell (1902–1945), who went on to become a missionary in China, once said, 'One word stands out above all others as the key to knowing God, to having His peace and assurance in your heart; it is obedience.' Obedience is so important in the Christian life. Every part of our lives now belongs to the Lord. He is our King and we are His servants. That may well involve us having to sacrifice certain things, but it is always going to be well worth it. John MacArthur writes in his excellent book *The Gospel According to Jesus*, 'Many stumble over the twin truths that although salvation is a free gift, yet it costs everything.'[2]

We shouldn't overlook the truth that if we are to obey all that Jesus Christ has commanded us, that includes His command to go and make disciples. In other words, part of the discipling that new Christians need to have includes how to go and disciple others. How much of a priority is it in our churches to train Christians to share the gospel and win others to the Lord? In 2 Timothy 2:2 a young pastor is exhorted by the apostle Paul, 'And what you have heard from me in the presence of many witnesses entrust to faithful men who will be able to teach others also.' Timothy was not only to teach others the Word of God; he was also to nurture others who could teach the Word of God. This is how the work of God has been perpetuated through the centuries, and the work is continuing still today.

The Lord Jesus makes it clear that the breadth of teaching that is to be passed on to others should be no wider and no narrower than all that He has revealed to us in His Word. There are so many things that disciples need to be taught, and, of course, learning the ways of godliness is to be a

THERE IS STILL MUCH TO DO!

lifelong activity for the Christian. Disciples need to be taught to live in a Christ-like way, to display Christ-like attitudes, to have Christ-like motives. These things are all of paramount importance. But we must also teach disciples to talk the talk. Both walking right and talking right are essential for the follower of the Lord Jesus. We need to make sure that we never allow ourselves to be persuaded that it should be one or the other. It should always be both. Seth Joshua became worried about this at a particular point in his ministry: 'My one fear is that many people are in danger of cultivating holiness at the expense of service. It would be a thousand pities to see people make holiness a substitute for work.' By 'work' he meant sharing the gospel.

I struggle with the famous saying of Francis of Assisi (1181–1226), 'Speak to others of Christ and if necessary use words.' It sounds very good on the surface—very pious, even. The sentiment is right that our lives should speak to others and that they should challenge others. But that on its own is not enough! Think about this for a moment: what do most unbelievers who look at the average Christian see? A moral person, a clean-living person, a religious person; more than that they don't see. What causes the Christian to be moral, to be clean-living, to be religious, they don't know. Words are needed to explain what the gospel is. It's a bit like the difference between general and special revelation. In a book entitled *The Glory Christian*, written anonymously, the author says of the Lord, 'His glory is seen in every springtide and every setting sun, but these do not convey the glory of Christ to the mind of an unbeliever. It is left for you and me to do this. We are Christ's witnesses.'[3] I recently read that

THERE IS STILL MUCH TO DO!

Francis did actually go around publicly exhorting people to trust in the Lord, which is very encouraging to know.

Sometimes it can take those of other faiths to motivate and challenge us. I read in the Barnabas Fund magazine about a manual to help Muslims achieve what is called *Dawah*, which is basically the Arabic for 'evangelism'. It means 'to invite'. It contained an eight-step approach. The final one was 'Mould the convert into becoming a "walking Koran" who can witness to Islam in every place and situation.' It made me think of what Christian disciples ought to be taught to be—those who know and love the Bible, so that they are equipped to go to others and share their faith likewise, 'in every place and situation'. Muslims are deadly serious about their desire to extend the tentacles of Islam as far and as wide as possible. We should feel challenged by their desire and their devotion. At the end of the day, what they have is completely false and absolutely hopeless, but what we have is the exact opposite. We have the true way of salvation which gives us two amazing blessings: the absolute certainty of sins forgiven and a home in heaven. No Muslim you ever meet will tell you he or she has either of those things.

It is vitally important, then, to give young Christians teaching about the Lord, but it is also vitally important to give them the opportunity to serve the Lord in our churches, with things like Sunday school, holiday clubs, children's meetings and open-air work. And if the opportunities locally are limited, opportunities further afield should be sought instead. We need to inculcate good habits of service and mission into the lives of young disciples. The earlier they get it into their blood, the better, which is one reason why

THERE IS STILL MUCH TO DO!

I love beach missions. These are great gospel opportunities, but also great training grounds! On the beaches we're seeking to make disciples, and as we do so, we're training others to make disciples.

My grandmother's brother, Jimmy Walkey, led a beach mission in Bude in the early 1920s. He worked as an evangelist for what is now Scripture Union. He later went to be a missionary in South Africa. My first taste of evangelism was on a beach mission in North Devon back in 1986. My grandfather had said to me one day, 'I think it will do you good to go to beach mission.' I wasn't very keen, but you didn't say 'no' to my grandfather! He was six foot four and had been a brigadier in the army. He was quite right, though. It did me great good. Now, not only have I been taking part in and leading beach missions ever since, but my two daughters have been involved in several as well. It's wonderful to think that the work is continuing down the generations. I know of a number of Christians who started off as teenagers on a beach mission and are now serving the Lord full time.

Being given opportunities for service needs to be part of the training of others for service, and for leadership too. Our churches need to let those who show keenness to serve to be allowed to have a go at something and see what happens. At times, we reformed people can be so insistent that everything is done just right that we are never willing to take any risks. You can usually tell quite quickly whether there is real potential for evangelism and ministry, so huge disasters can be avoided. How many great servants of God might have been overlooked if they were never given that first opportunity to speak in front of others!

THERE IS STILL MUCH TO DO!

May the Lord help us to be disciple-makers! It's the real fruit of evangelism. And may those disciples in turn be trained to be disciple-makers too!

Notes

1 Kent Hughes, *Disciplines of a Godly Man* (Wheaton, IL: Crossway, 2001), p. 170.

2 John MacArthur, *The Gospel According to Jesus* (Grand Rapids, MI: Zondervan, 2008), p. 147.

3 Anonymous, *The Glory Christian* (Marshall Brothers, 1925), p. 33.

6 Believing the promise

And behold, I am with you always, to the
end of the age. (Matt. 28:20)

The church of Jesus Christ has been given a commission. Not just that, but a Great Commission. Why is it so great? We've been trying to answer that question in the last few chapters, and not only that, but also apply it to ourselves. A final reason for why this commission is great is because it is accompanied by a great promise. This commission starts with Christ and it finishes with Christ. How wonderful that is! Where better could it start or finish? There is a lesson even in that: our evangelism, if it is to be anything at all, is to be Christ-centred. Not man-centred, not personality-centred and certainly not us-centred—no, not even church-centred.

OAM used to have an outreach event at Chester Races each May. One year I met a Roman Catholic couple who were very happy to chat. I asked them what they were trusting in for their salvation, and without any hesitation the man replied, 'The church, of course.' We might immediately think that we are a million miles from that position, and I hope we are, but we do need to ensure that our focus is always upon Jesus Christ and upon nothing and no one else. Just as salvation is Christ-centred, so His Great Commission is Christ-centred.

How encouraged we should be that the Lord Jesus Christ rounds off—or better still, crowns—His commission with a promise. David Livingstone described this promise as 'The words of a gentleman of the strictest and most sacred honour, and there's an end of it'. In other words, he was saying, because of who is saying these words, we can rely upon them completely and utterly. I suspect Livingstone also made this statement because he knew from experience just how true it was.

There's a lovely echo here at the end of Matthew's Gospel of what is made known at the beginning of the Gospel. The Son of God who was born in Bethlehem was 'Immanuel (which means, God with us)' (Matt. 1:23). This One who was 'God with us' at His incarnation is promising to stay with us always—to stay with us until His work in and through us is finally done! There is much work to be done, and He is going to be with His people to help get it done.

In the UK, and probably in many other countries as well, a promise is almost a dirty word in many quarters these days. In politics, for example, promises are not taken too seriously—except when there is going to be an election! In business, integrity has all but vanished. In marriage, the promise to stay together 'till death us do part' is sounding increasingly hollow. How good it is to know, therefore, that there is One who always keeps His promises. His book, the Bible, is a book of promises. The apostle Peter calls them 'precious and very great promises' (2 Peter 1:4)! And these promises have been 'granted to us'! They are for the church. They are for the people of God. They are for us!

So here, at the close of Jesus' commission, He gives one such promise. Yes, it is a great promise, a great and precious promise. In a sense, what more could He have given than a promise such as this! After all, He is promising nothing less than Himself. But is it really necessary to devote a whole chapter to this promise? Isn't it labouring the point? Yes, it is necessary! It's very important to spend time looking at this promise because evangelism can be very hard. There may well be times when we are labouring faithfully and nothing seems to be happening. No sign of any fish or any harvest. Even the Christians around us can become apathetic, and that can rub off on us. We may become discouraged and be tempted to give up.

There are even times when Christians can be downright discouraging about what we're seeking to do for the Lord. I once happened to be on my own preaching in Derby when a professing Christian who had been listening came over to tell me in no uncertain terms that he could give me five reasons why what I was doing was a complete waste of time. There's a sense in which it is far more painful to hear criticism from believers than it is to hear it from unbelievers. I listened patiently to his five points, but when I tried to respond he refused to listen and marched away. On the other hand, a few weeks later, an American lady stood listening to the preaching with tears in her eyes and came over to say how blessed she was to hear the gospel being preached on the streets of the UK. In times of discouragement the promises of God are what we have to come back to, and keep coming back to again and again. So we need to really know His promises and also to really believe them.

The Lord's final words on earth provide us with a very particular promise. We know that the Lord is always with His people in a general way. Hebrews 13:5 assures us, 'I will never leave you, nor forsake you.' This same promise will also be true when we face particular trials, as we read wonderfully in Psalm 23:4: 'Even though I walk through the valley of the shadow of death, I will fear no evil, for you are with me.' But here in the Great Commission we are told that He is with us at a specific time. When? When we go to others with the gospel message! He says He will be with His people when they go out with the gospel. So there's something very special about this promise: something very comforting and not to be overlooked, and something very challenging for each of us as well.

It begins with the phrase 'And behold'. The NIV translates this as 'And surely'. There are various things these words could mean: 'and notice this', 'and remember this', 'pay careful attention to this'. When my son Joshua was a bit younger he would always avert his eyes when he was being told off. My wife and I could often be heard saying to him, 'Josh, look at me.' We wanted to have his full attention. That way, Josh knew we were saying something important. And it's as if the Lord is saying the same sort of thing here: 'Look at Me. I want your full attention. This is vitally important.' And what is it the Lord wants us to know that is so important? 'You have an enormous task ahead of you. There is a huge responsibility to be faced! The chief business of the church has been set forth. It has been described for you clearly. And so, before you begin to carry it out, remember this, pay careful attention to this …'

Pay careful attention to what, exactly? Well, to something that had already been promised in the past, something that would be real in the present and something that was assured for the future. Let's think about these three aspects of this great promise.

THERE IS STILL MUCH TO DO!

1. PROMISED IN THE PAST

The disciples, who were the first to know of the Great Commission, already knew this promise from two sources of equal weight, which can encourage us just as they encouraged them. Firstly, they knew it from the Old Testament Scriptures. Many general promises were given to Israel, but specific promises were especially given to the nation, and to individuals from that nation, when they were called to go and serve the Lord in a special way. An example is Moses, when he questioned the wisdom of God's call to him to return to Egypt. In Exodus 3:12 the Lord simply yet powerfully answers his negativity by saying, 'I will be with you.' Could any excuse hold water when this promise was being made, particularly as it was made in emphatic language? The Lord was reassuring Moses that He was committed to being with him. Another example is Joshua, Moses' successor. He was quite fearful as he took over from his illustrious predecessor, so the Lord said to him, 'Just as I was with Moses, so I will be with you. I will not leave you or forsake you ... Do not be frightened, and do not be dismayed, for the LORD your God is with you wherever you go' (Josh. 1:5, 9). There was an awesome job ahead for Joshua that involved leading, governing, fighting and serving. He needed lots of courage to face it all. What would instil more courage in him than the assurance that the Lord would be there with him, every step of the way?

The Lord has never commissioned people to serve Him and then said, 'Off you go, then. Go and get on with it. I'll see you when you get back.' I had a dream about that when I was about to start at what was then London Theological Seminary (now London Seminary) back in 1987. In my dream, the Lord was leaving me at the gates of the college. They were very tall iron gates. It looked more like a prison than a Bible college. 'See you in two years' time,' the Lord said to me. The gates swung open and in I went, all on my own. I can assure you that that dream was no prophecy! Indeed, there aren't any gates at the seminary, iron or otherwise. The fact is, the Lord goes with us on each step of our Christian journey. He never sends us anywhere on our own. And without His presence it would be futile to go anyway!

Secondly, the disciples had themselves received this promise in the past from the very lips of the Lord Jesus Himself. Just a few weeks before the Great Commission was given, the disciples had been at that unforgettable occasion in the Upper Room. Jesus had announced that He was going to be leaving them. He knew it was crushing news, but He also gave them some very different news to make up for it. He told his followers that He, their present Lord, would soon be their 'omnipresent' Lord. Through His Holy Spirit, He would be able to be with all His people at all times and in all places. This was to be the special ministry of the Holy Spirit in relation to the redeemed people of God. The One who applied our salvation to us at a certain time in our history is also the One who will be with us for the rest of our history.

John 14:16–18 describes two great blessings for the Lord's people. The first is, 'He will ... be *with* you' (emphasis added). One of the names given to the Holy Spirit is 'Comforter', which in the original Greek literally means 'one who draws alongside'. Most people know of Liverpool Football Club. Like some other teams, their fans have a theme song. The

THERE IS STILL MUCH TO DO!

Liverpool one is very famous; it is 'You'll Never Walk Alone'. Jesus was reassuring His saints in that Upper Room with the promise that 'You'll never walk alone'. However tough it may get, He'll be there right alongside you.

The other blessing Jesus gave was 'He … will be *in* you' (emphasis added). The Holy Spirit would indwell the Lord's people. The equipping power that would be needed internally, as well as externally, would be given. The Holy Spirit would help them with the very words they would need to share the gospel with others. Have you ever been witnessing to someone and prayed for the Lord to give you the words to say? Did He do it? Did verses come to mind that you felt were clearly the Lord's leading? It's lovely when that happens.

I recall being at Hull Fair one year and sharing the gospel with a young man. At the end of what proved to be a profitable conversation he asked why we preached in the open air. Since he had said he had a Bible at home, I quoted some verses from Proverbs. He said he would look them up on reaching home. After he disappeared into the crowd, it came into my mind that I had given him the passage following Proverbs 1:8, when I had meant to give him the passage following 8:1. I rushed through the heaving crowds asking the Lord to help me find him. Moments later I spotted him and he appreciated my going after him with the correct reference. Phew!

There's an important question to ask about evangelism which is very relevant here. If we have this promise that the Lord is with us, should anyone else be with us as well? In other words, who should we work with in the cause of Jesus Christ? Now, sometimes we have to go solo in our gospel

THERE IS STILL MUCH TO DO!

labours. There may be times when no one else is able to go out with us. But even then we won't be on our own. The evangelists of OAM usually have the support of others with them, but occasionally they have to go out into an open-air situation alone. The wife of one of the men said to him once, 'Are you on your own today?' The reply came back from her husband, 'No, there are three others coming—the Father, the Son and the Holy Spirit.' He wasn't being facetious; he was reminding himself and his wife of a blessed truth, one that is truly incredible to think about.

The account of Paul in Athens in Acts 17 is an example to us of a man serving the Lord without any human accompaniment. He didn't take the day off while he waited for his friends to join him. Paul took a look round the city and was so burdened by the idolatry he saw everywhere that he felt compelled to begin preaching and witnessing in the busy marketplace.

It is interesting, when you talk with OAM evangelists, that their common experience during those times when they have to go out by themselves is that they feel the Lord's presence and help in a special way. It's as though the Lord makes up to us those times when no other believer is alongside us. A while back I was preaching on my own for an hour in Luton before others were able to come and join me, and it was such a blessing just to be out preaching the gospel. During that hour three different people came to ask questions, which was great. But should that be the norm that we are content with? The answer is very simple: no, it should not, because it is not the biblical norm. Remember that the Lord sent out His disciples two by two. Mark 6:7 says, 'And he called the twelve and began to send them out two by two.' That was very deliberate. The Lord knows what we need, and in gospel work we need one another.

In thinking about who we work with, there are two dangers that are worth thinking about: we can be either too narrow or too broad in our approach. An example of being too narrow is a church whose constitution states that members can 'do evangelism' only with other members of that same fellowship. They are potentially missing out on the blessing of working with other warm-hearted and like-minded believers from other churches. It's good that they want to evangelize, but rather sad that they insist on being so restrictive. OAM is made up of men who are quite a mixture, but I dearly love those men, even if we do differ from one another on certain secondary issues. I count it a privilege to stand with those who love the Lord, love the gospel and love the lost, and so should we all.

The other extreme is being too broad. The world-famous American evangelist Billy Graham is a sad example. Let me say, first of all, that undoubtedly many, many people have been converted through his ministry over the years. In June 1989 I had the opportunity to go and listen to him at Upton Park in London. This was the last time he visited the UK for gospel rallies. He preached on John 14:6 and it was a very clear gospel message. However, the trouble is the associations Billy Graham has had with others over many years, such as with men who believed different things about the Bible, different things about the cross and different things about salvation—in some cases, even different things about the person of Christ! Dr Martin Lloyd-Jones was much criticized

THERE IS STILL MUCH TO DO!

for standing apart from those rallies in the 1950s and 1960s, but he saw the dangers very clearly. For him, the truth of the gospel was at stake. Any unity not based on that, he said, is not real unity at all. He was absolutely right. Galatians 1:8 says in very strong language, 'But even if we or an angel from heaven should preach to you a gospel contrary to the one we preached to you, let him be accursed.' How can we possibly work with those who believe a different gospel? We cannot! We must not!

Perhaps we might be wondering whether there is any kind of benchmark to guide us in who we work with in gospel outreach. There is! That benchmark is the Word of God. We should refuse to work with those who believe less than its teachings, and, by the same token, we should refuse to work with those who believe more than its teachings. Some emphasize things like healing, which is growing in popularity on the streets in various places, but spiritual healing is far more important than physical healing, and our emphasis ought to be upon people's need to be saved and discipled. It can appear to be very kind to pray for people on the streets who may be ill, but it is far kinder to talk to those same people about the sin in their hearts and their need of the new birth.

2. REAL IN THE PRESENT

'And behold, I am with you.' In the Greek, 'I' appears twice, once as part of the verb and once as a separate letter: 'I, I am with you.' This is for emphasis. Physically, the Lord would not be present for much longer. It is interesting that the Lord appeared only intermittently to the disciples during the days between His resurrection and ascension. It was no doubt quite deliberate. Jesus was getting them ready for the time when they would see Him no more. Having said that, the apostles were still going to know the reality of the Lord's presence, but in a different way. What a blessing that would be to them! And this was not just a vague promise for the future, but one that was for now. That promise is wonderfully still true for us too in the twenty-first century. Not only does the Great Commission still stand, but this accompanying promise still stands as well, for those who will get involved in it.

There can be times when you go to serve the Lord somewhere that is pretty scary, even when you are part of a team. That was always true of Hull Fair that I mentioned earlier. The venue had quite a reputation. People could be very volatile there, even before the evening had worn on and some had had a large amount of alcohol to drink. As we took turns to preach, we stood on a small platform at the side of the road down which thousands of people passed every evening on their way to the fair. Missiles were fairly frequently thrown at the preachers. Burgers, screwed-up paper and coins were favourites, but once I remember a coconut being hurled at one of the men. It missed his head by only a couple of inches. The perpetrator thought it was a great joke and casually came and asked if he could have his coconut back.

Sometimes evangelism can take evangelists to much more dangerous places. I have a friend from Pakistan who pastors a church in East London. He was once escorted to witness to a Muslim he knew only vaguely. He ended up sitting at a table in a room with none other than the infamous cleric Abu Hamza. On the floor all around the room were Abu Hamza's disciples. My friend Elisha honestly thought he wouldn't

THERE IS STILL MUCH TO DO!

leave that room alive. But the Lord was there with him. He helped Elisha to speak, and in answering the questions put to him he was able to share the gospel very plainly. As he did so, Elisha noticed that the men sitting on the floor were visibly affected by the gospel. When Abu Hamza saw this, Elisha was asked to leave straight away. It was a very scary experience, but what a tremendous opportunity!

This teaches us that we can take great comfort in this promise that the Lord will be with us in every situation. The world might look on and ask, 'Why ever are you not afraid? Have you lost your senses?' Reason says that at times we should be terrified, but we walk by faith—faith in Him who has given us this great promise, 'I am with you always'. The apostle Paul was conscious of the Lord's presence when he stood alone before Caesar in Rome: 'The Lord stood by me and strengthened me, so that through me the message might be fully proclaimed' (2 Tim. 4:17).

Perhaps we question that at times: 'Is He really there with us?' It's perhaps not a bad thing to ask, because there may be times when He withholds that presence in a measure from us and, as a result, withholds His blessing. There are at least two possible times when this may happen that we need to be aware of. The first is if there is a lack of unity. One of the biggest problems we have to contend with in gospel work is, believe it or not, other Christians! This is one of the main reasons why missionaries give up and go home. This is terribly sad, but it is apparently true. In Matthew 18:19–20 the Lord Jesus speaks about the importance of unity. He uses the word 'agreement', which can mean unity, brotherhood or

THERE IS STILL MUCH TO DO!

accord. This word has reference to the harmony of different musical instruments playing together.

Some years ago my wife and I were invited to see a friend sing in a choir in Basildon that was accompanied by a full orchestra. I didn't view the prospect of the evening with a great deal of enthusiasm, but I confess that I found the whole event fascinating. I had been to a couple of concerts before, but this was the first time we had sat well above the musicians, which meant we could see them all clearly. It was so interesting to see the different sections all coming in at just the right moment, so that the music was flawless. That is how the life of the church is supposed to be. Often, however, there is much in our relationships which falls way short of the biblical standard that the Lord expects from us. There can be little harmony as a result. An audience won't stick around to listen to a discordant orchestra, so why should the world listen to us when it sees how we too often treat each other? Isn't it an awful thought that we may be the cause of holding back the Lord's blessing as a result?

Secondly, the Lord may withdraw Himself to a certain extent and hold back His blessing if there is sin among us. We can take comfort from the fact that the Lord will not close His heart to us—He will never do that—but He may turn His face from us at times. In Psalm 66:18 we read this admission: 'If I had cherished iniquity in my heart, the Lord would not have listened.' It is possible to grieve the Holy Spirit and to do so in different ways: by displaying wrong attitudes towards someone, by our general prayerlessness or by having some habitual sin we will not give up. If you are saddened by a lack of closeness to the Lord these days, that's good, because it means you want to do something about it. Another great promise that may help you is this: 'if anyone does sin, we have an advocate with the Father, Jesus Christ the righteous' (1 John 2:1).

There's a sense in which God's abiding presence as we serve Him is a two-edged sword. We rejoice, on the one hand, that He will be with us, but, on the other hand, the thought that He is with us should make us careful. We need to take care what we say and how we say it, so that we don't let Him down. The apostle Paul was very mindful of this: 'For we never came with words of flattery, as you know, nor with a pretext for greed—God is witness. Nor did we seek glory from people' (1 Thes. 2:5–6). To stand in front of other human beings and to preach is awe-inspiring in and of itself, but how it should affect us to know that the Lord is always in the congregation as well! Gospel labours are not about seeking to please men and women, nor about seeking their praise. Ultimately, we want to please God, and we should want any praise to be given to Him, not us!

If we want to stay united in our work for the Lord and to be pure in our work for Him, we need to pray for a greater measure of God's Spirit to be among us. That is needed in our individual lives and witness, but it is needed in the life and witness of our church as well. I don't mean what men can drum up, but what God can send down. This leads me to say something very briefly about revival. Please don't be one who says something like this: 'Let's wait for revival, then we'll go out to the lost. Let's pray for revival, by all means, but do nothing else!' That condition for evangelism is not part of the Great Commission the Lord Jesus gave to His church. No, it is nothing but an excuse for inactivity. The commission of the Lord says that we are to go now, whether revival comes or not. He commands us now and He promises to be with us now. We are to go now! We mustn't neglect evangelism because there is currently no revival. There is no biblical warrant for that kind of indolence at all!

One OAM evangelist was once preaching in Newport in South Wales on a hot summer's day. A man eating an ice cream came by, stopped and then interrupted the preacher, saying, 'What we need, brother, is revival!' He then just turned and went on his way, eating his ice cream. There was no thought to stop and help. What a discouragement! I'm not against enjoying ice cream, but shame on that brother in Christ! What a people we are if we try to justify what is ultimately laziness and indifference!

3. ASSURED FOR THE FUTURE

This promise has not run its course yet. It was given to last 'to the end of the age'. The disciples were to be sent out into a hostile world that was pagan and godless, so very similar to our own! What a tremendous difference it makes to know that, wherever you go, whatever circumstances you face, the Lord will be there with you. If we are living for Him and desiring to make Him known, we can be certain He'll be there with us. So here is what we need to take us on as servants of God: the sure and steadfast promise of the Lord, 'I am with you always.' None of us will outlive this promise, even if the Lord returns in our lifetimes; He will be with us then too.

It should give us confidence to do and be all we can for Him. We might wonder if, with the passage of time, we will feel that we can manage in gospel work without the Lord's help. No, we never get to that stage—certainly not if we preach in the open air. Any preacher will tell you that it never gets any easier, and I for one am very glad about that. You see, it means we still have to keep going back to the Lord and seek His help and pray His promises. If we ever feel we can go in our own strength, we had better not go at all.

We always need the Lord. Some of us need the Lord to stir us up in the first place. A man once asked a friend about D. L. Moody, 'Was he O and O?' Was he 'out and out' for the Lord? He wanted to know whether Moody was wholehearted, committed, fervent. Moody came to hear about this conversation, and this turn of phrase, 'O and O', greatly challenged him. In fact, he determined from that day onwards to be 'O and O', to be 'out and out' for the Lord. That phrase has gone out of common usage today, but perhaps we need to bring it back, and we certainly need to ask ourselves if it is true of us. Roger Ellsworth has written, 'Our profound regret when we are confronted with the glory of God will be that we only had one life on this earth with which to serve Him and we did not use it to its fullest.'[1] How that should challenge us to be out and out for our great Saviour, starting today!

The New King James translation of the Bible ends Matthew's Gospel and closes the Great Commission with the word 'Amen'. It's as though Matthew were responding to what has just gone before with the voice of the church: 'So be it, Lord.' Can we add our own 'amen' to it? Matthew Henry wrote that the 'Amen' to this promise turns it into a prayer. Is it our prayer? If so, are we prepared to be the answer to it?

It should go without saying that prayer is absolutely

essential when it comes to evangelism. However, there is a danger of viewing this promise in a presumptuous way, a way in which it was never intended. We might say something like this: 'The Lord will be with me, He has promised to be, so prayer to Him is not now that urgent.' That was not the attitude of the apostles, though they knew this promise of the Lord very well. There's a lovely illustration of that in Acts 4. Having faced opposition to the gospel in Jerusalem for the first time, did they immediately sit back and take it easy? No, they didn't. Did they just get straight back in there? No, they didn't do that either. They had a prayer meeting first, thanking the Lord for who He was and seeking His blessing as they went forward preaching the gospel.

These men were aware that they needed fresh supplies of the Holy Spirit's power and blessing. The Lord's promise to be with them did not discourage them from praying for Him to be with them. If we want His near presence, shouldn't we pray for it? If we want to be a blessing to others, don't we need a blessing ourselves? And doesn't God's blessing come from close communion with Him? We need to spend 'much time in secret with Jesus alone', as the hymn says, before we spend any time in public with others. When we look at the lives of those who were greatly used of God in reaching others for His kingdom, we see that they were men and women who placed a high value on prayer. We can't afford to do anything less.

I once read of a Dr Bachus, a former president of Hamilton College in the USA, who was lying in his bed very ill. On being told by his doctor he had only an hour to live, he said something that might surprise us: 'If that is true, then take me out of my bed and put me on my knees, and let me spend it calling on God for the salvation of the world.' How humbling to read that! His last hour on earth was devoted to praying for the lost. The famous British poet Lord Alfred Tennyson wrote, 'More things are wrought by prayer than this world dreams of. Wherefore let thy voice rise like a fountain night and day.' I don't know if Tennyson was a believer, but he certainly got that right. So this amazing promise the Lord Jesus has given should not lead to presumption; it should lead to more action, but more action fuelled by prayer.

One of the reasons why we need to be prayerful is because a harvest is coming. You know what that harvest is, don't you? It's the one that will arrive at the end of the age, when the reapers of souls, the angels, will come to gather and to separate. When will that be? When will the end of the age arrive? We don't know. Scripture does not tell us; and not only that, Scripture does not encourage us to waste our time trying to calculate when it will be. But one thing is quite possible: the end of the age may be nearer than we think! It is interesting that in Matthew 13:47–50 there is a fishing parable. But this one is not referring to evangelism. It is referring to the time when evangelism will be finished. This is the time when the fruit of evangelism will be gathered in, and when those who rejected the Saviour will be cast into the furnace of fire for ever. We haven't reached that great and terrible day yet, so how urgent we need to be.

The Great Commission urges us to see the importance of praying and of going. Yes, we need to pray for the work of the gospel, locally, nationally and internationally, but that alone, though commendable, is not enough. Someone once said, 'If

THERE IS STILL MUCH TO DO!

you do not wish God's kingdom to come, then don't pray for it. But if you do, you must do more than pray for it, you must work for it.' May we never grow tired of going! The Lord has made it abundantly clear that He will never grow tired of going with us! Amen.

Note

1   Roger Ellsworth, *Moses: God's Man for Challenging Times* (Darlington: EP Books, 2005) (2005), p. 41.

THERE IS STILL MUCH TO DO!

7 Reaching the locals

We will not hide them from their children,
  but tell to the coming generation
the glorious deeds of the LORD. (Ps. 78:4)

Most church buildings were erected with some sort of strategy in mind, and that strategy has usually been an evangelistic one. Our forefathers had a vision to reach those around them with the glorious gospel of the blessed God, and we need to catch something of that vision ourselves.

Whilst the church building is primarily the place for local Christians to gather for worshipping the Lord and hearing His Word preached, it is also a place from which gospel outreach can and should take place. In some places church buildings have been placed in the centre of town in order to be in a prominent position and also to try to draw people from a wide area. In other places they were built in suburban areas so the focus of witness could be on one locality in particular. To a certain extent, the location of our churches will affect the kinds of outreach we can attempt for the Lord.

It may be helpful to work through a number of different opportunities that could be taken. These may well be ones your church is already involved in, but perhaps one or two ideas might be new to you and could be thought about for your church setting. Let's start with the building itself and ask a question: are we maintaining it to the highest standards we can? If it looks tired and shabby, that may well be enough

THERE IS STILL MUCH TO DO!

to put off the casual visitor from crossing the threshold. Most of us spend time and money keeping our homes looking nice; we should definitely do the same with our spiritual home.

Then there's the noticeboard. I once heard of a church that was content to see its invitation to attend services on the noticeboard as the total extent of its outreach. How very sad that is! Having said that, our noticeboards are important because they are one of the chief means of advertising available to us. They need to be well maintained, preferably large, bright and up-to-date in all the information they contain. I once visited a church that had the name of the pastor on the board. There was just one problem: the pastor had gone to be with the Lord six months previously! If there is space, try to include a gospel text on the noticeboard, too. Never forget that God's Word is powerful (Heb. 4:12), so having a gospel text on display will provide a constant challenge to passers-by. Perhaps have someone in the church whose job it is to maintain the board and to change the gospel text on a regular basis. It rather amuses me that some churches like to put the name of the speaker on the board, as though that will draw unbelievers in; let's face it, since no one outside the church has heard of any Christian speakers today, there really isn't much point.

The other source of advertising is a church website. This is a must for the twenty-first century. Many of us, when we plan a holiday somewhere unfamiliar, will try to find a good church by using the Internet. What we find on a church website is likely to be sufficient to satisfy us either that it is a good place to go to or that it is one to stay well clear of. Make sure your church website is eye-catching, easy to navigate and has plenty of details about your activities, especially contact details. And make sure there is some gospel content on it, including audio messages. An unbeliever might visit your website without ever visiting your church, so it is important to have an evangelistic message of some kind on it for unbelievers to read or hear.

We now come to activities we could run in the church building. Let's start with the youngest and work upwards. You are probably expecting me to begin with Mums and Toddlers, but actually we're going to start with Bumps and Babes. This is a meeting for expectant mothers, some of whom would welcome friendship and advice as they prepare for what will be a life-changing event. Next is Toddlers. I call it that because these days it may not be simply mums who will attend with their little ones. It could be grandparents, childminders or even dads. Perhaps some imagination is required to come up with a catchy alternative name. The room or rooms you use for these events, as indeed for all invitational events, should be warm and bright and therefore welcoming. There should be plenty to entertain the children and nice refreshments for the adults. These meetings are a good opportunity to build relationships with unbelievers and they can also be a launching pad to a Christianity Explored course or a one-to-one Bible study. In our own church we have seen a number of mums come to Sunday services from time to time, especially the carol service just before Christmas.

Children's and young people's work is so important, especially as we live at a time when there is a desperate level of ignorance concerning the Lord Jesus and the gospel. A couple of examples should bring this home. A boy once wrote a

THERE IS STILL MUCH TO DO!

letter to a church in Llandudno where he had recently visited a Bible exhibition they were hosting. His name was Michael, and after expressing his appreciation he wrote, 'I never knew before that Jesus was alive from the dead.' We can take that piece of information so much for granted. Again, in the city of Lincoln one day, an evangelist was preaching in the busy pedestrianized shopping centre when a boy suddenly stopped and asked him, 'Hey, mister, why are you swearing?' The boy had heard the preacher mention Jesus, and in his young mind 'Jesus' was just a swear word. It may seem hard to believe that we have reached this point, but the truth is that we have.

The urgency of seeking ways to share the gospel with boys and girls cannot be overestimated. If you have a Sunday school and/or a children's club, do keep going, even if there aren't many children coming along or if there doesn't seem to be much fruit. We should always keep at the front of our minds that sowing the seed is our work and bringing in the harvest is the Lord's. These meetings should be fun, with age-appropriate activities and games and, it goes without saying, refreshments. There are lots of helpful websites where you can find good ideas for teaching, games and activities.

It is very important these days to ensure that all church helpers have had the relevant police checks carried out. We need to be above reproach as far as the world is concerned, as we never know when an accusation may be made against one of the team. Most churches will have what are called 'safeguarding policies', and these help us all to maintain the highest of standards in our dealings with children, and with vulnerable adults as well.

Something that shouldn't need saying, but perhaps does,

THERE IS STILL MUCH TO DO!

is that the leaders and helpers need to be committed to the meetings every week, if at all possible. The children will notice if you are not there, and consistency will mean a lot to some, as it is a way of showing an interest in them. We sometimes bemoan the fact that the children don't come every week, but we have no right to do that if we are not always there ourselves.

Teenagers' work is very important, not least because it will provide something to feed the children at the top end of the children's work into. Holding on to teenagers can be very challenging, as there are so many other things competing for their time and attention. The programme therefore needs to be as exciting as possible, peppered with trips out to places like bowling alleys and ice rinks. Lots of good material is available to provide help with the epilogues, which are so important. It can help to make the talks visual and even interactive. It can be profitable to hand all the young people a Bible so they can actually look up verses for themselves during the talk. If it is possible to arrange for the young people to attend weekend or even week-long camps, these can be a great blessing to them. To be away from home in a Christian environment can speak volumes to those from non-Christian homes, in addition, of course, to the Bible teaching they will receive.

Many churches put on special events for children, such as Bible exhibitions. OAM has three of these: 'Journey through the Old Testament', 'The Life of Christ' and 'The Amazing Acts'. It also has one on the story of *Pilgrim's Progress*. Churches book to have one of these, usually for a week's duration. Many find it beneficial to have these on an annual basis and either invite local schools to come in and see them, or, as an alternative, take them into the schools. Each exhibition has light-weight Velcro boards with pictures on. A guide will take a class at a time around the boards, and every so often they will stop to meet one of the characters, such as Abraham, Daniel or Mary. Members of the church dress up in appropriate costumes and then tell their story in the first person. At the end, the children do a quiz and then have refreshments. Around five hundred children will come into a church in the course of a week, so it really is a tremendous opportunity. Often, someone from the church will go into the schools the following week with prizes, and this provides an opening to take regular assemblies.

Assemblies are themselves great opportunities. If your church already has a contact with a local school, that person may be able to arrange for you to meet the headteacher and enquire about the possibilities. If not, perhaps one of the church elders could write to or phone the school for the same purpose. Sometimes schools are a little wary of people or groups they are not familiar with, so if an invitation is given to lead an assembly, it is probably best to tread gently by gradually introducing more in the way of gospel application as you go back for future visits. Some pastors and evangelists have an open door into their local schools, taking not only regular assemblies, but also RE lessons. At two local schools where I take assemblies I am invited each year to be interviewed by their year classes about what a Christian is. It is great to be plied with questions for forty-five minutes about all sorts of things. These openings can provide opportunities to advertise events at the church, such as holiday Bible clubs.

THERE IS STILL MUCH TO DO!

Many churches run holiday clubs on an annual basis for several days at a stretch. These can be a very good means of helping to boost the regular children's work that goes on. Activities such as games, crafts, singing, quizzes and stories are the norm. A good team of helpers is needed to run a holiday club, as they are hard work, but at the same time they are very rewarding. Again, you can find plenty of materials online to provide inspiration for themes and activities. Some churches, particularly those in Northern Ireland, run what are known as 'five-day clubs'. These are very similar to holiday Bible clubs, except that they take place out of doors, usually in local parks or on patches of grass at the end of a street. A gazebo is put up as a focal point with a banner advertising the church, and local children are invited to attend. They have the usual mix of singing, quizzes and a Bible story.

Moving on to other outreach events: those with food can often be an attraction. We might say that the motives of those who come are not very pure, but my response to that is, 'So what!' Many people have been converted at meetings they didn't really want to attend or maybe attended 'by accident'. An associate evangelist with OAM was once preaching on the streets of Bristol. It began to pour with rain and it seemed that it had been a waste of time. The preacher curtailed his message and ran, along with his two co-workers, to the car that was parked nearby. After a few minutes there was a knock on the car window. A very excited man was standing there. He explained that he was a mechanic and had been lying under a car within earshot of the preaching, and he had trusted the Lord through what he had just heard. He wanted to share the good news with the preacher, who was stunned but overjoyed. Years later, the same preacher attended a service in Bristol and was delighted to see the mechanic again, fervently going on with the Lord. The point is that God is sovereign in salvation, and so the thing we should always be working towards is people coming under the sound of the gospel. That includes, of course, the need to be building up relationships with them.

Coffee mornings can be good opportunities to invite people to, especially in town centre churches. It can help to have a small team outside the church with simple invitations to invite people inside. This can be particularly useful on a rainy day. Coffee mornings are social events that are a positive means of meeting people and getting to know them. Have Bible verses on the walls and literature available for people to take with them.

Lunches or suppers can be very profitable ventures, both for older folk and for other age groups. These can be good to mark special occasions, such as harvest, or maybe to celebrate national events such as the Queen's birthday or some other major anniversary. Some churches in multi-ethnic areas put on international evenings, where there will be a diverse range of food and attire. Other ideas include fondue evenings, or, in the summertime, barbecues. Do ensure that the food is good: once again, as it is at home, so it should be at church! Always try to have a gospel epilogue or at least a testimony at these events. If you place the testimony after the sweet and before the coffee, it will serve two useful purposes: people will not leave before the message, and it will mean that during the coffee there may well be the chance to discuss what has been said. Do have literature available and possibly invitations to church services.

Afternoon or evening meetings can be good for senior citizens. Meetings for men and ladies are more common now than they used to be. Many older people have very few reasons to leave their homes, so a 'Friends and Neighbours' type group can give people a real lift. They are a good means of Christian fellowship, but also of sharing the gospel.

Sometimes it can be effective to host a meeting at a neutral venue. This is being mindful of those who may view the church threshold as a chasm that they are not ready to cross, whereas a meeting in a town or village hall would seem far less daunting. A creation meeting could be good. There are a variety of subjects under this orbit that could be attractive to either people we know or 'the man in the street', such as 'Is God past His sell-by date?' or 'Hasn't evolution disproved God and the Bible?' Another very topical issue is the subject of suffering. Invite a guest speaker who is well qualified to handle such a subject and who is willing to answer questions afterwards. Public meetings like this could be advertised in local secondary schools and the local paper, as well as among our regular contacts.

Another means of reaching the locals is by engaging in door-to-door work. There's no point making any bones about the fact that this is far from being an easy form of gospel outreach. But then again, overseeing a hall full of lively children isn't exactly an easy prospect to most of us either. Going on the doors is hard because by doing it we are going onto other people's territory and we are also interrupting their day. The exciting thing is that, at times, we will meet those who are very happy for their day to be interrupted. Many people in those houses are hurting and have questions to which they want answers. Others are lonely and will just appreciate a conversation.

The work can also be hard if you are in an area where the Jehovah's Witnesses or Mormons are very active. That was the case where I lived in Loughborough many years ago, such that many front doors had a card saying, 'No JWs!' Our small team regularly felt compelled, when people opened their doors, to assure them that we were not JWs. That backfired on me on one occasion, though. I said to a lady, 'Don't worry, madam, we aren't JWs.' 'Well I am!' she indignantly replied.

Another reason why we can find this particular work hard is because at each door we knock on, we have no idea what will face us on the other side. Will there be a ferocious dog that just loves Christian meat? On a serious note, it is overwhelmingly the case that dog owners keep their animals back when they go to the door, so this is something we need not be overly concerned about. Mind you, the immediate response of the home owner may be just as hostile as an aggressive dog, but we are there to represent the Lord Jesus Christ, and during what may be only a fleeting conversation we can at least offer a gospel leaflet.

Some churches will simply deliver leaflets around their locality. This doesn't usually yield much response, but of course we shouldn't in any way despise it, as it is something God can and has used. It is better, though, to visit the homes with the aim of knocking on the doors and speaking to people.

It is wise to go around the doors in pairs. The Lord sending out the disciples two by two (Mark 6:7) was no accident. He knew that His servants would need both encouragement and accountability in their work for Him. It is important from the start to introduce who you are and give the name of your church. That will differentiate you from a door-to-door salesman, a cult member or someone collecting for charity. Most people will be more at ease if they know you haven't come to persuade them to part with any money. If the door stays open, you could perhaps ask something like, 'Have you ever given any thought to Jesus Christ and why He came into the world?' Mentioning the Lord Jesus usually provokes some kind of reaction, favourable or otherwise. A question like that can well lead to a conversation. Take it in turns to speak to people, so that the load is shared; or if one of you is less experienced or even out for the first time, just listen and chip in only as and when you feel able to do so.

You will soon identify whether a person is willing to have a conversation or not. Even if someone clearly doesn't want to engage, still offer that person some literature, as most people are likely to receive it, and at least they have met a friendly face from the local church. Make sure you have at the ready gospel leaflets and something giving the details of your church. It can be useful to take around invitations to any special events you are having at the church. At the very least, you are showing a willingness to be a part of the local community.

Always be friendly and courteous, irrespective of how people may be towards you. Try to take a varied selection of leaflets and booklets with you, and at the end of a conversation always try to leave something to help people to think through further what has been discussed. Also—

THERE IS STILL MUCH TO DO!

and it may sound very obvious—do make sure you are familiar with the contents of anything you offer, in case you are asked what it contains. You might also like to take a few CDs or even DVDs. It is surprising how many people don't read, won't read or can't read, so it is good if you have an alternative for them.

Other possibilities that can take us out of our buildings include old people's homes. Often, they will warmly welcome church groups to come and take a monthly Sunday afternoon service. As well as these being good opportunities to share the gospel with those who are in their latter years, they are a good training ground for would-be preachers. I spoke in public for the very first time at a home in Wendover in Buckinghamshire in the summer of 1986. I remember speaking on the parable of the Pharisee and the tax collector, and my talk lasted a grand total of two and a half minutes. It might be just a bit longer than that now!

If a church is in the vicinity of a prison, that too could be a place for a gospel witness. It can take a long time for an application to be processed so that you can visit, but it is usually well worth it. A retired pastor in Manchester, for example, has been into his local prison every Monday evening for many years. Bible studies have been held with inmates who volunteer to attend. The turnover of prisoners is quite high, but this has meant that many men have come into contact with an evangelical Christian who has been sharing the gospel. An OAM evangelist who for a number of years has taken meetings in a prison in Oxfordshire often comments that you are one step ahead in your presentation in a prison, because the men there already know that they are sinners. They don't usually need convincing of that fact, which is so different from most other people.

I am conscious that many churches would love to be involved in a great deal more outreach, but their problem is a lack of workers. This can be both frustrating and discouraging. Obviously it is something to make a matter for prayer, and it is worth saying that it is not something to feel guilty about. Perhaps at a church members' meeting you could discuss very frankly what manpower you do have and how that could be used to maximum effect for the Lord. Another thing you could consider is asking another local church if a joint venture could be attempted. That might well be a means of mutual encouragement.

Finally, as we're thinking about reaching the locals, we need to say something about personal contacts. After all, if we don't have these, we won't have anyone to invite to our church-based meetings. The phrase that we often hear today is 'friendship evangelism', and we should certainly all be seeking to foster friendships with unbelieving people—whether that is with relatives, work colleagues or people we have got to know in a variety of other contexts. The question is, do we see these individuals who cross our paths as those with whom we can share the gospel?

Often just inviting someone for a coffee is a good way to get to know that person. Hopefully, as we give others the opportunity to talk about themselves, they will give us the opportunity to talk about ourselves, and that should afford an opening to begin to share our testimony of what the Lord has done for us. As time goes on we can be praying for openings to share more, and then, when it seems right, to invite them

THERE IS STILL MUCH TO DO!

to a gospel meeting. I would say that, in the context of getting to know our neighbours, asking them too soon to come to a meeting at church could scare them off. I've learnt this the hard way. It is better to establish the relationship first. In the next couple of chapters we are going to look more closely at personal conversations.

THERE IS STILL MUCH TO DO!

8 Getting the knowledge, part 1

… always being prepared to make a defence to anyone who asks you … (1 Peter 3:15)

Anyone who wants to become the driver of a black taxi cab in London first has to 'get the knowledge', as it is called. This means that that person has to learn the location of every street and landmark in the city and then pass a stringent exam at the end. It can take years. You'll be glad to know that there is no exam at the end of this book, but having said that, we do need to get the knowledge in a number of areas if we are going to be prepared to share with others the message of the gospel.

I will try to make what I say here relevant to all aspects of personal work, whether it's street work, door-to-door work or 'friendship evangelism'. The passage from which the verse at the head of this chapter comes, 1 Peter 3:13–17, is very helpful in this area. So, with the thought in our minds of getting the knowledge so that we are ready for the task of personal evangelism, let's highlight a number of things that it would be helpful for us to know:

1. KNOW YOUR PRIVILEGE

If we are believers in the Lord Jesus, we are not only servants of God, but we are also His ambassadors. To be an ambassador in any context is to hold a very honoured position. We've been given the honour of going to another country and representing our King and His country. This earth is not our country; our home is heaven; we are citizens there (Phil. 3:20). As Christians we are the representatives of the Lord Jesus here on earth. We stand in for Him. What greater privilege could we ever have than this, even if we come across opposition, rejection and persecution! However hard it may be to talk to others about the Lord, never forget what a privilege it is to be able to talk about the divine Saviour of sinners. Specifically, according to verse 15 of our passage, we are to share 'the hope that is in [us]'. That hope is a living hope in a living Saviour!

We know we are living in a hope-less world, one that is surrounded by so many hope-less people, and whether they realize it or not, we have what they need: we have the gospel. And we have the honour of being able to share that gospel of hope. Many of us would have to confess that there have been times when we've been embarrassed to speak for Him, or we couldn't find the right words to say anything, or maybe we just couldn't even be bothered to do so. We need to remember what He was willing to do for us. He died for us, so can't we at least live for Him? And living for Him includes speaking for Him as opportunities arise. This is our great, great privilege!

2. KNOW YOUR RESPONSIBILITY

Someone once said that 'A saved man is an ungrateful creature if he has nothing to say about what the Lord has done for him'. We know that the Lord has done so much for us, and not only that, we also know that the world needs to hear the gospel. It constantly hears so much that is trivial at best and downright evil at worst. What people need to hear more than anything else is the gospel! Charles Spurgeon once said, 'Soul winning is the chief business of the Christian minister, indeed, it should be the main pursuit of every true believer.' Is that true of our church leader or leaders, and is it true of us all?

J. C. Ryle once said something very succinct but very challenging: 'God has no dumb children.' All of us can speak for Him. All of us should speak for Him. All of us must speak for Him. Perhaps we need to pray a lot about this matter. Maybe you feel you're not able and at times not willing. We can pray that the Lord would help us to be both. Amy Carmichael (1867–1951), the famous missionary to India, once wrote a parable called 'Thy Brother's Blood Crieth' that describes people rushing headlong over a ravine into eternity. There were sentries along the edge of the ravine who were there to warn the people, but there were not enough of them, so there were large gaps between them. While this was going on there were those who just sat making daisy chains, unmoved by the plight of the lost. You can find the full text online; it is very striking and very moving. It finishes with this plea: 'God arouse us! Shame us out of our callousness! Shame us out of our sin!' We can so easily be indifferent to the lost, but we can thank the Lord that the person who told *us* about Jesus was not indifferent, and that should be a great challenge.

3. KNOW YOUR PRIORITY

We have already said that the definition of 'evangelism' is 'sharing the good news', telling others about the Christian message, about the Lord Jesus and, specifically, pointing them to the Lord's death and resurrection. That is the primary issue we should want to get to in any conversation and then focus on. It's often been said, but it's worth repeating, 'Keep the main thing the main thing!' At times the people we're speaking to will focus on secondary issues, and we need to be aware of that and, when it happens, try to get back to the primary things again as quickly as possible. Some will ask questions, such as, 'Why are there so many church denominations?' or 'Where do animals go when they die?' Whatever people may bring up, we need to get them back to the gospel, stay with the gospel and leave them with the gospel. Secondary issues can be a big distraction in evangelism, and in more ways than one. We may meet believers when we are out seeking to evangelize, and we can start to discuss our differences. We might begin to want to win them to our position. That's all very well, but it's not evangelism, and we have allowed ourselves to be diverted from it. If you are that keen, and if that believer needs spiritual help and guidance, arrange to meet up for coffee to discuss such things if you want to, but don't waste time on the doors or on the street talking with believers. And do remember this, too: sheep-stealing is not evangelism.

I was with a friend preaching in Northampton some years ago on a rather cold and miserable day when a young man interrupted me with the question, 'Have you got the gifts?' I explained that we were there to preach the message of salvation to the lost and our focus was on pointing people to the Lord Jesus. He replied, 'That's good, but have you got the gifts?' I have to admit that I became quite annoyed at this point and I rebuked him for being taken up with something that was secondary. I repeated the fact that we were there to

THERE IS STILL MUCH TO DO!

reach the lost. He eventually went away, but it was with a heavy heart that I had that interaction with him.

4. KNOW YOUR BIBLE

There are two main reasons why we need to know our Bibles: for ourselves and for others. Firstly, we ourselves need the equipping that can only come from God's Word. For example, we need courage, something that many of us know we don't have naturally. Even the great apostle Paul asked for prayer for this in Ephesians 6:19–20: 'and [pray] also for me, that words may be given to me in opening my mouth boldly to proclaim the mystery of the gospel ... that I may declare it boldly, as I ought to speak'. If he needed to ask for it, we surely need to as well!

We can be afraid of different things. For example, we can be afraid of how people will react to being asked about the gospel. On my very first beach mission in Ilfracombe, while we were on the seafront one evening, I was standing at the edge of the open-air meeting offering tracts to passers-by. I noticed a very big-looking man coming down the promenade. He seemed to have muscles on muscles. I began to wonder if I had the courage to offer him a leaflet as he approached, and I prayed for the courage to do so. How surprised I was at his reply to my offer: 'Oh yes, please, I'd really like to read one of those.' I learnt a valuable lesson that day; and since then, whenever giving out tracts, I have made a point of always offering them to the biggest and nastiest-looking people who come along, because they usually do accept!

Remember how scared Jeremiah was at the start of his ministry: 'Ah, Lord God! Behold, I do not know how to speak, for I am only a youth' (Jer. 1:6). Do you remember what the Lord said to reassure Him? 'Do not say, "I am only a youth" … Do not be afraid of them, for I am with you to deliver you, declares the LORD' (vv. 7–8). However frightening people may look to us, we should not let that put us off.

An aggressive young man called Jake came up to listen to an OAM evangelist in Brighton. The Mission used to have a week of outreach in Eastbourne, but we always spent one day in Brighton. The chap had long hair and a number of piercings. Tattooed down one leg was the word 'rebel'. On the surface, who could be less likely to be interested in the gospel than him? However, looks can be deceptive, as someone once rightly said. Jake was actually very open to thinking about the claims of the Lord Jesus. He stayed and had a long conversation with the preacher, and went away at the end expressing deep appreciation for the time spent with him. It can be a big mistake to judge by outward appearance.

Several years ago a small team of us were invited to Albania to introduce a number of churches to open-air evangelism. I spent four days in the capital, Tirana. We did a seminar in the church on the Saturday and then on the Sunday afternoon we did an open-air right in the centre of the city. It was an encouraging time as a number of people stopped to listen. We, of course, preached through interpreters, as our Albanian was limited to about ten words. Among the team from the church who came out with us was a twelve-year-old girl called Lydia, who I noticed was fearlessly approaching people and giving them literature. Afterwards I went to commend her for being so brave, but she replied, 'I just want to tell everyone about

Jesus.' What a delight it was to hear that from one so young, and what a challenge she should be to all of us as well!

Sometimes we can be afraid of what people might say. Once on a church holiday we had a men's Bible study during which we discussed witnessing. The overwhelming reason given for holding back was the fear of messing it up and not knowing how to answer people. After all, the people we talk to may be dismissive or may ask very hard questions. Actually, there are certain questions that come up time and again, which we'll come back to later. In Ezekiel 2:6–7 the Lord said to the fearful prophet, 'And you, son of man, be not afraid of them, nor be afraid of their words ... you shall speak my words to them.' We are in good company if we admit that we need more courage. So we need to know the Scriptures that tell us that courage is available when we seek the Lord, and we need to realize that a lack of courage is not a legitimate excuse for staying silent. Puritan Thomas Watson (1620–1686), who was the master of the spiritual one-liner, once asked, 'Does Christ appear for us in heaven, and are we afraid to appear for Him on earth?'

As well as courage, a second thing Scripture gives us is confidence. We must not apologize for what we believe! We must speak with humility, but we should at the same time speak with authority. In Titus 2:15 Paul encourages his friend, 'Declare these things [gospel things]; exhort and rebuke with all authority. Let no one disregard you.' These are instructions we need to follow when serving the Lord. Sometimes, when we talk with people we know about what we did at the weekend, 'church' may come up. That's good, but we need to get beyond that. Some people can be very

THERE IS STILL MUCH TO DO!

friendly asking about church—they may be churchgoers themselves—but it is when we move from church to Christ that we find out whether we can proceed further or not. A person can change dramatically when we begin to talk about Jesus. His name nearly always has an effect for good or ill. Some people are often quite happy to talk about the sin in the world, but they are far less keen to face the sin in their own hearts. The state of the country, or of the world, can be a deflecting tactic that some will use with us. We need to have the confidence to bring them back to where they stand with the Lord.

Another reason why we need to know the Bible is because it declares itself to be our weapon. Hebrews 4:12 says, 'For the word of God is living and active, sharper than any two-edged sword.' We don't have any other weapons, but we do have the Word! I always have my small Bible with me in the open air. It was once stolen from my display board in Leicester. I prayed that it might be returned, and a few minutes later two cheeky teenage boys appeared and tried to sell me my own Bible. I eventually managed to persuade them to give it back.

You never know what opportunity there may be to refer to the Scriptures or to quote from them. In conversation it's good to show verses to people so they can see that our views are found in the Bible and that we haven't made them up. Even better is to get people to read the verses for themselves. This is especially good to do with Muslims. Even though they believe that the Bible has been changed, they will usually still show respect for the copy you hold in your hand.

This brings us to the second main reason why we need to know our Bibles, and that is for others. You don't have to

THERE IS STILL MUCH TO DO!

be a Bible expert to witness for the Lord, but the better we know it, the better we will be able to share it with others. We ought to be lifelong students of the Word, but the following are key gospel verses that perhaps we could learn by heart: John 3:16; Romans 3:23; 5:7–8; 6:23; Ephesians 2:8–9; and 1 Timothy 1:15. Of course there are many others, but these are a good place to start. But a word to the wise at this point: witnessing is not just stringing texts together. We must be reasoned in our approach, as 1 Peter 3:15 encourages us: 'always being prepared to make a defence to anyone who asks you for a reason for the hope that is in you'. We are to present a reasonable message. When Paul stood before Governor Festus, he was accused of being mad. Paul responded, 'I am not out of my mind, most excellent Festus, but I am speaking true and rational words' (Acts 26:25). If we had to summarize our message in three words that make sense and flow from one to the other, those words would be *God*, *sin* and *salvation*. They are the essence of our message.

5. KNOW YOUR OPPORTUNITIES

First Peter 3:15 urges us to 'always [be] prepared'. The first time I worked on a beach mission team in Tenby, on the first evening, the leader announced that we all had to join the RFA squad. We were quickly enlightened as to what that stood for: 'Ready For Anything'! Being part of that squad kept us on our toes throughout the week. We all need to be on our gospel toes every week. After all, we never know when an opportunity may arise.

We may feel that we are not gifted in doing personal evangelism. It may surprise you, but even the great missionary

THERE IS STILL MUCH TO DO!

William Carey (1761–1834) felt like that. In a letter to Andrew Fuller back in England he wrote, 'I have not resolution enough to reprove sin, to introduce serious and evangelistic conversation in carnal company, especially among the great to whom I sometimes have access. I sometimes labour with myself long, and at last cannot prevail sufficiently to break silence.' If we feel similarly to Carey, perhaps a few tips on starting conversations would be helpful.

By the way, this is one of the great advantages of open-air work. We put up a board and a preacher stands by it, using it for his presentation. We have a team standing listening. This encourages others to stop and listen. If someone stops, we let him or her listen, and only approach that person as he or she is moving away from the meeting. We can then ask something like this: 'I noticed you were listening to my friend preaching. Could I ask you if you have ever thought about these things before?' This will often lead straight into a conversation. You haven't got to try to bring the conversation round to spiritual things because you're on topic straight away. That person's mind is already on the gospel.

But how can we get started in conversation? Most of us manage fine in general conversation. We all know we can fall back on the weather when we meet someone. (It must be terrible living in Spain: whatever do they have to talk about when it's sunny every day?) But we need to try to move from ordinary to spiritual issues. For example, if you were standing at a bus stop and someone said, 'What a beautiful day!' you could simply reply, 'Yes, God is very kind to us in giving us a day like this.' Making that very simple statement is like throwing out your fishing net. You wait to see what will happen. Will you 'get a bite', as fishermen say? You will find out soon enough whether things are going to develop from there.

There are some people we see once and others that we see from time to time, and this may give us the chance slowly to build up a rapport with them. Three times a year a window cleaner comes to our house. His name is Michael. He tends to be quite chatty, and when we first met he told me about his son, who was suffering from cancer. Every time since I have asked him about his son, and Michael has always appreciated the interest shown. He once asked me what I do for a living, and this led very naturally into a spiritual conversation. Michael is a cynical Roman Catholic, with no time for organized religion, which he feels is full of hypocrisy. He is happy to talk about that, and sometimes he'll make a comment that lends itself nicely to bringing in the gospel. He once stated, 'The church lays a guilt trip on people.' To which I replied, 'Of course—we're all guilty before God, aren't we? And that's why He sent His Son to die on the cross.' Michael can't ever talk for long, but he has taken several pieces of literature over the years.

If you get the opportunity, it is good to identify yourself as a Christian, as this can help to turn a conversation to spiritual things. Usually, when you tell someone that you are a Christian, you get some kind of reaction. It is surprising how many people have a Christian connection of their own. It's becoming less the case, but often people will tell you if they have a relative or friend who's a Christian, or, in the case of older people, if they once went to Sunday school. Then you will have a natural link to take the conversation further.

THERE IS STILL MUCH TO DO!

Sometimes, though, it is hard even to find the right moment to tell someone you are a Christian. Back in 1990 I started work as a postman. I found it hard to start a conversation in the sorting office, so much so that I decided to wear a small fish on my jumper. I was glad I did as several conversations developed through that. I was surprised how many people knew it meant I was a Christian. Mind you, it meant I always had to be prepared, and that was quite a challenge, especially very early in the morning. I well remember a chap called Nigel, who asked me one morning at 5 a.m., 'How did you get into religion, then?'

There may be other things you could try. In your room if you are at university or on your desk if you are in a place of work you could put a Bible in a visible place, or put up a calendar showing a Bible text. Another idea is to put a sticker on your car with a Bible verse—but only do that if you intend to keep to the speed limit at all times, otherwise it will mar your testimony. Following these little suggestions almost forces you to have to be ready for the next opportunity that comes along. For the majority of the time, especially in the workplace, at school or in college, there won't be time to start conversations. You have to be wise anyway, because you don't want to be witnessing when actually you should be working. Opportunities may come when others make a comment or ask you a direct question. That can be the best time—when someone else has initiated the conversation.

It is good to have Christian leaflets with you which may be appropriate to offer to someone. Keep them in a pocket or bag, as you never know when you might be somewhere where an opportunity presents itself. These can be a good way into

THERE IS STILL MUCH TO DO!

a conversation as well. We find this very much the case when in the open air. Sometimes people going by will ask what we're giving away. OAM produces many leaflets, and they all have questions on the cover; for example, 'Are you good enough to get to heaven?' 'Is there life after death?' 'What do you think about the cross?' 'Will you consider Jesus?' 'Where will you spend eternity?' 'Will you think about your future?' 'Is the Bible true?' We also have a booklet called *Why All the Suffering?* That is the number one question we are asked on the streets. It comes up time and again on the doors as well. Sometimes people are impressed by the booklet just because they are surprised that Christians have an answer to that question. At some open-airs we have a literature table. It can be amazing how people will be drawn to come and have a look. Again, this can be a great means to start spiritual conversations. You can often have tables at fairs, fetes, carnivals, agricultural shows, as well as in your local high street. Preaching may not always be possible, especially if there is no pedestrianized precinct, but a table may work well. One crucial thing is that you don't cause an obstruction, as this is likely to bring the local authorities down on you.

It is good to have tracts and other literature in your home that can be passed on to those who knock on your door. I have a little pile sitting ready and waiting on top of the electric meter. It's nothing to hand a delivery driver a gospel leaflet. A couple of years ago, a man came to read the meter. I offered him a tract, upon which he said he was a Muslim from Turkey. Three months later he called again, so I asked him if he had read the tract. He stayed to talk and accepted a John's Gospel. I wondered afterwards whether an Anglo-

THERE IS STILL MUCH TO DO!

Saxon meter reader would have been so happy to talk about spiritual things. It's good for Muslims to meet real Christians, as they tend to think everyone in the West is a Christian, and therefore how worldly Christians are. So it is good for them to meet those who are genuine followers of *Isa al-Masih*, Jesus the Messiah.

Sometimes the Lord will bring about new gospel opportunities for us, for which we again need to be prepared. A friend of mine was due to go into hospital for a minor procedure for two days. He is one who is always on the lookout for a chance to witness. After he came home he told me with great excitement, 'I prayed for two people to speak to about the Lord, but He gave me nine!' He was prepared. In the Lord's providence we might be directed to meet all kinds of people. We need to have it in mind that perhaps a particular providence was ordered just so we could say a word for the Saviour to a certain person. I once broke down on the M1. It seemed such a pain at the time. However, it gave me a half-hour opportunity to speak with the pick-up truck driver who took me home. He happily received a John's Gospel when he dropped me off.

Sometimes the Lord may lead us to what will be only a very brief opportunity. The first time I took my two oldest children to watch an Aston Villa match (I'm a third-generation Villa fan!), the man sitting behind us started swearing at the referee. Both another parent nearby and I asked him to stop. It was quite amusing that for the rest of the match we could hear him growling whenever the referee made a controversial decision. He was doing that instead of swearing. At the end of the match, I felt I ought to thank him for not swearing. I asked him his name and he said it was Chris. He was just about to go off in a different direction, so I said to him, 'Chris, if you trusted in Jesus as your Saviour, you wouldn't ever want to use bad language again.' With that we parted company. I will probably never see him again, but who knows what that one sentence might do in his life.

Sometimes out of nowhere we can feel compelled to do something, though it may seem a very small thing. A few months ago, while making a cup of tea in our kitchen, I noticed two Mormons waiting for the bus opposite our house. They both had suitcases with them, so I guessed they were about to return to the USA after doing their year over here as missionaries. Knowing that the bus would come at any minute, I rushed over the road and said, 'This may sound strange, but when you get the chance, take out your Bible and read Hebrews 1:1.' They politely thanked me and I went back to making my cup of tea. I've no idea what good, if any, that did them. Only the Lord knows. And that is often the way with our witnessing. We cast our bread upon the waters and we have to leave to the Lord what will become of it.

Finally, the Lord may lead us to what can be very unexpected opportunities. We may be in a place where the last thing we expect is a chance to witness for the Lord. One Saturday evening I was about to go out jogging. It was around 7.30 p.m. However, my wife Ruth asked me to bath the children, so I didn't get out until 8 p.m. I had run about three miles and was heading into Dunstable town centre. Up ahead were three young men who seemed to be larking around. I decided to avoid them, so I crossed the road. However, almost straight away, they too decided to cross over. This meant I had to jog through them.

To my great surprise, one of them started to jog alongside me. We started chatting and I discovered that his name was Craig. He invited me to the party he and his friends were heading to, assuring me that there would be plenty of booze. When I said, 'Thanks, but I don't drink', he asked if I was religious. This led to a lovely gospel opportunity. Eventually we reached the road where he was turning off for his party. I stopped and we shook hands, and I urged him to think about what we had talked about. He thanked me, turned and went. I floated, rather than jogged, the final mile home! I was so thrilled by this providence, which had so clearly been orchestrated by the Lord. How important it is that we are prepared to speak, and what joy it gives us when we have done so!

THERE IS STILL MUCH TO DO!

9 Getting the knowledge, part 2

… and you will be my witnesses. (Acts 1:8)

We're still thinking about the knowledge we need to get in order to be prepared to witness for the Lord. The next point is this:

6. KNOW YOUR GEOGRAPHY

Open-airs in town centres have the advantage of taking place in neutral territory. The high-street witness allows us to identify those who have a certain level of interest. This is particularly so if they come over to listen to the preaching or engage in conversation. We might see a sea of faces and wonder which of them might be interested in the gospel, but an open-air witness will help us to find out those who would like to know more.

There are certain groups of people for whom church would be a complete no-no. Take Muslims, for example. Very few would ever go to a church service; however, they are usually very happy to stand in the street and talk about religious things. A neutral venue gives them the liberty they might not feel in another context. OAM evangelists speak to hundreds of Muslims during the course of a year; how thrilling it is when they are prepared to accept a copy of John's Gospel!

There are others for whom a shopping precinct is a good place to talk as well. I remember meeting a young Hindu woman named Kiren in Derby. She had loads of questions.

THERE IS STILL MUCH TO DO!

When I suggested a local church she could attend, she made it clear that there was no way her father would allow her to go. Thankfully, she knew of someone at college who was a Christian and she could go and talk to him. Sometimes Roman Catholics are unwilling to enter a 'Protestant' church, but again, they are very happy to talk on the streets.

Thinking about geography, here's a question: is anywhere out of bounds for the believer who wants to witness to others about the Lord? We should be willing to go where people are—perhaps willing to go even to the roughest of housing estates or outside the worst of nightclubs. If you're going to witness outside a nightclub, though, it's probably best to go earlier in the evening, before people have had too much to drink. But what about inside a nightclub: should we venture in there too? I feel that some places are both dangerous for us and potentially damaging to our witness. Nightclubs are full of temptation, no matter who we are. We are all weak, and these are places of excess of every kind. Did you notice that the first part of 1 Peter 3:15 says, 'But in your hearts honour Christ the Lord as holy'? How can we do that if we're putting ourselves in harm's way? Also, won't we risk giving the impression that, actually, we're no different from anyone else if we're happy to be in such an environment?

I feel the same way about pubs, although I know some Christians will disagree. Yes, you can say that you'll only have soft drinks, but you are identifying yourself with what goes on there, and supposing someone sees you who doesn't know what you're drinking? What message does that send out? The unbeliever thinks, 'Christians are no different from me!', while a younger Christian perhaps thinks, 'It's all right for me to drink alcohol because he is.' Whatever your view on these things, make sure you have thought it through; don't just go to a place because others are going there.

I once heard of a Methodist church in Northern Ireland where, on one occasion before the evening service, a lady offered a man who looked unwell some alcohol that she had in her car. The man accepted it. The next day he went and bought his own, and before long he was hooked. Tragically, he soon became an alcoholic. We never know what effect our actions can have, so we must be very careful indeed.

7. KNOW YOUR TESTIMONY

To be a witness, we must have seen something. The Lord Jesus has called us to be witnesses for Him. You may be asked about this. What do you believe, and why do you believe it? You might find it helpful to write your story down. It can be useful to have an ordered account of how you came to know the Lord. A helpful summary could be based on these three questions: (a) What were you? (b) What happened to change you? (c) What are you now? People will often be interested in your answers to these questions. Sometimes at open-airs we have people sharing their testimonies. Often this is done as a question and answer session. In some church services space will be given for testimonies, which can be very profitable.

Do remember, though, that ultimately our testimony is an opportunity not to glory in our former sins or just talk about ourselves, but to honour our Saviour and talk about Him. A lovely example of that is a seven-year-old girl who trusted the Lord on a beach mission in Woolacombe in North Devon. She wrote to the evangelist leading the team to express her appreciation and simply said, 'I feel new on the inside.' Even a young girl can have a testimony of the Lord's dealings with her.

8. KNOW THE USEFULNESS OF YOUR TESTIMONY

Paul's example to us should be instructive. He shared his testimony on a number of occasions, two of which are recorded in the book of Acts (chs. 22 and 26). Paul knew that his story of God's work of grace in his heart could impact others for the Lord, and ours can do so too. John MacGregor, the OAM founder, once said, 'This is the answer of Christianity to every form of doctrine opposed to the gospel—see what it has done!' Sometimes in our witness people will want to argue with us. They may put forward their views but not listen to our responses. In such cases it's good just to tell them what God has done for you.

Whatever others may think of it, your experience is your experience. In Reading once, a man named Donald came to argue with the team of preachers who were in the town centre. He was a chemist and expressed very strident views on evolution and the Big Bang. One of the team then asked Donald if he would listen while he shared what God had done in his life. Donald agreed to do so. When he had heard the testimony, Donald was ready to admit, 'I can't argue with that!' and he went on his way in a subdued frame of mind. We found out later that Donald had a Christian friend at work, which was really encouraging.

9. KNOW YOUR CULTURE

There are three things to say on this subject. The first is the

THERE IS STILL MUCH TO DO!

importance of appropriate behaviour. The best practice when doing open-airs is for men to speak to men and ladies to ladies. If a conversation takes place in a home or church and a man is talking to a lady, make sure it is done so that others can see. We must be above reproach in our service for the Lord. We must also behave in a way that will avoid offence.

When in Albania a few years ago, we went to do some evangelism with a church in the city of Fier. My interpreter was the wife of a local pastor. We were out in a park where a large number of men gathered to read their newspapers and to play chess most evenings. I got into conversation with one elderly man, but because everything I said had to be translated, I said to the pastor's wife, 'I think it would be easier for you to have the conversation with him.' 'No, carry on,' she said. 'I'll explain why later.' When we arrived back at their home, the pastor's wife told me that Albania is a very patriarchal society, and most men don't want to know what women have to say, but they will listen to other men. If we plan to go and serve the Lord in another culture, there are clearly lots of things we will need to learn.

As we have so many people from other cultures in the UK today, there are things we need to learn here as well. For example, if we are standing in a street giving out tracts and a Muslim couple approach, we should always offer the literature to the man. It would be considered offensive to speak to the woman first.

We also need to know what others believe, as another reason for not giving offence—not that we should hold back from sharing the truth, but so we can be sensitive to others nonetheless. One day we were preaching during a week of outreach in the city of Londonderry. A seventeen-year-old girl named Shona stood for about fifty minutes listening to one preacher after another. At one point she asked me, 'What about Our Lady?' I knew what she meant, and it wasn't a surprise in a place that was overwhelmingly Roman Catholic. She was basically saying, 'You have spoken so much about Jesus and salvation, and yet you haven't once mentioned Mary.' I could have responded to Shona's question by telling her that she risked going to hell for worshipping Mary, but what good would that have done her, especially as she was obviously a very sensitive soul? We always need to avoid being harsh, as I sought to do that day. People will remember our words, but they will also remember how we spoke those words. I simply explained that we need only Jesus to be saved and that, if she hadn't done so already, she should call to Him to be her Saviour. Shona came back the next day to hear more and had many of her questions answered.

The second point about culture is the need to be aware of the activities of others. In other words, who else is active in 'evangelism' in the area? If Mormons are active in your town, don't dress really smartly when you go on outreach, or people may think you are one of them. Having said that, don't dress really scruffily either, as we don't want our attire to create a barrier between us and those we want to reach. If you have a town-centre witness, try to avoid standing where the Jehovah's Witnesses put up their board, as again some might think you are one of them, which we want to avoid at all costs.

Thirdly in relation to culture, you need to be able to answer questions. Where people are at spiritually, or what background they are from, or what religion they belong to, will affect the kinds of things they ask. The most common questions that are asked are things like: 'How can you prove God's existence?' 'Hasn't evolution disproved the Bible?' 'Why would a God of love allow all the suffering?' 'Isn't death the end?' These all come up time and again. To be able to answer them we have to do some preparation. The same is true if you have people around you with different beliefs. You will be the most help to them if you know something about where they are coming from. For example, if you have a neighbour or a colleague at work who is a JW or an evolutionist, find out what they believe. Two very helpful books are *Truth Under Attack* by Eryl Davies (in three volumes) and *The Creation Answers Book* by Don Batten, David Catchpoole, Jonathan Sarfati and Carl Wieland. By knowing what others believe, we will hopefully be kept from saying or doing something that will harm and not help our witness.

10. KNOW YOURSELF

Firstly, our lives must match our words. This is so very important. We come back to 1 Peter 3:15 again, where it tells us, 'In your hearts honour Christ the Lord as holy.' The NIV 1984 put it like this: 'In your hearts set apart Christ as Lord.' I once met a man from Nottingham who said he was saved through a man preaching in the centre of the city. He added: 'It wasn't anything that the man said that I remember and which so challenged me. It was the way he spoke; it was his demeanour.' That is a very powerful challenge to all open-air preachers. Someone once asked, 'If you were arrested for being a Christian, would there be enough evidence to convict you?' I hope there would be plenty of evidence to convict all of us.

Sometimes we miss gospel opportunities. We've all been guilty of this, haven't we? Have you ever wondered why that happens? Often it is because we weren't walking with the Lord as we should have been. Many of us have had times when we have allowed opportunities to slip through our fingers. Perhaps sinful thoughts were in our minds and so we felt something like this: 'I'd be a hypocrite if I witnessed to that person.' So, ultimately, we weren't ready! Verse 16 of the 1 Peter 3 passage begins, 'having a good conscience'. That is surely crucial to the Lord's work! But it's no good beating ourselves up over past failures. We must get the matter dealt with. Say sorry to the Lord and ask for determination from Him not to make the same mistake again. Praying for readiness is something we should regularly be doing as well. It is something we should do before, during and after our witness, asking the Lord to lead us to those to whom we should speak, granting us the wisdom to know what to say and blessing the seed that has been sown.

Secondly, our demeanour is very important, and there are various aspects to that:

(a) We need to be natural when we witness
We need to just be ourselves—and since a Christian is a huge part of who and what we are, that shouldn't be a problem for us! I once heard of a preacher who spoke from the pulpit in a very affected voice. There is no place for affectation in the work of the Lord. People will respect us more for being ourselves than for trying to be something or someone else.

THERE IS STILL MUCH TO DO!

(b) We need to be friendly

This can help break down barriers with people, which is especially good if an angry person is in front of us. Proverbs 15:1 states, 'A soft answer turns away wrath, but a harsh word stirs up anger.' When I joined OAM I spent a week with a senior evangelist in Kent called Ken Weaver. One day as he was preaching in Maidstone a furious man came and stood right in front of him expressing his disdain. The evangelist stretched out his hand and very warmly said, 'How do you do? My name is Ken.' The other man simply melted and a positive conversation ensued.

It is so important that, if someone addresses us angrily or arrogantly, we do not respond in kind. First Peter 3:15 finishes with the clause 'yet do it with gentleness and respect'. We're not superior to anyone, after all, and in our street preaching we will often make the point that we're not saying we're better than anyone else. We are sinners just like our hearers. The only difference is that we've been forgiven by the grace of God. We were once children of wrath, but now we enjoy peace with God through our Lord Jesus Christ.

(c) We need to be good-humoured

Sometimes a sense of humour can be a good ice-breaker—but having said that, we mustn't get carried away. Witnessing is a serious business.

(d) We need to be gracious

There may be a difficult person in front of us, but that person may be difficult simply because we've challenged him or her. Most people are not likely to admit that they have been challenged. They may instead come back to us defensively, if not angrily.

A devout Sikh named Hiren was on holiday with his family in Llandudno in North Wales. He came across the beach team preaching on the promenade one evening. He began a twenty-minute conversation with the team leader, who felt at the end of it that he hadn't got anywhere with Hiren. However, three months later, that same team leader was preaching one Wednesday afternoon in Leicester, and who should approach him but Hiren! He immediately embraced the preacher and said, 'I've become a Christian, and I'm so glad to be able to tell you. It all started when I spoke with you that evening in Llandudno. God began to speak to me through what you said.' Wow! What a blessing that was! Hiren went on to make a clear stand for the Lord in his family, even though there was a high price to pay. Hiren's father-in-law was a Sikh leader, who was so incensed by Hiren's conversion that he forced his wife and children to leave the family home for a time.

That story should remind us that the work of the Holy Spirit is largely secret. In Luke 17:20 we read, 'The kingdom of God does not come with observation' (NKJV). Outwardly, it may appear that nothing is happening, but the Lord may be at work in a wonderful way.

Thirdly, we are to know our weaknesses. We all have them. For example, some of us enjoy debating, but it is possible to enjoy it too much at times. On one occasion at Hull Fair during my first year in the Mission I was debating with a man and we were going back and forth. Suddenly, and to my shame, one of the senior evangelists pulled me away, saying, 'You've told him all he needs to hear; best leave it now.' He was right, and I felt quite ashamed that winning the argument had been more important to me than winning the man. It is surprising where self can rear its ugly head, even when we are serving the Lord.

At times, pride can be there too. For example, we might try to blag it when in conversation and we don't know the answer to a particular question. The right thing to do—and the humble thing—is to be honest enough to say we don't know the answer. Most times people will respect us more for being honest. Actually, it can be useful to be able to say something like this: 'I don't know the answer, but I will find out. How about letting me email you what I find, or how about meeting up again and I'll try to have an answer for you.' This way it can become a good opportunity to make further contact.

11. KNOW YOUR CONTACT

There are two aspects to this. Firstly, we must listen. The Lord gave us two ears, but only one mouth. Sometimes we can be a little too keen in our witness! We can be so enthusiastic about what we have to share that we don't give the other person the chance to say anything in reply. That person may have a particular burden to share, a problem with a particular issue to ask about, or just general questions about what we have said. We need to be good listeners, then, as well as good talkers. Listening is an important way of showing the other person that we are interested in and concerned for him or her.

Listening early on in a conversation is also important because it will help us to learn where the person is coming from in his or her beliefs or non-beliefs. Once we find out where that person is at, we are better equipped to take him

THERE IS STILL MUCH TO DO!

or her forward from there. People are usually happy to share what they believe, and that will then be our starting point.

Something else we should be sensitive to is when we reach the point where we have said enough and the enquirer can't take any more. Remember, we don't have to tell a person everything there is to know about the Bible in one go. Leave the person wanting more, rather than exhausting him or her.

Secondly, we must ask questions. It's so easy for us to go on the defensive, but instead we can go on the offensive. Asking the enquirer questions can get that person to think. This can be a great way of changing hostility to curiosity, and it can get a person to evaluate how solid or otherwise is his or her belief system. We could ask those who claim they don't believe in God, 'Why are you an atheist?' If they come back with, 'Well, I can't see God, so He can't be there', you could say, 'Do you really only believe in things you can see?' You could then give examples of all the things we do each day without needing to see what makes them work—for example, the engine of our car. We set off on a journey without feeling the need to check under the bonnet each time to make sure the engine is still there. So faith is not nonsensical; we exercise it many times every day of our lives.

I once spoke with a militant atheist in Sunderland (there seem to be more and more of them around). His name was Gary, and he was completely hung up on evolution, which to his mind was a cast-iron fact and proved there is no God. I tried to show him the holes in the theory of evolution, but he didn't seem to accept anything I said. Then he suddenly remarked about evolution, 'It's what the scientists believe is true, anyway!' Here was my opportunity. Here was a chink in Gary's armour. So I said to him, 'So you're the same as me then, Gary.' He was far from happy with this suggestion. I think that the idea that he was anything like this weak-minded Christian before him was almost beyond the pale. He liked what I told him next even less: 'Yes, Gary, you're a man of faith, just like me.' He stormed away, muttering angrily. My words had hit a very raw nerve, but perhaps they would get him thinking that the 'facts' of evolution are no such thing. We'll come back to dealing with atheists in the next chapter.

On another subject, an increasing number of people are stating something like this: 'Jesus didn't even exist.' To which we can reply, 'Really? Why, then, are there so many first-century historians, with no sympathy with Christianity, who said that He did?' (There's quite a list of such historians.) The date on any coin can also be used to good effect with this sort of person. We can ask questions about that and then proceed to suggest that possibly the truth is that he or she simply doesn't want Jesus to exist because of the claims He made and the demands He has put upon us.

A favourite statement we hear when doing open-airs is, 'The Bible is full of contradictions!' To this we throw questions back to try to get the person to think. For example, 'That's funny, I've been reading it for years and I haven't found any. Can you show me one, please?' Usually people have never read anything of the Scriptures, so they come unstuck at that point. We can then ask them if it's wise to judge a book without giving it a fair hearing (or reading).

Some people will ask about the hypocrisy they perceive in the church, which again we can throw back to them. I once met Michael Jackson in Doncaster (no, not that Michael Jackson!). He told me, 'Half the people who go to church are hypocrites!'

I said to him in reply, 'Do you realize what that means?'

'No, what?' he asked.

'That the other half are not hypocrites. They're the real thing.'

That led to a very worthwhile interaction.

We will often meet people of one religious persuasion or another. I have found that you can use the same approach with a Muslim as you can with a Roman Catholic. It comes down to showing the person that in Christ we have something better—far better. You can say to the person, 'Can I just ask you two very important questions? Are you sure your sins are all forgiven? And are you sure of going to heaven [paradise for the Muslim] when you die?' The answer will always be 'no' to both questions. We can then tell the person humbly yet confidently that for us the answer is 'yes' to both questions. As we share that we are sure of both these things, and why, we'll be sharing the gospel and pointing to our unique and wonderful Saviour and Lord.

If you meet someone who says he or she is a Christian, and you think the person is probably only a nominal Christian, you can ask, 'It's great to hear that you are a Christian too. Can I ask how long you've been one?' The usual answer that comes back is either 'All my life' or 'I was born a Christian'. Both of these give the game away. So we can take this person straight to John 3. Some will be very uncomfortable at this point, but others will say, as an elderly lady once said to me, 'I've never heard about being born again before!' That might

THERE IS STILL MUCH TO DO!

shock us, but there are so many churches in the UK where conversion and the new birth are never taught.

Sometimes we will meet those who don't want the gospel light to shine too close to home, so they may try to throw in a red herring. This was what the Samaritan woman did when asking about worship in John 4:20. Don't get sidetracked by the red herring. Bring the focus to the person's sin and to his or her personal need of a Saviour. The JWs are masters at trying to jump from one thing to another. If you are focusing on the deity of Christ and you get JWs on the ropes, they will try to wriggle onto another topic, but don't let them. Keep them on the ropes to help them see they have a wrong interpretation of who Jesus is and the way of salvation. Dr Peter Masters has written a book entitled *Biblical Strategies for Witness* which analyses people in different spiritual states. There is also an excellent book by Gregory Koukl called *Tactics: A Game Plan for Discussing Your Christian Convictions*, which is very helpful in suggesting different questions we can use depending on the different situations we might find ourselves in and the different types of people we may encounter.

12. KNOW YOUR FOLLOW-UP

It is always good to give the person some literature, so that he or she can consider things further. Perhaps a Gospel or some other booklet and maybe a card with your church details may be appropriate. Carmen was spoken to during an open-air in Bracknell. She had come from Italy to improve her English and was working as an au pair, but was very unhappy. She was from a Christian family, who must have been praying hard for her while she was so far from home. Carmen was invited to the local church on Sunday, but she didn't come. Two weeks later, however, she did. In her broken English she said afterwards that she had enjoyed the service and would return the next week. She did return, and what a surprise! On arriving at the church this time, she was full of joy and shared that during the week she had come to know the Saviour. Her parents must have been thrilled when they heard the news.

If a conversation has gone well, you may feel that you could give the person an invitation to meet up for coffee, or at least swap contact details. It is always good to try to get the name of the person you are speaking to—if possible, early on in a conversation. That makes it less formal. Also, if you have the person's name, you will find that it helps you to pray for him or her. If you are doing gospel outreach regularly, you can build up a list of people for whom you can pray.

Finally, reporting back to the church should be an integral part of gospel outreach. It's what Paul and Barnabas did at the end of their first missionary journey: 'And when they arrived and gathered the church together, they declared all that God had done with them, and how he had opened a door of faith to the Gentiles' (Acts 14:27). This will be an encouragement to the church and to you, and it will also be an opportunity when more prayer can be made for those who have been contacted. We should remember that those who pray for the work back at home are just as much a part of the gospel team as those who go out to where the people are. There will be those who are now too infirm to be on the front line, but their prayer support is still absolutely vital if there is to be blessing upon the work.

During a week of outreach in Reading we used to visit an

elderly lady called Marjorie, who always kindly served us with tea and crumpets. I remember her saying once rather disconsolately, 'Of course, I can't be involved in the work any more.' We assured her that she could still pray, and that was a vital part of the work of the gospel.

13. KNOW YOUR EFFECT

Witnessing can have a threefold effect. Firstly, it can bring opposition. That was the experience of virtually every Christian mentioned in the book of Acts. If we expect it, which we should, we won't be put off standing for the Lord (1 Peter 4:12–14). Perhaps you were opposed to the gospel at one time and yet the Lord dealt graciously with you. Let us pray for those who may persecute us—perhaps someone at work or school, or maybe someone we meet in the street.

When I worked as a postman, a massive chap called Neil used to shove me every time he walked past. Thankfully, the Lord helped me just to smile and walk on without a word. Far more recently, I was walking back to our church in Dunstable after an open-air outreach in the town centre when a man who had earlier been trying to aggravate us came past and spat at me. I simply told him that that wasn't a very nice thing to do, and he went away rather sheepishly.

Secondly, witnessing will bless us, just as preaching blesses a person. I experienced that particularly after speaking with that chap while jogging, but it always has this effect to a greater or lesser extent. It is a joy to speak of the Lord Jesus Christ! It warms our hearts, and that is particularly so when we have spoken with someone who seems genuinely to be searching.

THERE IS STILL MUCH TO DO!

This was true of a Chinese student in Luton named Hugo. He listened to the preaching and then came to say he wanted to talk. He shared that he was weighed down by sin because he had mistreated his grandmother back in China, but she had died, and so he felt there was no way of being forgiven. He said he felt so bad that he had even contemplated committing suicide. 'I feel utterly condemned,' he said. What a lovely opportunity it was to open the Scriptures and share the gospel with him! Hugo was amazed to hear that he could be forgiven and have peace with God. He took several items of literature and before leaving said he would start attending the Christian Bible study that he knew took place on the campus. What an encouragement to meet someone who was so concerned about his sin! The Lord was clearly dealing with him.

Thirdly, witnessing works—just as preaching works and literature distribution works. Our trouble is that we don't always believe that, and that may well be because we don't always see the fruit of our labours. Let's remember that we don't know the Lord's mysterious workings in a person's heart. Perhaps one day we shall see the full results of our feeble efforts to make the Lord known. And that's just the thing: our work is to point people to Jesus Christ and then to point people to the church of Jesus Christ, and leave the Holy Spirit to do the rest.

THERE IS STILL MUCH TO DO!

10 Scratching the itch

*In the beginning, God created the heavens
and the earth. (Gen. 1:1)*

According to census figures, between 2001 and 2011 there was a significant decrease in people who identify themselves as Christians (from 71.7 per cent down to 59.3 per cent). At the same time, there was an increase in those reporting no religion (from 14.8 per cent to 25.1 per cent). This means that a quarter of people in the UK would now class themselves as atheists. That is an awful lot of people, and we are likely to know some of them and even have the opportunity to witness to them. Given that this is a growing number, it warrants a whole chapter to think about our engagement with them, the main point simply being that we need to start with people where they are. That is just what Paul did when he was invited to speak to all the intellectuals of Athens, as we'll see shortly.

Since we know that there is an abundance of evidence to demonstrate God's existence, it might be worth beginning by asking: what causes people—an increasing number of people—to reject God and embrace an atheistic position? In one word, the answer is 'evolution': the view that this world came into being and came to be as it is today through nothing more than chance random processes that took place over billions of years of time—or as someone has quipped, 'we have evolved from the goo, via the zoo, to you'. That is the foundation upon which atheists take their stand. The teaching

THERE IS STILL MUCH TO DO!

of evolution has been very successfully disseminated through our entire education system and through every type of media outlet, not only in the UK, but throughout the Western world. We increasingly seem to live in an evolutionized world. You can't even go into a museum without Darwinian evolution being foisted upon you somewhere along the line. As a result, we have reached a position where people on the street confidently tell us that evolution is a proven fact (which actually is very far from being the case) and that therefore God doesn't exist.

An example of where the higher echelons of academia are today is a quotation from William Provine, who is professor of biology at Cornell University in New York State in the USA. The following quote should at the very least help us to realize that the subject of evolution is not a side issue when it comes to our task of evangelism. Provine writes, 'Let me summarize my views on what modern evolutionary biology tells us loud and clear: There are no gods, no purposes, no goal-directed focus of any kind. There is no life after death. When I die, I am absolutely certain that I'm going to be dead—that's the end of me. There's no ultimate foundation for ethics, no ultimate meaning to life.'[1] When eminent men make these pronouncements, it shouldn't come as any surprise that many of us lesser mortals tend to bow to their mastery. This is especially true when the media blindly accept these pronouncements and the so-called evidence that goes with them, such as the supposed millions of years needed for fossils to have evolved. Even when something turns up that ought to challenge their thinking, they seem totally unable to

THERE IS STILL MUCH TO DO!

take off their evolutionary glasses through which they see the world and everything in it.

Take Dr Mary Schweitzer, a molecular palaeontologist at North Carolina State University, and her team, who in 2005 found what they viewed as the seemingly impossible— soft tissue preserved inside the leg of an adolescent *Tyrannosaurus rex* unearthed in Montana. This proved to be very controversial, because the prevailing view was that no soft tissue could be preserved from a creature that had lived 68 million years ago. Scientists had thought that proteins that make up soft tissue should degrade in less than one million years in the best of conditions. In most cases, microbes apparently feast on a dead animal's soft tissue, destroying it within weeks. In 2007, Schweitzer and her colleagues analysed the chemistry of the T-Rex proteins. They found that the proteins really did come from dinosaur soft tissue, but what never seemed to occur to them was the possibility that this find could be indicative of the fact that dinosaurs may have lived much more recently. It would seem so obvious to throw that suggestion into the equation, but no, not for card-carrying evolutionists.[2]

How sad it is that there are many Christians who are very keen to stand with those who believe in millions of years of slow evolutionary change. I spoke to a young man who once rang the OAM office and wanted to discuss these issues. He claimed that it actually brought more glory to God to suggest that He created the world over billions of years than for Him to have done so in six days. I find that very bizarre. Usain Bolt didn't win all his Olympic gold medals and gain all the glory he has from them by running his races over the longest times possible. When Mary Berry bakes a cake on television, she doesn't leave the cake in the oven all day in order to gain the best result. She'd look pretty foolish if she did so.

God's glory literally shines through in the creation the Bible describes Him bringing into being, because Genesis 1:3 records, 'And God said, "Let there be light", and there was light.' What mind-blowing power the Lord must have exerted! But that is just what He did, and just by speaking. The foundation upon which we as Christians are to take our stand is the Bible and nothing but the Bible. Someone once said that the meaning of everything is tied up in its origins. That is most definitely true of God's Word.

Creation writer and speaker Dr Carl Wieland, for many years the director of Creation Ministries International, was an atheist while at university. He would sometimes be approached by Christians wanting to share their faith with him. He found that they hadn't thought through the implications of what Genesis taught about creation. He said to a Christian on one occasion, 'Why should I listen to what the Bible says about eternal life if what it says about how we got here isn't true?' Sadly, the Christian had no answer. What he was basically saying was that we need to be able to trust the Bible from the beginning if we are really to trust the rest of it. In other words, if we can't trust the Bible on the topic of history, how can we trust it when we come to theology? As the Lord Jesus said to Nicodemus, 'If I have told you earthly things and you do not believe, how can you believe if I tell you heavenly things?' (John 3:12). We need a consistent position on the whole of the Bible if we are going to witness both faithfully and effectively.

THERE IS STILL MUCH TO DO!

It is totally wrong to try to argue that it doesn't matter what we believe about Genesis as long as we can get people to read the Gospels. The Gospels come in a context, a context of history. Isn't that what we like to emphasize so much about the Lord—that He was a real person, who really lived on Planet Earth two thousand years ago, really did do those miracles, and really did die upon that cross and then rise again on the third day? History is of paramount importance and the Lord's history fits into History—the history of the world. Jesus was real and He said that Adam and Eve were real; not only that, but He was crystal clear about when in history they lived. In Matthew 19:4 the Lord asked a group of Pharisees, 'Have you not read that he who created them from the beginning made them male and female?' God didn't make them billions of years after the beginning, but 'from the beginning'. Mark 10:6 puts it even more clearly: 'But from the beginning of creation, "God made them male and female."'

Have you ever considered that trying to fit millions of years into the text of Scripture means having to put the curse before sin, and yet, according to Genesis 3, the curse came as a result of sin? The organization Answers in Genesis has produced a humorous picture of Adam and Eve: in the top half of the picture they are standing in the Garden of Eden and saying to each other, 'The world really is very good, just as the Lord said.' But in the lower half of the picture, lying beneath the ground, we see that they are standing on layers and layers of dead animals killed because of either violence or disease. The picture highlights the fact that it wouldn't be a very good world if disease and death came before God's curse upon the world. The foundational events of God making a perfect world followed by the first Adam's sin give meaning to the central events of Jesus Christ's death and resurrection for sinners. As 1 Corinthians 15:21 says, 'For as by a man came death, by a man has come also the resurrection of the dead.' The lesson is surely that we must be faithful to the infallible Word of God and not feel pressured to fit in with the prevailing views of fallible men.

The alternative, compromising on the early chapters of Genesis, is to risk finding ourselves coming unstuck, as demonstrated by these famous words from Sir David Attenborough:

When Creationists talk about God creating, they always instance hummingbirds, or orchids, sunflowers and beautiful things. But I tend to think instead of a parasitic worm that is boring through the eye of a boy sitting on the bank of a river in West Africa, a worm that is going to make him blind. And I ask them, 'Are you telling me that the God you believe in, who you also say is an all-merciful God, who cares for each one of us individually … are you saying that God created this worm that can live in no other way than in an innocent child's eyeball? Because that doesn't seem to me to coincide with a God who is full of mercy.'[3]

The truth is that God created a perfect world with no sin and death, but because of Adam's disobedience, sin and death entered the world and as a result everything came under the curse of the Almighty. The good news that we can then launch into from this in our conversations with people is that Jesus Christ entered this world in order to take that curse upon Himself, and He did so as He hung upon the cross. Paul tells us the marvellous truth that 'Christ redeemed us from the curse of the law by becoming a curse for us' (Gal. 3:13).

THERE IS STILL MUCH TO DO!

We can go on to say that if we have received the forgiveness of our sins through what Jesus accomplished in our place, we can look forward to that world to come where there will be no more curse. In John's vision of eternal glory he writes, 'No longer will there be anything accursed, but the throne of God and of the lamb will be in it, and his servants will worship him' (Rev. 22:3).

We need to appreciate the danger of driving a wedge between one part of Scripture and another. A well-known American atheist called Frank Zindler said,

The most devastating thing that biology did to Christianity was the discovery of biological evolution. Now that we know that Adam and Eve were never real people the central myth of Christianity is destroyed. If there never was an Adam and Eve there never was original sin. If there never was original sin there is no need of salvation. If there is no need of salvation there is no need of a saviour. And I submit that that puts Jesus, historical or otherwise, in the ranks of the unemployed.[4]

Zindler is right about one thing: by implication he says that you can't marry up evolution with biblical creation and, by extension, the gospel. It's one or the other!

We may be guilty of thinking that atheists are people who won't ever budge from their position so there is no point talking to them about spiritual issues. We need to know that that is a huge mistake. Some of my best friends were once atheists, but now they love the Lord and His Word, the Bible. An awful lot of people who claim to be atheists are those who simply haven't ever thought through the weakness of their position. They have just tended to go along with the crowd. Over the years I have had a number of conversations

THERE IS STILL MUCH TO DO!

164

with people who started out claiming to be atheists, but after only a few minutes came to realize that they were really agnostics—which means they had moved from saying there is no God to saying that they were not sure whether or not there is a God. That makes them more open to considering why they can actually be sure that there is a God, and hopefully even being willing to consider what that God has revealed about Himself.

An example of someone like that was Mark, a middle-aged man in Kendal who spoke to Mission evangelist Keith Bullock, who is now with the Lord. Keith wrote about this encounter:

He fiercely challenged me about the existence of God. Eventually he calmed down and we spoke at length. Mark confessed that he had lied to me and that he wasn't an atheist after all, but rather an agnostic. He said his father was hard and had instilled atheism into him, but was now dying and terrified of death. Mark had challenged his father as to why he should be afraid of death if there was nothing beyond the grave. The way his father struggles with death had disturbed Mark and caused him to think that perhaps there was life after death and a God to face. He willingly took literature and said he would read it. He thanked me for my patience and kind response to his initial rudeness. First impression—an atheist! Conclusion—a seeker!

So do we need some special technique in order to speak to atheists about the Lord in the most profitable way? In one sense, no, we don't. Our aim is to point them to Jesus and His death and resurrection, just as it is with every other unbeliever we may meet. However, in another sense, we do need to make sure we start where these people are. This will

THERE IS STILL MUCH TO DO!

help us to bring them in the most reasoned way to Calvary, so yes, we need to scratch where they itch, just as the apostles were so adept at doing.

When Peter preached on the Day of Pentecost in Jerusalem, his hearers were those who already knew the foundational truths of the Old Testament Scriptures. It meant that when they heard that Jesus, whom they had crucified, was the long-awaited Messiah, many of them were convicted of their sins: 'Now when they heard this they were cut to the heart' (Acts 2:37). It was as though they just needed the missing piece in their theology, which was that Jesus had come to be the ultimate sacrifice for the sins of His people.

How different it was for Paul when he visited Athens, when he spoke both in the marketplace and in the Areopagus (the gathering place for the city's intellectuals). A few of those intellectuals or philosophers, on hearing Paul in the market 'preaching Jesus and the resurrection' (Acts 17:18), said to him, 'You bring some strange things to our ears' (v. 20). Paul knew his hearers had no biblical foundation and as a result would react to the message of the cross in a very different way from Jewish congregations. As Paul wrote to the Corinthians, 'Jews demand signs and Greeks seek wisdom, but we preach Christ crucified, a stumbling block to Jews and folly to Gentiles' (1 Cor. 1:22–23).

So what did Paul do when he was invited to address the Athenian intelligentsia? He used a different strategy. He started by introducing his hearers to the Creator God. Very cleverly, Paul gave them an object lesson which at the same time was a helpful point of contact. He directed his congregation to their statue to the unknown god, which he had noticed during an earlier tour around the city. It was as if the pagan Greeks had made up this god just in case they had left someone out of their plethora of self-made deities.

Paul was able to use this unknown god to say to them that actually they were right: they had indeed missed someone out. They had missed out the one true living God. He is the great Creator of all things in heaven and on earth. He is the One to whom we owe our very lives. He is the self-sufficient One. He doesn't need us to give Him anything; instead He is the One who gives us everything. He is also omnipresent. He is not some local god whose power extends only to one sphere of life. He is the Creator and sustainer of all life, and not only that, He is also the judge of all. Hence there is a pressing need for all to repent. The positive proof that there will be a judgement is the fact that the One appointed to be the judge has been raised from the dead. The doctrine of resurrection was something that Greek philosophy rejected; hence it was at this moment that many refused to hear Paul say any more.

However, this was very far from being a wasted opportunity. Acts 17:32 indicates that the interest of some was sufficiently aroused that they were willing to hear more from Paul, but better than that was that 'some men joined him and believed' (v. 34). Two people are then mentioned by name as having been converted through the message they had just heard. Some have criticized Paul's approach, but it was exactly the right one. Perhaps the reason why there was not the same response in Athens as there had been in Jerusalem was that Paul was starting from scratch, having to build a foundation to give meaning to the central events of the gospel. That may well be just the approach we need to take

THERE IS STILL MUCH TO DO!

with atheists. We may have to spend time seeking to break up the false foundation of paganism, so that we can then build the solid foundation of the gospel.

Starting with Jesus and the cross may make little or no sense to a person who doesn't even believe in God. So we have to start at the very beginning and tell such a person about God. We have to give a reasoned defence for His existence. The design argument is perhaps the most straightforward one. A cake needs a baker, a house needs a builder, a painting needs an artist, and so a world that is infinitely more complex than any cake, building or painting needs a Creator. We can then use examples from nature, from the solar system and from the human body to point to design.

There is a huge amount of irony in Professor Stephen Hawking's words, 'We have just one life to appreciate the grand design of the universe, and for that I am extremely grateful.'[5] Aren't we left asking: but who is the designer, and who is he grateful to? Or what about these words: 'The complexity of living organisms is matched by the elegant efficiency of their apparent design. If anyone doesn't agree that this amount of complex design cried out for an explanation, I give up.'[6] Would you be surprised to know that they come from arch-atheist Richard Dawkins in his famous book *The Blind Watchmaker*? Of course, he draws the wrong conclusions, but he does, perhaps unwittingly, speak of 'complex design'. Mentioning such quotes in either our preaching or our conversations is like what Paul did in Athens. He quoted from two Greek poets (Epimenides and Aratus), which perhaps helped Paul to build up a certain rapport with his listeners. It no doubt helped his credibility, and so it will do for us if we can show that we are aware of the big names of atheism in whom many put such confidence.

The complexity of design is another area to challenge atheists about. In his famous book *Darwin's Black Box*, Michael Behe, professor of biochemistry at Lehigh University in Pennsylvania, argues for what he calls 'irreducible complexity'. To put it simply, he claims that biochemical systems have a complexity that cannot be reduced beyond a certain point in order for them to work. He uses the example of a mousetrap. Without all the necessary component parts the trap will not work, and this indicates that it must be the result of intelligent design, which of course it is.

Michael Denton, who has both a doctorate in biochemistry and a degree in medicine, in his book *Evolution: A Theory in Crisis* estimated that if we knew how to build a machine as complex as the (once thought of as simple) cell, it would take at least one million years to build—working day and night, and churning out parts on a mass-production basis. Charles Darwin, who published his infamous book *On the Origin of Species* in 1859, believed that the single cell was merely a microscopic lump of jelly-like substance that is destitute of texture and organs and with no trace of organization. Now we know differently. It is a highly complex machine, and even children know that machines do not come into being by chance; they need intelligent design.

There are a number of other important arguments we can put to atheists:

1. 'THE ANTHROPIC PRINCIPLE'

This phrase was coined in 1974 and basically describes the

THERE IS STILL MUCH TO DO!

fact that the entire universe is finely tuned for life—human life. There is so much evidence for that, including the earth's size, its tilt and its distance from the sun.

2. THE CONSCIENCE

In his book *Candle in the Wind*, Gary Brady says of the conscience, 'God has a spy in every heart, a preacher on the inside.'[7] Evolution has no explanation for the existence of the conscience.

3. THE HUMAN PERSONALITY

Evolutionists are at a loss to explain this. Francis Schaeffer once said, 'No one has presented an idea, let alone demonstrated it to be feasible, to explain how the impersonal beginning, plus time, plus chance, can give personality. We are distracted by a flourish of endless words, and lo, personality has appeared out of the hat.'[8]

4. THE ORIGINS OF INFORMATION

With this and all the other issues we can go on the front foot with our atheistic friends. We can ask questions like: where did information come from if the universe started from nothing? We all know that information can come only from intelligence. No wonder Dr Stephen Grocott, Fellow of the Royal Australian Chemical Institute, concluded, 'I am afraid that as a scientist I simply cannot say strongly enough that spontaneous generation of life is a chemical nonsense and, therefore, I am left with no alternative but to believe that life was created.'[9]

Some will try to argue that science and religion are in conflict with each other. It can be helpful to introduce

THERE IS STILL MUCH TO DO!

atheists to the fact that many of the greatest scientists in history were Christians. I strongly suspect that most people don't know that men like Johannes Kepler, Robert Boyle, Sir Isaac Newton (I don't think he was a born-again Christian), Carl Linnaeus, Michael Faraday, Samuel Morse, Charles Babbage, James Joule, Louis Pasteur, Lord Kelvin, Joseph Lister and James Clerk Maxwell were all Bible believers. These were men who made a tremendous difference, several of them responsible for the saving of countless lives through their discoveries. The findings of French scientist Pasteur, for example, helped establish a new branch of science, that of microbiology. His developments in pasteurization, bacteriology and immunization transformed medicine.

True science and faith are not in opposition to one another. We have to be honest with people and say that both involve faith as well as facts. A lesser-known scientist named Sir William Henry Bragg led a team which won the Nobel Prize for physics in 1915. This was for their work on X-ray crystallography. In a lecture he gave at the Royal Institution in London a few years later, Sir William stated, 'Sometimes people ask if religion and science are opposed to each other. They are—in the sense that the thumb and fingers of my hand are opposed to each other. It is an opposition by means of which anything can be grasped.'

There is also the important point that, whatever people may say, deep down in their hearts they know there is a Creator. As Paul instructed the Roman Christians, there is no excuse for claiming there is no God (Rom. 1:20). Douglas Wilson, in his book *Letter from a Christian Citizen*, has written, 'Mankind was created by God, and despite

THERE IS STILL MUCH TO DO!

man's sin, we cannot shake the reality of that created-ness from ourselves.'[10] It's not always worth starting with this argument, as it may only succeed in winding up an ardent atheist, but it is a valid point to make. A famous preacher and hymn-writer, Dr Philip Doddridge (1702–1751), had a little daughter nicknamed Tetsy. On one occasion she was observed trying to teach the family dog about the existence of God. The poor creature placed its tail between its legs when frustrated Tetsy exclaimed, 'You, Dr Doddridge's dog, and you don't know who made you!' On relating this anecdote, Doddridge said to a class of theological students, 'And if so much is expected from my dog, what may be expected of us?'

In his helpful book *Has Science Got Rid of God?* John Blanchard relates the following anecdote:

Madalyn Murray O'Hair, founder and president of American Atheists Inc., famously filed a lawsuit which in 1963 resulted in the US Supreme Court banning organized prayer in public schools. Dubbed 'the most hated woman in America', she and her two children disappeared (along with over $500,000 of American Atheist funds) and six years later her burned and dismembered body was found on a remote Texas ranch. She was renowned for her bitter and crude attacks on Christianity, spoke of 'the insanity of believing in God' and said, 'There's absolutely no conclusive proof that Jesus ever really existed.' Yet in her diary she repeatedly wrote, 'Somebody, somewhere, love me!'[11]

What a terrible irony that she so vehemently rejected the One whose love for sinners is so great and so wonderful!

Sir Isaac Newton wrote in his book *A Short Scheme of the True Religion*, 'Opposite to godliness is atheism in profession and idolatry in practice. Atheism is so senseless and odious to

THERE IS STILL MUCH TO DO!

mankind that it never had many professors.' Tragically, we have to face up to the fact that there are now many professors of atheism. We must equip ourselves to meet them head-on and lovingly seek to share the good news of salvation with them.

Notes

1   Quoted in John Blanchard, *Why Are You Here?* (Darligton: Evangelical Press, 2014).

2   Dr Jonathan D. Sarfati, 'DNA and Bone Cells Found in Dinosaur Bone', *Creation Magazine*, December 2014; http://creation.com/dino-dna-bone-cells.

3   Radio interview with Andrew Denton, *Enough Rope* (ABC), episode 28 (broadcast 22 September 2003).

4   Debate with William Craig, *Atheism v. Christianity* (video; Zondervan 1996).

5   *Curiosity*, Discovery Channel (2011).

6   Richard Dawkins, 'Preface', *The Blind Watchmaker* (London: Penguin, 1991), p. 1.

7   Gary Brady, *Candle in the Wind* (Darlington: Evangelical Press, 2014), p. 49.

8   Francis Schaeffer, *The God Who Is There* (Wheaton, IL: Crossway, 1990), p. 95.

9   Quoted in John F. Ashton (ed.), *In Six Days: Why 50 Scientists Choose to Believe in Creation* (Green Forest, AR: Master Books, 2001).

10   Douglas Wilson, *Letter from a Christian Citizen* (Braselton, GA: American Vision, 2007), p. 102.

11   John Blanchard, *Has Science Got Rid of God?* (Darlington: Evangelical Press, 2004), pp. 119–120.

THERE IS STILL MUCH TO DO!

11 Acting the part

I have become all things to all people, that by all means I might save some. (1 Cor. 9:22)

You can go to seminars to learn how to do all sorts of things under the guise of 'evangelism' today. Gospel magic, for example, is popular—doing clever tricks with paint and water and a host of other things to help draw a crowd in the open air or to keep the interest of a congregation inside a church. There is an aspect to these tricks that should trouble us, though. They are usually used in a rather deceptive way to attract people. This is especially true in the context of the street. It is normally the case that the evangelist will make no mention of who he is or of what he is really doing. Not, that is, until a crowd has gathered. Only then does he begin to introduce the purpose of his presentation. God, Jesus, sin and the gospel are kept out of the way up to that point, as it is thought that they may hinder people from stopping and paying an interest if introduced earlier.

I have to be honest and say that I have grave concerns about this style of evangelism, and for two specific reasons. Firstly, I am concerned because it is using methods that are totally alien to those of the apostles and their successors, and secondly, and more seriously, because of the element of deception about the whole thing. The devil's work is deception; ours as Christians is to be the very opposite. In 2 Corinthians 4:1–2 it says, 'Therefore, having this ministry by the mercy of God,

THERE IS STILL MUCH TO DO!

we do not lose heart. But we have renounced disgraceful, underhanded ways. We refuse to practise cunning or to tamper with God's word, but by the open statement of the truth we would commend ourselves to everyone's conscience in the sight of God.' These are surely very important verses to carry with us into our work for the Lord! The phrase 'open statement' literally means 'uncovering'. How ironic that some would cover up before people who they are and what they are doing, in order to then supposedly uncover the gospel message!

Using magic, therefore, begs the question: in what are we putting our confidence when we evangelize? That is surely a vital question for us to be concerned about, and one that we should keep coming back to again and again. A verse that is used to justify things like magic and indeed drama is 1 Corinthians 9:22: 'To the weak I became weak, that I might win the weak. I have become all things to all people, that by all means I might save some.' We need to discover exactly what it is that Paul is meaning by these words.

Paul is saying that his focus is on doing all he can to get alongside his hearers so that any hindrance to the gospel is removed. There are two famous missionaries who come to my mind as I think about this. The first is Hudson Taylor, who controversially adopted both Chinese dress and a Chinese hairstyle while serving the Lord in China. He did this because he realized that his western attire was putting up a barrier between him and the people he was seeking to reach for the Lord. To Taylor, then, the 'all things to all people' meant the willingness to adapt culturally for the sake of the gospel, despite what others may have thought of him.

THERE IS STILL MUCH TO DO!

This was also the case with our second missionary, Mary Slessor. It was said of her,

> Other missionaries considered Mary foolish for flouting the European way of dressing; going bareheaded in the tropics, barefooted through the forests and abandoning her Victorian petticoats to cope better in the climate. Her motive was simply to remove any barrier that got in the way of communicating the gospel, which she shared with anyone who would listen.[1]

For a woman to dress differently, and perhaps it was considered less modestly, was even more radical, but Mary could see the sense of it and eventually others would follow. It is so important for missionaries to appreciate that they go to other countries and cultures, not to turn people into Westerners, but to turn them to the Lord Jesus.

So where does this leave something like drama, which is also popular as a means of evangelism? Rather than listening to someone just speaking, these days people want something more entertaining. Drama is increasingly squeezing out preaching in many churches today. It is worth giving space to look at this, not only to show what we should perhaps avoid doing, but also, positively, to show what we should be doing instead.

There is no doubt that those who advocate the use of drama are very sincere in their desire to reach people for the Lord. I simply want to argue that there is a better way. Please notice the following points:

1. PAUL DOESN'T MENTION DRAMA IN THIS CHAPTER
This point is surely very significant. We should focus on what Paul does mention in 1 Corinthians 9, as it is quite revealing. He mentions preaching the gospel, and does so no less than

four times. Paul was a preacher. That is what he loved to do, and without a doubt he loved it because he saw it as the most effective way of sharing the gospel.

2. PAUL DOESN'T EVER REFER TO DRAMA BEING USED

Paul doesn't refer to using drama either to teach Christians or to evangelize the lost. It is important, when broaching the subject of drama, that we not only check the context of this chapter, but we also widen it out to the context of the whole of the New Testament. When we do so, we fail to find any reference at all in the book of Acts to Paul or any of the apostles ever using drama. We also fail to find any supporting references to drama in any of the letters of Paul or in any other New Testament writer. We must also state that there are no references whatsoever to the Lord ever using drama in his ministry. Yes, He did things that were dramatic, such as cursing the fig tree outside Jerusalem, but that is a world away from gospel truth being acted out. However, the New Testament is not silent on the preferred way of evangelizing: it is clearly preaching and witnessing.

3. DRAMA STILL REQUIRES FURTHER EXPLANATION AND APPLICATION

I once saw a performance on the streets of High Wycombe and the message was so indistinct that I had to ask someone afterwards what it was they were seeking to convey. Even good drama needs preaching to back it up. However, good preaching does not need anything to back it up.

4. DRAMA RISKS TRIVIALIZING THE SERIOUSNESS OF THE GOSPEL

James Stewart wrote, 'The old-fashioned method of evangelism

THERE IS STILL MUCH TO DO!

was to make people weep, but the modern Hollywood way is to make people laugh.'[2] However, the supreme emphasis in communicating the gospel must be a sense of seriousness. After all, life-and-death issues are being dealt with. Matters of eternal significance are being addressed. Paul writes, 'I charge you in the presence of God and of Christ Jesus, who is to judge the living and the dead, and by his appearing and his kingdom: preach the word' (2 Tim. 4:1–2a). Acting out a funny sketch just seems so out of place.

5. THE CHURCH ONLY INTRODUCED DRAMA AT A TIME OF SPIRITUAL DECLINE

This was true of what were called the 'mystery plays' during the Middle Ages. These were performances that usually represented biblical subjects. They developed from plays presented in Latin by churchmen on church premises and depicted such subjects as the creation, Adam and Eve, the murder of Abel, and the last judgement. During the thirteenth century, various guilds began producing the plays in the vernacular at sites in the open air. Under these conditions, the strictly religious nature of the plays gradually declined, and they became filled with apocryphal and satirical elements which were designed to mock physicians, soldiers, judges and even monks and priests.

6. THE DRAMA USED DID NOT REVERSE THE SPIRITUAL DECLINE

It was preaching that the Lord used to reverse the decline during what became known as the Reformation from the sixteenth century onwards. Even before then, the Lord used preaching to reach people. John Wycliffe (1320–1384), who was known as 'the morning star of the Reformation', sent out his Lollards in the fourteenth century. 'Lollard' was a term of contempt, by the way. It meant 'mumbler'. They were regarded as heretics by the church! They still went out faithfully, though, with tracts, sermons and copies of the English Bible Wycliffe had translated. They were poor priests, often uneducated men. But they were men sent out to preach the gospel—not only in churches and churchyards when necessary, but also in markets, fairs and other open places where people congregated. They were times of spiritual famine, but they knew what the antidote for that famine was: the preaching of the Word of God. We're living in increasingly similar times. God has committed to us the very same antidote of public proclamation of the truth.

Brian Edwards, in his very helpful little book *Shall We Dance?*, makes a very powerful point regarding church history. When the church has gone down the visual road, it has lost the spiritual road. When the church has been strong, there's been strong preaching, both as cause and effect. When the church has been weak, there's been little or no preaching. We should heed the warning!

7. IT IS PREACHING THAT THE WORD OF GOD ENCOURAGES OVER AND OVER AGAIN

We find this to be the case throughout the Bible. There is a very real sense in which we can say that good preaching should be drama enough! If a man is taken up with the grandeur and glory of his message, he should be demonstrating that in how he expresses himself. Dr Martyn Lloyd-Jones said that true preaching should be 'action, action, action'—not dreary, not dull and stoical, but bright, energetic, enthusiastic and fervent.

8. MISAPPLYING PAUL'S WORDS COULD OPEN THE DOOR TO THE WORST OF EXCESSES

There are those who see that phrase of Paul's, 'all things', and understand it to mean doing whatever takes our fancy in order to evangelize. Surely, though, it cannot be right to step outside the orbit of what Scripture encourages in our methods of seeking to reach the lost.

Some might ask, 'What about the parables? Aren't they full of drama?' Yes, indeed they are, but they are real-life illustrations told as stories and not performed sketches. The Lord never got the disciples to act them out for people to watch. The parables had a twofold purpose—to clarify the truth for some, and to hide the truth from others. Drama does not have that twofold purpose.

Perhaps you wonder about the use of puppets in children's work. They are no doubt entertaining and usually give people a good laugh, but I cannot help feeling that they are an inappropriate means to share the gospel. We are seeking to convey to people the reality of gospel truth, but doing so through non-real characters must send out mixed messages. Have we lost confidence in the art of story-telling? A Bible story told well will hold children's attention just as well as any puppets.

Let's turn our attention to why preaching should have a prominent place in our gospel outreach:

1. PREACHING HAS BEEN ORDAINED BY GOD

A man just standing and speaking may seem a bit lame today.

THERE IS STILL MUCH TO DO!

Even the church in many quarters has precious little time for it. Some years ago, I read in a Christian magazine an article that described preaching as 'outmoded and ineffective'. If that is correct, we ought to be able to come up with something better, something that will bring more success in reaching modern men and women and producing better results. After all, we want to do our best for the Lord, so we want to do all we can to reach the lost, and to feed the saints as well.

Don't be alarmed—I'm not going to suggest we jettison preaching! Far from it! John Wycliffe said nearly eight hundred years ago, 'Preaching is the highest service to which man may attain on earth.' I think he was right, and even after all these centuries he is still right. (I later cancelled my subscription to that magazine, by the way.) Yes, preaching can be hard. Indoor preaching can be hard. Few may come in to listen, or, on the other hand, many may come in, but they may not listen. Open-air preaching can be very hard. There's often so much apathy and indifference to the things of God and the good news of the gospel.

So when the discouraged preacher returns from a meeting that seemed to produce no visible effect on any of the hearers, should he say to himself, 'I need to find a better way of sharing the gospel than this'? No, he should not. If he should be saying anything at all, it is this: 'I need more of God in my preaching. I need more of Him before, during and after, so that His Word will be a blessing to others.' In Paul's letter to Titus he makes an important statement about preaching and its significance in the work of God in the world: 'God … has in due time manifested His word through preaching, which was committed to me' (1:2–3, NKJV). God had instructed Paul that his main vehicle of communication was to be public preaching of the Word of God.

We need to remember that neither our churches nor the Church Fathers came up with the idea of preaching. If they had, it would be a type of evangelism that is merely cultural, which would mean that at some point it would run its course. Actually, though, preaching is something that transcends culture and is therefore vitally relevant for today. But how do we know that? For at least two reasons:

(a) God ordained preaching from the earliest of days

Do you know who the first preacher was? 'Noah,' you might say. Peter tells us that Noah was 'a herald of righteousness' (2 Peter 2:5). But you are wrong: he wasn't the first preacher; God was. It was in the Garden of Eden, in his question to Adam and Eve: 'Where are you?' (Gen. 3:9). That question is still an integral part of our gospel preaching today, asking unbelievers to search their hearts as to where they are with God.

This is very instructive for us. Ever since that first sermon, Almighty God has been communicating with mankind through words. Yes, He has also done so, and continues to do so, through visual aids like stars, the skies, landscapes, flowers, organs, cells. Through these He reveals something of 'his eternal power and divine nature' (Rom. 1:20). But He reveals so much more about Himself through His Word—that living Word, the Lord Jesus, and that written Word, the Bible. God communicated His word first through His prophets. We can think in the Old Testament of Noah, Moses, Samuel, David, Ezra, Isaiah and Jeremiah, to name but a few. The Lord commissioned Jeremiah to 'Proclaim all these words in the cities of Judah and in the streets of Jerusalem' (Jer. 11:6). How interesting that, even when in a different culture, as Babylon certainly was for the Israelite exiles, preaching was still God's way of declaring His will to His people. We can read about Ezekiel to be sure of that. The Lord said to his servant, 'You shall speak my words to them, whether they hear or refuse to hear' (Ezek. 2:7).

And finally, God's word would come through His Son. Of all the activities listed in the Gospels that Jesus was engaged in, preaching or teaching always topped the list: 'And Jesus went throughout all the cities and villages, teaching in their synagogues and proclaiming the gospel of the kingdom and healing every disease and every affliction' (Matt. 9:35). The apostles and others after them were commissioned by the Lord to preach among Jews and Gentiles in many different cultural settings. That's why Paul, at the end of his life, was so fervent in exhorting Timothy to 'Preach the word' (2 Tim. 4:2).

(b) God ordained preaching for dark days and light

'Preach the word; be ready in season and out of season,' Paul urged. This word 'season' is not a reference to sport or gardening. Paul is saying that the gospel message must be preached both when it is popular and when it is unpopular. The eighteenth-century Anglican minister and evangelist John Berridge was challenged by his bishop for preaching outside his parish without permission, something that is prohibited in the Anglican Church. Berridge replied something like this: 'But I have only preached twice—in season and out of season.' We could ignore that and just wait for Christianity to come back into fashion, but that risks never sharing the gospel with anyone. At the end of the day, it isn't preaching that people don't want, so much as the message itself. They don't want to hear about the living God and the demands He makes upon their lives to repent and believe—the very things they so need to hear of and do.

Many churches are ignoring these words of Paul in the Bible completely. They have developed the mindset that when the Word of God is out of season, we shouldn't preach it. A couple of years ago, a student in Exeter hindered other students from listening to the street preacher by saying loudly, 'This isn't the right way to reach people!' It turned out that she was a born-again Christian. She missed the irony that quite a crowd was actually standing there, listening to God's Word! Keeping on 'out of season' is hard, but it's very sad when that difficulty is made harder by Christians. It can be very tough, but we must keep going. There's a sense in which the response is irrelevant anyway. A famous theologian and preacher from the fourth century, John Chrysostom, who was the Archbishop of Constantinople, said, 'Just as the fountains, though none may draw from them, still flow on, and the rivers, though none drink of them, still run, so must we do all on our part, in speaking, though none give heed to us.' Yes, preach the very best we possibly can, but nonetheless our work is to do just what the Lord said to Ezekiel as already quoted: 'You shall speak my words to them, whether they hear or refuse to hear' (2:7).

2. PREACHING IS SOMETHING GOD USES

THERE IS STILL MUCH TO DO!

When God has a means, you can be sure He has an end in view! That end is the saving of many, many lost souls. We're living in days when we long to see more souls saved and brought into the kingdom. We long to see God using preaching far more—of course we do! We long to see God using it as He did in what we affectionately call 'the olden days'. I'm only fifty, but according to my children I've lived in 'the olden days'. I've had to point out several times that I've only lived in 'the newen days', not 'the olden days'.

When we think of the real 'olden days', our minds may go back to the eighteenth century and to the enormous crowds that gathered around men like George Whitefield and John Wesley in England and Howell Harris and Daniel Rowlands in Wales. Even as recently as 1915 large crowds of soldiers gathered around the OAM evangelists as they preached in garrisons like the one in Frimley near Aldershot. At this venue, the congregation was almost entirely made up of German prisoners-of-war! The OAM Annual Report for that year records, 'Colonel Douglas-Jones interpreted the secretary as he preached to over twelve hundred men. The prisoners themselves provided a platform, bringing a trestle-table for that purpose. The hearing was truly wonderful. At the close, huge numbers of Testaments were distributed. The gratitude of the prisoners was profoundly touching.' Large crowds of British troops would gather in many other garrisons and other open-air venues during the First World War.

There's power in this old gospel, isn't there? From time to time it can still be seen. A few years ago, three of us from the Mission went to survey the centre of Manchester to see if it would be suitable for an outreach event. We set up the display board and one of the evangelists began preaching. It was a message he had used many times before. However, on this occasion, a large crowd gathered to hear him. I stood back and counted. There were fifty people who allowed their day to be interrupted for a few minutes to listen to a man holding a Bible and preaching a message from it. It was a glorious sight!

Powerful preaching can do two tremendous things: reach the lost and feed the sheep. Our focus is on reaching the lost. Some reading this can no doubt testify that it was through the agency of preaching that God graciously brought them to Himself. It was through preaching that God first spoke to you and saved you. Let me give you a couple of examples of the Lord doing just that elsewhere, one from indoors and one from the open air.

An evangelist was preaching at a gospel meeting in a church on one occasion. At the end he approached a lady in the congregation to make conversation.

He asked, 'Are you a Christian?'

'Yes,' she said.

'That's really great!' he replied, before probing a bit further: 'How long have you been a believer?'

The reply was very surprising, but very wonderful: 'Oh, about ten minutes!'

An OAM associate evangelist was preaching in the open air in Pontypridd about eight years ago. An eleven-year-old girl stood and listened for about fifteen minutes. She was approached afterwards to see what she thought, whereupon she volunteered the following statement: 'I never became a

Christian till I heard you telling the gospel.' He had a little talk with her and it seemed that she had responded in her heart while she was listening.

We mustn't give up on preaching as somehow outmoded and of no real use any longer. It is still God's way! It is still God's means! Modern man is not so modern that he won't listen to preaching when God is speaking.

But we need to know what energizes that gospel power so that God is heard to speak. The answer is that it's not a 'what' but a 'who'. It is the ministry of the person of the Holy Spirit. We have been promised by the risen Lord Jesus that we shall receive power when the Holy Spirit comes upon us. That is what the church needs more than anything else in this generation. However naturally gifted a man may be, however great his wealth of experience, God must come and anoint his preaching if he is going to see people being saved. How we should be praying for the power of the Holy Spirit to come upon our meetings, whether indoors or in the open air! Without the Spirit of Jesus we can do nothing, we can achieve nothing. We need Him in our midst; we need Him speaking through us, to the minds and hearts of our hearers.

3. PREACHING HAS AUTHORITY

We live in a day which is anti-authority. People don't like to be told, 'This is the way, walk in it!' It is probably one reason why preaching is viewed negatively in many quarters—preaching has authority. The preacher is a herald delivering a message, and because that message has come from the King it has authority. Rather than hear that message and then humbly respond to it, people at worst dismiss it or at best want to have their say about it. The trouble is, 'having our say' all too often leads to 'having our way'.

Does a man convey that what he has to share is from the Lord, rather than just from him? Is he just bringing instruction from the Word of the Lord, or is He bringing a message from the Lord of the Word? There is a difference! If you saw the order of service I have in front of me when I lead a service, you would see that I never include the word 'sermon' on it. Never. This is the definition of a sermon: 'a spoken or written discourse on a religious or moral subject.' Now that is part of the preacher's job, but preaching is surely something far more than that. On my order of service I always have the word 'message' before the final hymn. My supreme joy, blessing and responsibility is to share a message which I earnestly believe is from God to that congregation. If any man comes to a congregation, whether it's indoors or in the open air, with a message to communicate that has come from God, that should show—and very clearly!

4. PREACHING HAS GRAVITY

When we think of the momentous subject matter of the Bible and the tremendous themes of the gospel, there should be a certain gravitas about making those things known, and that must include the 'what' of our message as well as the 'how'. There can be a real temptation to give the hearers what we think they want, rather than what we know they need. In 2 Corinthians Paul warns the Corinthians about false prophets who were hard at work trying to infiltrate the church: 'For we are not, like so many, peddlers of God's word, but as men

THERE IS STILL MUCH TO DO!

of sincerity, as commissioned by God, in the sight of God we speak in Christ' (2:17). Paul draws a clear distinction between himself and them.

Peddlers of the gospel have always been around. Back in fourteenth-century England there were many friars whose itinerant ministries were supposed to involve gospel preaching. John Wycliffe said of them, 'They peddled anecdotes and fables.' Peddlers were known to be dishonest. They talked up their whole stock, irrespective of whether what they sold was good quality or not. There are peddlers today, too. They are mainly heard emphasizing all the benefits of salvation, while neglecting the cost of discipleship! In effect, they are treating their hearers as consumers! Isaiah 1:22 speaks of those who mixed their wine with water. A watering-down of the gospel message is very common today. Some portray the Lord as nothing more than a kind of cosmic sugar daddy. He's waiting with a blank cheque book to give you whatever you want. Such preachers may be genuine in their motives, but they are genuinely wrong and damaging in their results. Yes, the Lord certainly is a heavenly Father to those who trust in Him and submit to Him, but He is no sugar daddy!

We are not to be guilty of cheapening God's revelation, His truth. Several times over the years I have been challenged in the open air for preaching about sin and its consequences: 'You need to just preach on the love of God.' The thing is, although that is a tremendous part of the gospel, it is not the entirety of it. Someone once responded to that way of thinking by saying, 'If you only tell people that God loves them, they will just smile and go on sinning.' We need at all costs to be faithful to the One who has entrusted to us the message to share. Paul stated that he was commanded to preach, and to preach God's Word! The gospel message is not something to tamper with in order to make it more attractive. It is already attractive enough. The Lord says,

Come, everyone who thirsts,
    come to the waters;
and he who has no money,
    come, buy and eat!
Come, buy wine and milk
    without money and without price. (Isa. 55:1)

The Lord Jesus said, 'Come to me, all who labour and are heavy laden, and I will give you rest' (Matt. 11:28). What a glorious offer!

5. PREACHING SHOULD GRIP US

Yes, we should be gripped by the need to preach. Preaching the gospel is a task that must be done. 'For if I preach the gospel, that gives me no ground for boasting. For necessity is laid upon me. Woe to me if I do not preach the gospel!' (1 Cor. 9:16). Why did Paul write those words? Because he knew that preaching was the best way to fulfil Scriptures like Proverbs 24:11: 'Rescue those who are being taken away to death; hold back those who are stumbling to the slaughter.' We should therefore be passionate about seeing preaching done, and done well. And a part of that ought to include passion in the preaching itself. We need to preach with passion. After all, we're sharing the greatest news in the world! Hymn-writer Edward Burns put it like this:

THERE IS STILL MUCH TO DO!

We have a gospel to proclaim;
Good news to man throughout the earth.
The gospel of a Saviour's name:
We sing His glory, tell His worth.

How can preachers not get excited about that! How can preachers not be fired up about this incredible message to undeserving sinners! Richard Baxter once wrote, 'I marvel how I can preach to people coldly; and how I let men alone in their sins; and that I do not go to them, and beseech them, for the Lord's sake, to repent, however they may take it, and whatever pain and trouble it may cost me.'

A pastor of twenty-eight years went through a spell of ill-health and was unable to preach for quite some time. He later wrote an article with his reflections on that time. He said this about preaching:

After many years of doing, the call of it, the weight of it, the privilege of it and the accountability of it struck me as even more demanding. Now what a thing is this—a mere man called to tell others the way of life! If public prayer seems audacious, what shall we say of preaching? Has not that man enough to do to guard his own soul and behaviour, without being so presumptuous as to take it upon himself to teach others? O how we need God the Holy Spirit to fill the man and feed the people. Preaching! The unspiritual mind has always despised it—the Bible said it would—yet it is the God-ordained means whereby sinners are converted, believers are built up and God is glorified. Not surprisingly, surely, I pondered once more how any man can dare to climb the pulpit steps![3]

He was absolutely right! Of ourselves, we're not worthy of it—in fact, we're not up to it on any level. Basically, it is too much for us on our own. That is why what we need in our

THERE IS STILL MUCH TO DO!

preaching is the Lord: His help, His enabling, His blessing! Prayer and preaching, then, must go hand-in-hand every step of the way if the Lord is going to use it!

Notes

1 Dr Sid Garland, *Evangelical Times*, January 2015.

2 Quoted in R. Stanley, 'Holy Spirit: A Luxury or a Necessity?' SermonIndex.net.

3 Alun T. McNabb, 'The Preacher in the Pew: A Fresh Look at Old Things', *Evangelical Times*, 5 May 2002, https://www.evangelical-times.org/26739/the-preacher-in-the-pew-a-fresh-look-at-old-things/.

12 Preaching the gospel

... to testify to the gospel of the grace of God. (Acts 20:24)

I wonder what you think about the place of the gospel in Sunday services. By 'the gospel' I mean evangelistic or gospel preaching on the Lord's Day. What is gospel preaching? We need to be clear on that since there are some different views around. For me, very simply, it's preaching that is specifically addressed to the unbeliever; preaching that seeks to persuade the non-Christian of his or her need of Christ. My contention in this chapter is that the gospel message does need to be preached in our churches and probably far more than it is. If the gospel really is 'the power of God for salvation' (Rom. 1:16), we should be absolutely thrilled at the prospect of it being preached. If preaching the gospel is God's mechanism to bring people to Himself, it must be preached often—even, dare I say it, weekly!

Some might respond like this: 'Well, you would want to emphasize the gospel wouldn't you. You work for an evangelistic agency. But don't you realize that God's people need teaching as well? The sheep need to be fed as well.' Yes indeed, 'as well' is exactly right, but not 'instead'. This was something that Paul addressed on many occasions in his letters both to churches and to individuals like Timothy and Titus. An example was when Paul was in a place called Miletus, where he called the Ephesian elders to come and hear him for the very last time (Acts 20). He had spent three years preaching and teaching God's Word in the church and in their city. He was now on his way to Jerusalem, anticipating persecution and possibly death. So this was going to be his last opportunity to pass on some helpful spiritual advice to leaders in the church, and he wasn't going to waste it!

Paul said that, while he was in their city, he had preached 'the whole counsel of God' (v. 27). Yes, if Christians are going to grow, like children, they need to be fed. There's no doubt about that at all. Good teaching in our churches is absolutely essential! But there is something else that will feed and benefit believers as well as hearing good teaching. What is it? It is hearing good gospel preaching.

Yes, of course, unbelievers need to hear it. They need to be challenged about their standing with God. They need to be urged to repent and believe in the Lord Jesus.

A lovely example of this happening was back in 2008 with a man named Ivan, who walked down George Street in Luton. It was a Thursday, the day when OAM holds its weekly outreach meeting there. As Ivan drew near, he stopped to listen to the preaching of the gospel. When the preaching stopped, someone approached Ivan and began talking to him. Ivan was invited to a local church on the following Sunday. Ivan accepted this invitation and went along for several Sundays. During one of the services where the gospel was preached, Ivan accepted Jesus Christ as his Saviour, and he joined a local homegroup. A few weeks later he met with the pastor to discuss baptism. Subsequently Ivan was baptized after giving a testimony of his salvation. He continued to attend church regularly. The only time he missed it was when he was away visiting relatives in either Ireland or London. Ivan invited a friend to church who also went on to be saved.

THERE IS STILL MUCH TO DO!

Sometime later, Ivan had to be admitted to hospital, but he seemed at first to be responding to the treatment. However, in March 2009, Ivan went to be with the Lord.

This leads me to say that if we have unbelievers in our congregations, it would seem rather strange to ignore them. I have been troubled to sit in church services where the preacher, in all he said right through the service, assumed that everyone in the room was a Christian. Since I have known full well on those occasions that that wasn't the case, I have wondered whether the preacher either didn't ask about it beforehand or just wasn't especially interested to know. Some have argued that the preacher just needs to proclaim the Word of God anyway and people will be saved. Yes, the Lord is sovereign, He can if He chooses save a person through a message that is directed at Christians. Having said that, why not preach messages that address the people in front of you? It is not hard to choose subjects that will be relevant for both believers and unbelievers. And even if we think everyone in the room is a Christian, especially if we are visiting preachers, we should always have a word of challenge for the unbeliever, just in case.

If we are planning to preach an evangelistic message, there are a few things we should try to keep in mind:

1. TIMING

Some preachers seem to think they are above needing to stick to the time they have been asked to speak for, but if there are unbelievers present at a meeting, they may not be used to a forty-five-minute message, so the preacher will have been asked not to exceed thirty minutes for a reason. If you are in your own church, you will know the length of message that people are used to sitting through. If it is a special meeting to which unbelievers who don't normally attend any Christian meetings are likely to come, we have to accept that they are probably not used to long talks, and if we want to see them again we need to keep our message to an appropriate length. Half an hour provides ample time to include plenty of the precious truth that will do souls much good.

2. SIMPLICITY

I don't think the need for simplicity in gospel preaching today can be stressed enough. We must do all we can to speak in simple language from the pulpit as much as when in one-to-one conversation. If we are going to use words that we know so well, such as 'justify' and 'redemption', we must define them. Even words like 'sin' and 'gospel': though they are perhaps fairly familiar to people, most do not know exactly what they mean. Lamentations 4:4 says, 'The young children ask for bread, but no one breaks it for them' (NKJV). Breaking that gospel bread into manageable chunks is the job of the preacher.

3. DIRECTNESS

Too many speakers today preach about the gospel, but don't actually preach the gospel. Preaching the gospel means being direct; it is addressing the people who are before us and not just talking in generalities. Paul urged in 2 Timothy 4:2, 'Preach the word ... reprove, rebuke, and exhort, with complete patience and teaching.' It is not enough to tell unbelievers something like this: 'People need to believe in

THERE IS STILL MUCH TO DO!

Jesus if they are going to be saved.' Rather, we should be saying to them, 'You need to believe in Jesus if you are going to be saved.' We thereby aim our gospel arrows straight at the target instead of just firing them into the air. Since the Lord Jesus was very direct in His preaching, as were John the Baptist and the apostles, we need to be as well. A. W. Tozer once wrote, 'We are not diplomats but prophets, and our message is not a compromise but an ultimatum.' How right he was!

4. HUMOUR

There is surely a place for humour in our preaching—so long, that is, that it is kept in its place. A light sprinkling can be used to good effect. Charles Spurgeon wrote in his book *The Soul Winner*, 'I would sooner use a little of what some very proper preachers regard as a dreadful thing, that wicked thing called humour—I would sooner wake the congregation up that way than have it said that I droned away at them until we all went to sleep together.' Stuart Olyott, in his excellent book *Preaching Pure and Simple*, lists a number of uses for humour: 'It can relieve emotional pressure, help concentration, capture those who are hostile to us, assault hypocrisy, show how ridiculous some ideas are and prove to our hearers that we are human.'[1] There is plenty there to indicate its usefulness, but we must take care that humour doesn't come to dominate our messages. John Piper says in his little book *The Supremacy of God in Preaching*, 'It is a sign of the age that we are more adept at humour than tears ... laughter seems to have replaced repentance as the goal of many preachers.'[2] What a tragedy

THERE IS STILL MUCH TO DO!

it is that this is true! Preachers are not stand-up comedians; they are heralds of the cross.

5. VISUAL AIDS

If a church is quite happy for you to use visual aids, a PowerPoint presentation can help with the message. John Bunyan spoke about the value of eye-gate as well as ear-gate. Visitors may not be used to long sermons, so a visual presentation can help their concentration. A warning note that needs to be sounded is not to allow the presentation to be so amazing that it drowns out the message. As with illustrations, visual aids are to be windows on the truth, not shutters.

6. CONTENT

Last but by no means least, preach from a text or passage that naturally lends itself to the gospel. If you are preaching evangelistically on a regular basis in the same church, use plenty of variety. Preaching through any of the Gospels is ideal. Another option is to deal with topical issues or seek to answer hot-potato-type questions. One of the benefits to the preacher of being out on the streets on a regular basis is that he keeps in the loop with what people are thinking and talking about. Being relevant to our hearers is vital. Finally, aim to get to the cross as quickly as you can—after all, that is the centrepiece of the Christian message—and always give a clear challenge at the end. In other words, tell people how to become a Christian and explain why it is so urgent.

It is also worth dwelling on the fact that, while the gospel is being preached to the unbeliever, it can do much for believers.

THERE IS STILL MUCH TO DO!

It will do believers an awful lot of good to hear the gospel on a regular basis. Here are eight ways in which it will do us good:

1. IT WILL SHARPEN OUR FOCUS

The gospel, which is good news concerning the life, death, burial and resurrection of the Lord Jesus Christ, is absolutely central to all that we believe and all that we now are as Christians and as churches. Here's a lightning-quick survey of the Scriptures as a reminder of that.

The Old Testament contains at least one prophecy making clear that the very first element of Messiah's work would be to 'bring good news to the poor' (Isa. 61:1). The first four books of the New Testament are called 'the Gospels'. They are the written accounts of the good news of salvation in Jesus. The word 'gospel' appears in the New Testament no less than 104 times. In Mark 1:1 we find the declaration, 'The beginning of the gospel of Jesus Christ, the Son of God.' Then the first recorded public words of Jesus are, 'The time is fulfilled, and the kingdom of God is at hand; repent and believe in the gospel' (Mark 1:15).

Matthew sums up the public ministry of the Lord Jesus as follows: 'And he went throughout all Galilee, teaching in their synagogues and proclaiming the gospel of the kingdom' (Matt. 4:23). An almost identical statement is in 9:35: 'And Jesus went throughout all the cities and villages, teaching in their synagogues and proclaiming the gospel of the kingdom.' Then at the end of the Lord's time on earth, He commanded His people to be involved in this very work. Just before He ascended back into heaven He told the disciples, 'Go into all the world and proclaim the gospel to the whole creation'

(Mark 16:15). And that is exactly what the apostles then went and did. In Acts 8:25 it says, 'Now when they had testified and spoken the word of the Lord, they returned to Jerusalem, preaching the gospel.'

There are six other occasions when Luke specifically draws attention to the fact that the apostles were spending their time proclaiming the gospel, the final one being the little phrase used by the apostle Paul in Miletus, when he makes it abundantly clear how important the gospel was to him and his ministry. Paul reminded the Ephesian church leaders about the importance not only of preaching the Word, but also of preaching the gospel: 'to testify to the gospel of the grace of God' (Acts 20:24c). Paul saw that as his absolute priority. Nothing was more important!

There may be much going on in our churches—I hope there is—but the gospel should be at the heart of every activity, including what is preached from the pulpit on Sundays. Is it right to think that we can move on from the gospel? Someone rightly said, 'The gospel is not just the ABC of the Christian life, it's the A to Z of the Christian life.' Not quite convinced? Romans 1:8 says, 'your faith is proclaimed in all the world.' Boy, what a church they must have been! So what makes up the majority of the content of that great letter Paul is writing to such mature and godly Christians as the Romans were? He explains the gospel to them. He does so in greater detail than is found anywhere else in the Bible, and he is extremely keen to come and do so in the flesh as well. In Romans 1:15 Paul writes, 'So I am eager to preach the gospel to you also who are in Rome.' If believers with a glowing reputation like theirs needed to hear the gospel, then so do all of us!

THERE IS STILL MUCH TO DO!

2. IT WILL HUMBLE OUR PRIDE

What is the biggest problem Christians have? 'I have many problems,' I hear you say. Yes, so do I. But what is the biggest one? It's pride! God may have dealt it a huge blow when we became Christians, but it's still there, isn't it? There are times when it is given another big knock. We may not like that, but it's good for us when it happens.

A few years ago we went on a church holiday to Cloverley Hall in Shropshire. During the free time there were always lots of games available. A lady called Mina said she wanted to play me at Scrabble. She's from the Philippines and had been in the UK only for about four years. Tagalog is her first language, so I thought our game would be very one-sided. It was, but not in the way I had expected. Imagine how I felt when she beat me! That certainly dented my pride!

So our pride takes hits from time to time, but it isn't dead yet, is it? We know only too well that it is still there. Someone rightly said, 'It still lurks through the corridors of our hearts.' We can still think we are better than we are. We can still think we are better than others are. We can think that, although we weren't saved by what we do, somehow we are kept by what we do, and we earn favour by what we do. These thoughts are so wrong, but they can cause pride to surface. So anything that squashes our pride has got to be a good thing. And what better to do that squashing than the message of the gospel, 'the gospel of the grace of God'? The message of salvation by grace alone, grace alone from beginning to end? The message that we don't, and won't and can't, ever deserve anything from God at all?

We probably know well the line of the hymn, 'Nothing

in my hand I bring'. Isn't that our testimony still today, as much as it was at our conversion? We need reminding that our hands were and are empty, in and of themselves. And we need to be pointed to the cross so that our love, our affection, our confidence, our motivation, our boasting, will be on that and nothing in ourselves. To put it another way: it will be on the One who went to that cross for us, in our place, and who stayed there, in our place, until He had fully paid our debt; until He had fully atoned for all our sin; until God the Father's anger against us had been fully poured out on Him. It was all of grace! And it still is.

Isn't that what we need again and again so much: to have the flames of our pride doused with the water of the message of the cross? That being preached directly to the unconverted will not pass us by, as something no longer relevant, will it? Instead, it will remind us, better than anything else can do, just what we were, and just what God has so graciously done for us in His Son, Jesus!

3. IT WILL INFORM OUR MINDS

Proverbs 15:28 says, 'The heart of the righteous ponders how to answer.' If we are those who want to be used by God to tell others about Him, we need help to do that well. Yes, instruction is needed in order to be able to pass on the message to others! One of the places that instruction can be received is from listening to the gospel being preached, listening to men explaining the way of salvation to others. And there are many different ways in which that can and should be done. Before a new house can be built, you often have to remove the rubbish from the site. There are many false teachings being put out today, some of a very fundamental nature. They need to be refuted. For example, there are those who are known as 'the new atheists', who are becoming increasingly vocal and even aggressive in their tone. They are vigorously challenging the very existence of God. Gospel preaching must answer them. We need to show people that God is, and only the fool will deny it!

There are also many false gospels being espoused—ones that are works-based and religion-based. They come under a host of different names, but at heart they are all the same. The preacher will have to spend some time explaining why they don't and can't work. That may involve stripping away the debris of atheism and evolutionism, plus lots of other 'isms' as well, so that a biblical foundation can then be laid.

There are many questions that will need to be answered to that end: about the meaning of life, the existence of God, the existence of truth, the suffering in the world, the reliability of the Bible, the number of religions. Then there are questions relating specifically to the Lord Himself: did He really live? If so, wasn't He just an ordinary man? What was so special about His teaching? How can anyone live a perfect life? Why did He die on the cross? (What an enormous question that is to answer!) But it doesn't end there: did Jesus really rise from the dead? Will He come back to earth? Why is He coming? When will it be?

As well as there being false gospels to refute, there are also what we might call 'modern takes' on the gospel that also need to be exposed. For example, there is a popular one that sees people as deprived but not depraved. It claims that we need 'stuff' to make us happy, such as money and

THERE IS STILL MUCH TO DO!

possessions. Actually, the 'stuff' we need more than anything is the forgiveness of our sin. It is sin that separates us from our Maker and sin that ultimately makes us miserable.

When the gospel is being preached there will also be explanation, as well as refutation. The preacher will explain *what* the gospel is, *why* it is needed, *how* it works, *what* it does, and *what* the results are, in this life and the next. As we listen to all these issues being dealt with in gospel preaching, we will be being equipped to face those we come into contact with who ask these questions and raise these issues.

4. IT WILL WARM OUR HEARTS

Hearing the gospel will affect more of us than just our minds. It will affect our hearts and our affections as well. Our hearts can so easily grow cold! What's the best remedy to heat them up again? Surely it's hearing the gospel. Haven't you known many times when you have sat listening to the gospel message and it has really blessed you? Sometimes we may even have said something like this afterwards: 'If I wasn't a believer already, I would be after hearing that!' Perhaps that's not very theologically correct, but we know what we mean.

Yes, you are hearing the same truths that you have heard over and over again down the years, truths that some reading this may even have preached over and over again down the years. But it greatly blesses you to hear them yet again. In a very real sense, we should be blessed every time we hear the gospel. After all, it never stops being good news! I've been married for twenty-six years, but I never get tired of Ruth telling me that she loves me. I've never reached the stage where I've just got fed up with it. I may get fed up with some other things she says to me, but never of hearing those words: 'I love you.' In a way, that is what is happening when the gospel is preached. God is telling us again that He loves us and what He's done to prove it. Can we ever tire of being reminded of that? Shouldn't we actually feel rather ashamed if it doesn't warm our hearts again and again?

This is the greatest message in the world. It should mean the world to us. We should simply love hearing it! The old hymn testifies,

I love to hear the story which angel voices tell,
How once the King of glory came down on earth to dwell.
I am both weak and sinful, but this I surely know,
The Lord came down to save me, because He loved me so.

(Emily H. Miller)

But some may want to protest and say, 'But I would get tired of hearing the ABC of the gospel, of hearing John 3:16, preached every week.' I suppose we all would. But that isn't what it has to be. It's been said that the gospel is a bit like a large and beautiful diamond. It has many sides to it, and when lifted up in the sunlight it sparkles with amazing lustre from all its various angles. Would the owner of a huge diamond tire of looking at it, enjoying it, basking in the blessing of it, the glory of it, the worth of it? I don't think so! And neither should we tire of hearing the gospel!

The preacher's job is to show those many sides of that gospel diamond. As well as all those questions we mentioned earlier, he can preach on so much else: on the Old Testament story of redemption, on the men and women of faith in the Old Testament, on the types of Christ in the Old Testament, on

THERE IS STILL MUCH TO DO!

prophecies about the Lord that abound in the Old Testament. Then there's the life of the Lord in the Gospels, the parables of the Lord, the teaching of the Lord, the miracles of the Lord, the passion narratives. He can preach the great gospel sermons in Acts, the wonderful conversion stories in the Acts, and the great gospel doctrines in the epistles. The range and variety available is immense!

5. IT WILL THRILL OUR SOULS

Isn't this the same as warming our hearts? No, because what I mean here is that the gospel should thrill our souls if we are aware that we are not the only ones in the room hearing this wonderful message. When we are sitting in the congregation and someone is preaching the gospel, we should be doing two things as well as listening:

(a) Rejoicing

We should be thanking God that there are unbelievers in the room who are hearing the message that can transform their lives. We should be rejoicing that non-Christians are listening to the gospel of the grace of God! We should be thrilled that those who otherwise might never hear the precious truths about the Lord Jesus are hearing them right now. Hungry people are being offered the bread of life. What could make any of us happier?

And that leads me, very naturally, to the second thing.

(b) Praying

We should be praying for those who are hearing the gospel. That is surely part of our responsibility, our role, in what is going on. We're not bemoaning the fact that this isn't for

THERE IS STILL MUCH TO DO!

us—it is for us, as the other points have tried to demonstrate. But this is for others as well. And we know that God is pleased, in some mysterious way, to use our prayers, as well as gospel preaching, to draw men and women, boys and girls, to Himself! Knowing that He does that is thrilling too.

We know, of course, that we can't save the unbelievers who are in the room with us, but, equally, we know the Lord can! We should be so burdened for them that in those moments we should be doing the only thing for them we can: praying for them; praying that the Lord would open their eyes to the truth of the gospel and enable them to respond in faith to what they are hearing!

6. IT WILL QUELL OUR DOUBTS

Let's be honest, we all have doubts from time to time. Surely nothing is so helpful at removing those doubts than being reminded of gospel truth, of the things that really did happen outside those walls of Jerusalem all those years ago, of the things that Jesus did for sinners, even the very worst of them, as he hung upon that terrible cross. We have solid facts of history on our side, and being reminded of them will do us all good. A lawyer once said to a colleague, 'Why do you go to hear that evangelist D. L. Moody—you don't believe as he does, do you?' The reply came back, 'No, but he believes what he preaches with all his heart, and it is well to meet such a man in these days of doubt and uncertainty.' Oh, to hear preaching like that and also to be a preacher like that! To be those who are known to have such conviction, so that we will be of maximum help to those who may be doubting!

THERE IS STILL MUCH TO DO!

7. IT WILL LIFT OUR SPIRITS

There are many reasons why a Christian may become discouraged or downcast. What a blessed help it will be in those times to be reminded of the glorious gospel of the blessed God. The apostle Paul wrote many of his letters to churches that were going through tough times. Again and again he pointed them back to the beloved Saviour who was crucified for them. Hearing the gospel will help to keep us near the cross, and that is the place to be when we are feeling low. In his lovely little book entitled *Spurgeon's Sorrows*, Zac Eswine writes, 'Jesus Christ knows all your troubles, for similar troubles were His portion too.'[3] This is the reason why we need to have our minds and hearts turned to Him and to His sacrifice again and again.

8. IT WILL RENEW OUR ZEAL

How we need this again and again! When we remember what the Lord Jesus was willing to endure for us, what He went through, all that He suffered, can it do anything *but* stir us up to want to serve Him with all of our hearts? He has done so much for us; can it be right that we have done so little for Him? This particularly needs to be the kind of question regularly asked by pastors and evangelists, and indeed by all of God's people. Hearing the gospel will surely, more than anything, bring us back to where we need to be.

An Army Scripture Reader named Harry Wisbey, who served the Lord on the front line in France during the very early part of the First World War, would rise in the morning and say, 'Another blessed day before me, with many opportunities for doing service for God. Oh, that I may just

THERE IS STILL MUCH TO DO!

seize them—every opportunity!' Everyone he met he sought to tell about Jesus. Oh, for more of that zeal in me! Thomas Watson wrote, 'Zeal in the ministry is as proper as fire on the altar.' If it is lacking in us, how we need to beseech heaven to send it down!

Yes, it is profitable for Christians to hear the gospel being preached—to sharpen our focus, to humble our pride, to inform our minds, to warm our hearts, to thrill our souls, to quell our doubts, to lift our spirits and to renew our zeal. There's really no end to the benefit of hearing the old, old story of Jesus and His love. And at the same time, who knows what blessing it will be to the unbeliever who hears it proclaimed?

Notes

1 Stuart Olyott, *Preaching Pure and Simple* (Bridgend: Bryntirion Press, 2005), p. 132.

2 John Piper, *The Supremacy of God in Preaching* (Grand Rapids, MI: Baker, 1990), p. 58.

3 Zac Eswine, *Spurgeon's Sorrows* (Tain: Christian Focus, 2014), p. 32.

THERE IS STILL MUCH TO DO!

13 Calling the unchurched

And he went about among the villages teaching. (Mark 6:6)

Thomas Watson was never one to hold back from challenging the Lord's people. He once wrote, 'Christ's ministers must embrace every opportunity of doing good to souls.' He was urging preachers to be looking for occasions and locations where they could be sharing the gospel with the unchurched. It may be that some men have never given any thought to the possibility of preaching anywhere but inside their churches. But praise God, He has given us many very good locations which are in the open air. Now, of course, the church is a very good place to preach the gospel, but there are so many people who have not ventured, and perhaps never will venture, into our churches. We need to understand, therefore, that we cannot afford just to wait for them hopefully to see sense and come in to us; instead, we must go out to them.

For several reasons there are some who have decided that open-air preaching is not a valid form of outreach in the twenty-first century, but I would humbly urge them to think again. If the Bible is to be our manual for evangelism, then open-air preaching is actually the most valid form of evangelism in any century. We are on very dodgy ground if we try to say that, although it was appropriate in a bygone age, it is not so today. The words of the Lord Jesus make that crystal clear.

THERE IS STILL MUCH TO DO!

In Mark 13:10, describing the events leading up to the Second
Coming, He says, 'And the gospel must first be proclaimed to
all nations.' The Greek word translated 'proclaimed' here is
kērusso, which specifically means public proclamation. Surely
what the Lord is saying is that the preaching of the gospel will
not go out of fashion, as far as He is concerned, until His return.
That being the case, it must not go out of fashion as far as His
church is concerned, either! Since the Lord hasn't returned yet,
we mustn't stop preaching where people are.

Matthew 24:14 records the Lord expanding a little on this
and using the same verb as in Mark 10: 'And this gospel of the
kingdom will be proclaimed throughout the whole world as
a testimony to all nations, and then the end will come.' If we
think that the Lord's return is near, we might be wondering
what it is important for us to be doing. But now we know: we
should be preaching the gospel to people where they are! Our
great God has commanded it.

Sadly, there are excuses given for not wholeheartedly
supporting the work of open-air preaching today. For
example:

1. IT IS UNDIGNIFIED

Some preachers feel it is somehow undignified to preach
outside. It is interesting that the only man in the whole of
the Bible who is known as an 'evangelist', Philip, did not feel
this way! That's exactly what he did in Samaria, and much
blessing was upon his ministry there. Acts 8:5 reports, 'Philip
went down to the city of Samaria and proclaimed to them the
Christ.' What follows in terms of the response makes thrilling
reading. After his encounter with the Ethiopian eunuch we're

told that 'as he passed through he preached the gospel to all the towns until he came to Caesarea' (8:40).

Surely what is undignified is preaching to lots of empty seats every week! I don't say that to mock those who are perhaps very busy and very diligent in seeking to fill those seats. But we should be concerned if there are many who are doing very little to bring people under the sound of the gospel. Too many have convinced themselves that evangelism is a church-building-based activity and limit themselves to that. Yes, we have special services at Christmas, Easter and harvest, and maybe at other times too. We have meetings with food to entice people in. These are all well and good, but there is something wrong with the mindset that sees evangelism and preaching as happening only within the four walls of a building. After all, lots of people won't come to meetings even when a lovely free meal is available for them.

The question we should ask ourselves is: is this 'indoor mentality' to be found in the Gospels? The answer is 'no'! Is it found in the book of Acts, then? No! Is it taught in the Epistles? No again! What about in church history? Well, yes, some men had very firm views. Take John Wesley. He wrote in his journal on 31 March 1739:

In the evening I preached in Bristol, and met Mr Whitefield there. I could scarce reconcile myself at first, to this strange way of preaching in the fields, of which he set me an example this Sunday; having been all my life so tenaciously of every point relating to decency and order, that I should have thought the saving of souls almost a sin, if it had not been done in a church.[1]

However, the influence of his good friend George Whitefield

brought about a radical change in Wesley's thinking, so that just a few days later, on 2 April 1739, Wesley wrote, 'At four o'clock in the afternoon, I submitted to be more vile, and proclaimed in the highways the glad tidings of salvation.' That was the first time in what was going to be fifty-one years of blessed open-air preaching (they called it 'field preaching' in those days) all over the British Isles.

2. IT IS UNCOMFORTABLE

Let's be honest, we would all prefer the warmth, comfort and safety of our church buildings. We talk today of our comfort zones. In the work of the Lord Jesus He very often takes us outside these zones, and we should be willing to go where He leads. To quote John Wesley again, he once wrote in his diary, 'What marvel the devil does not like field preaching. Neither do I. I love a commodious [spacious and comfortable] room, a soft cushion, a handsome pulpit.' That was his natural inclination, as it is ours, too. But Wesley went on, 'But where is my zeal, if I do not trample all these under foot in order to save one more soul?' This brings us back to our concern or otherwise for the lost. If, as is the case, so many people are never hearing the gospel, and this is one way that enables more to do so, surely we should be motivated to go to them and call to them, like the heralds of old, and urge them to seek the Lord while He may be found.

George Whitefield was often barred from preaching in churches because of his evangelical theology. Maybe one day that will be our experience where we are called to minister the gospel. Whitefield's response was telling: 'If the pulpits be shut, blessed be God! the fields are open. I can go outside the camp, bearing the Redeemer's reproach. I am used to this and glory in it.' Here was a great man of God who wasn't at all bothered about the location, so long as he could preach the gospel to those who needed to hear it.

3. IT IS UNACCEPTABLE

This has been the view of some who have wrongly interpreted verses of Scripture such as Matthew 7:6: 'Do not give dogs what is holy, and do not throw your pearls before pigs.' I suppose the thought is that by going into open-air situations we may be speaking to 'dogs' and 'pigs'. Over the years I have undoubtedly met people who fall into this category. They hate the gospel and make it known very readily and in an arrogant and rude way. When we meet such people, we must undoubtedly give them short shrift and move on to speak to others. But how terribly wrong it would be to suggest that everyone we come into contact with in the open air falls into the category of 'dogs' or 'pigs'. Most people are not such, and in fact some are very keen to hear the gospel of Jesus Christ. When we stand before a crowd of people to declare the gospel, we never know whether among them there are sheep whom the Lord intends to bring into His fold. The Lord Jesus Himself regularly preached in the open air, not to mention the Old Testament prophets and the New Testament apostles; so to try to argue that it is unacceptable is in itself unacceptable—not least because it is something the Lord blesses. And by the way, that quotation from the Lord Jesus above is from the Sermon on the Mount, the most famous message ever preached. Where was it preached? In the open air!

THERE IS STILL MUCH TO DO!

In July 2008 a young man called Keith from a Roman Catholic background stood at a distance listening to an OAM evangelist in Windsor. It took him a while to pluck up the courage to go over and speak. He eventually did so and a brief conversation ensued. Keith was slightly autistic and didn't show much emotion as he asked about sin and forgiveness. Four weeks later he returned and greeted the evangelist warmly, and during the conversation it was noticeable that Keith's understanding of the gospel was clearer. Eight months later Keith returned again, but this time it was to say that he had become a Christian three weeks previously. From the way he spoke it was clear that he had been saved. Keith lived in Slough and said he had already found a good church. It was great that he had seen the importance of that without being told. I had the privilege of meeting him a few months later in Slough. He was carrying a good Christian book that he was reading; it was great to see that he had a real spiritual desire.

4. IT IS UNNECESSARY

This might be the view of the pastor of a large church: 'I am preaching to several hundred every Lord's day, so why do I need to preach outside?' The answer is very straightforward. However many hundreds are there on Sunday, they constitute only a tiny fraction of the number of people who live in our towns and cities. What about the huge numbers of people who never have the privilege of hearing even the slightest bit of the gospel message? Even if we were to say that every member of that large church was regularly witnessing to five people—which is being pretty generous—it would still leave the overwhelming majority of local people not hearing the gospel. Let's remember too that very often our congregations are made up mainly of fairly middle-class people, whereas we are called to reach all kinds of people: people from every class in society. The benefit of going into a shopping precinct to evangelize is that every kind of person will be found there, from the richest to the poorest, and everyone in between.

Perhaps we need to make sure that it isn't pride that is keeping preachers fast bound in their pulpits. The truth is, the streets are good pride-killing venues, and since pride is the biggest problem we all have as Christians, we should for that reason alone find open-air ministry very appealing.

Others see street preaching as unnecessary because they would rather use other means on the streets to try to reach people. However, the emphasis of the New Testament is always upon preaching the message: 'And how are they to hear without someone preaching?' (Rom. 10:14). Paul never advocated actors, or mime artists, or dancers, or escapologists, or prayer tents or even singers, but preachers.

I was once preaching with a small team in the centre of Bristol. A student from a local Bible college stood watching and then came over to ask me why we still preached in the open air in this day and age. My answer was short and to the point: 'If preaching was good enough for the great apostle Paul, should it not be good enough for us?' The student's response was, 'Yes, you have a very good point there!' In the Foreword to David Eby's challenging book *Power Preaching for Church Growth*, John MacArthur plainly states, 'Since it is the Lord alone who adds to the church, our focus in church growth ought to be the means He has ordained'[2]—the chief means being preaching, followed by personal evangelism.

THERE IS STILL MUCH TO DO!

What we find again and again is that preaching is like a fishing net that draws people in so that we can then have personal conversations with them.

5. IT IS UNEDIFYING

John MacGregor once said, 'The willing are not able and the able are not willing.' He was drawing attention to two things: firstly, that at times it is those who are most gifted to preach who are least willing to do so in the open air; and, secondly, that often it is those who are least gifted to do street preaching who willingly engage in it. So our problem here may well be that we have seen street preaching done badly: perhaps a man wearing a dark suit standing on his own in the middle of a street, holding a large Bible and shouting in a strident and even harsh way. I totally agree: that really doesn't commend the gospel at all well.

There is a good way and a bad way to do everything; so just because we have seen something done badly, should we write it off altogether? Lydia, the younger of my two daughters, does quite a lot of baking. There have been times when she hasn't been very careful in the quantities she has put in the mixing bowl, and the result has been a pretty untasty cake. However, when I have taken a bite, I have never decided, 'Right, I'm not going to eat her cakes ever again!' When she has been careful with the ingredients, she has baked some lovely cakes. More of the same, please! The lesson to learn is to do the very best you can—and we can apply that to street preaching just as much as to anything else. It has always been the aim of OAM to do open-air preaching in the very best way possible. This is why we run seminars for churches: to help others do the work and to the highest of standards. One of the things we find a great help in the open air is to use a display board. On the upper part of the board we place the bare bones of the messages we preach, and on the lower part we display free literature. Perhaps this would be a good point to draw attention to the fact that a board like this is useful for a number of reasons:

(a) It provides a focal point for the witness
Passers-by can see that something is going on and may be drawn to have a look to see what it is.

(b) It helps to advertise who we are
We always ensure that we have on display the name, address and website of either the local church or the Mission. That gives a sense of accountability and may also reassure people that we are not a strange cult that has just arrived from over the pond.

(c) It can help the listener
To see the headings going up one by one is useful for people, especially those who may come along part-way through a particular message. It means they can pick up the thread of what is being said without difficulty.

(d) It can help the preacher
As we always try to keep eye contact with people, it is not really appropriate to have notes when preaching out of doors. The headings that go up on the board are therefore a very useful aide-memoire for the preacher.

THERE IS STILL MUCH TO DO!

(e) It displays the Word of God

We always include verses of Scripture among our headings. It is more important for people to read these than anything we have come up with ourselves.

(f) It can continue to speak after the preacher has finished

It is regularly the case that when no one is preaching, people will stop to read what is on the board. This will often lead to useful conversations. At holiday destinations, overseas visitors will often photograph or even video what is on the board. Who knows who will end up seeing the content in the future!

6. IT IS UNINSPIRING

This is the final excuse some Christians try to make. You may have seen an open-air meeting and wondered what on earth was being achieved for the kingdom of God. This was a question I was once asked one Thursday afternoon in Luton. Three girls were on an evangelism training day at a local church and came to chat. Two of them quickly expressed their disdain for open-air preaching, although the third girl was very encouraging. I politely explained that, right at that moment, the pastor of a local church was in conversation with a man who had stopped to listen to the preaching. I had no idea at the time what was being said, but afterwards I found out how profitable it had been. The man's name was Jaffa. He was so ashamed of his life that he had changed his name, thinking that would help him to have a new start. Jaffa was a recovering alcoholic and said that he was amazed to hear that God could be interested in someone like him. Contact details

THERE IS STILL MUCH TO DO!

were exchanged and the next day the same pastor paid Jaffa a visit in his flat.

During that conversation Jaffa said he found it hard to accept that someone else could be punished in his place. Literature was left with Jaffa and a few days later he wrote to the Mission office to say he had trusted the Lord. The pastor went back to visit him and later reported the following: 'Jaffa has been converted. What a difference there was in him! He is so full of the joy of the Lord.' This story reminds us that we just never know what the Lord may do through our witness. I often wish I'd been able to share Jaffa's story with those two girls who thought street preaching was a waste of time.

Charles Spurgeon was a great supporter of open-air preaching. In his tremendous book *Lectures to My Students* he devotes two chapters to the subject and even mentions John MacGregor and OAM. One challenging comment is as follows: 'No sort of defence is needed for preaching out of doors; but it would need very potent arguments to prove that a man had done his duty who has never preached beyond the walls of his meeting house.' In another place Spurgeon wrote about the early apostles of the Lord Jesus, 'those who went from city to city proclaiming everywhere the Word of the Lord Jesus would never have turned the world upside down if they had felt it needful to confine themselves to iron rooms adorned with the orthodox announcement, "The gospel of the grace of God will (D.V.) be preached here next Lord's day evening."' In other words, preachers should be greatly inspired to get out among the people and preach the glad tidings of salvation.

In the main, we do see people stop and listen to the gospel message being preached. There are times however, when

THERE IS STILL MUCH TO DO!

there doesn't seem to be anyone listening, and that can be a little discouraging. However, the Lord often gives us surprises in the work. I remember preaching in Luton one very cold February afternoon, having gone out with very low expectations of what would happen that day. I preached a whole message with, it appeared, no one stopping at all. When I finished, someone tapped me on the shoulder. A young Muslim man had been sitting on a bench behind me all the way through. It was barely above freezing, but he stayed to talk for forty-five minutes and only left because he had a job interview to attend. We had a very good discussion and he received a Gospel of John before hurrying away.

Sometimes we hear of even more unusual incidents which remind us of the benefit of open-air preaching, even when it might seem otherwise. The following letter was received from a lady called Debbie:

Last summer I was passing by on the Cornhill in Ipswich one Tuesday lunchtime when I heard a man preaching the gospel message. No one seemed to be listening so I said a prayer and moved into Lloyds Bank to complete my business. As I walked up the stairs to the first floor I remember saying to the Lord, 'That guy is wasting his time.' Our Lord was to teach me a lesson! I went over to the counter and waited to be served. I waited, and waited, and waited. It was a hot day and all the upstairs windows were open to let in the breeze. I was slightly irritated since there were three young ladies apparently having their lunch break who had no interest in serving me at all. I then noticed that they were all thoroughly engrossed in a certain gentleman and his talk that was coming clearly up into this upstairs room. Eventually I was spotted and served, and as I came down the stairs I apologized to the Lord, who told me firmly, but gently, that He doesn't send people out to waste their time and that He knows exactly what

THERE IS STILL MUCH TO DO!

He is doing. I was humbled, but also pleased that the preacher had an audience, even though he could not see them. May he be greatly blessed for being obedient enough to scatter the seed even on stony ground, and may there be a good harvest.

Brian Dee, who was an Associate evangelist with OAM for many years, was the preacher. Brian is now with the Lord.

The danger with all of the above reasons is that really they can be excuses for our not using our preaching gift to the full by being willing to speak out of doors. Perhaps our problem is a lack of zeal. The following description was given of C. T. Studd:

> He saw men and women going in their millions to hell. And he always said that that is all the preparation a man needs for preaching the gospel, if it be a dozen times the same day. 'Don't go into the study to prepare a sermon. That is all nonsense. Go into your study to go to God and get so fiery that your tongue is like a burning coal and you've got to speak.'[3]

If we had more of that fire, would we not be more willing to go wherever the opportunities are and make Christ known?

Now that we've tried to address the negative matters relating to open-air preaching, it would be good to cite the positives:

1. IT IS A MEANS FOR PEOPLE TO LISTEN

It is the usual practice of OAM not to use amplification when preaching in the open air. Really loud preaching tends to annoy people who don't want to listen and also has the effect of pushing people away from us, when our aim is to seek to draw them in. We therefore rely just on the strength of our own voices, but try very hard not to shout, as this usually comes across as being aggressive, which again we want to avoid at all costs. We always encourage local Christians to support the open-air work, as the larger the team, the better the opportunity. The team will stand around in front of the preacher to support him and be on the lookout for anyone listening. Once a person listening moves away from the meeting, the nearest team member will then approach that person to try to engage him or her in conversation. It is thrilling to return to the church after the meeting to discuss all those who have been spoken to, for encouragement and also for prayer.

2. IT IS A MEANS FOR PEOPLE TO ASK QUESTIONS

Sometimes questions will be asked publicly by those we refer to as hecklers. They can be very useful, as a vocal questioner will often catch the ears of other passers-by who will stop to find out how the preacher will answer. This can sometimes lead to others asking questions, and if people are polite enough to wait for the answers, it can encourage more and more people to stop. Sometimes, if a heckler is quite aggressive, this can also help to draw a crowd. The preacher needs a lot of wisdom at those times to keep charge of proceedings and always to respond in a gracious way. From time to time someone will ask a question that is very heartfelt. That was the case in Leicester once, when an elderly man interrupted the preaching by asking, 'I'm ninety years old; am I too late to be saved?' Four or five others who had been listening were able to hear the preacher warmly explain that 'No, you are not too late to be saved!'

THERE IS STILL MUCH TO DO!

3. IT IS A MEANS FOR PEOPLE TO TALK PERSONALLY

Very often, people have questions that they want to ask privately. This leads to one-to-one conversations, and these can be immensely profitable. It can be a great privilege to talk to people individually because at times people will bare their souls and share things that are very private. I suppose they feel that, because this Christian is outside their circle, they have the liberty to open up. Sometimes people who are deeply troubled will come to talk. How we need prayerfully to seek to direct them to the Saviour and, if necessary, point them to a relevant public body such as social services for help.

We can also sense the privilege of talking to people when we identify that the Lord is obviously working in them. Such was the case with Dan, whom I met at Speakers' Corner in London during an OAM outreach event. He was on his way home to visit his mum, who he said was a born-again Christian. Dan shared that he was a bit of a prodigal. He had been involved in all sorts of things, including drink, drugs, witchcraft and even Mormonism. However, he had come to realize that none of these things was of any real benefit to him. During the twenty-minute conversation Dan said longingly, 'If only I could be sure that what you are talking about, Jesus and stuff, is real.' I simply replied by asking him if he thought it was real for his mum. 'Yes, it is,' he said. Dan then said something which is a huge mistake that many make: 'I need to get myself sorted out and then I'll turn to Jesus.' I explained to him that it needed to be the other way round: he needed to turn to Jesus so that he could get his life sorted out. He left with a warm handshake, and I felt glad that he was on his way to see his mum, who would further direct him to the Lord.

THERE IS STILL MUCH TO DO!

4. IT IS A MEANS FOR PEOPLE TO RECEIVE LITERATURE

Very often, people don't have time to stop, but they may well be happy to accept a gospel leaflet. Sometimes these go all over the world and we have no idea how they ended up there. Take Lawrence in Zambia, who wrote to the OAM office having found the Mission address on the back of a leaflet. This prompted him to ask a number of questions about salvation. We wrote back to him, sending some helpful booklets and encouraging him to keep in contact. Some weeks later Lawrence sent the following reply: 'Thank you very much for the help you gave by answering my questions. I thank God that you are there to help us understand God. I want you to know that I am no longer the person I used to be. I have come to know God and Christ through your help.'

5. IT IS A MEANS FOR PEOPLE TO BE SAVED

That should be our prayerful expectation every time we go out. It is good to remind ourselves that nothing is too hard for the Lord. Charles Spurgeon once said, 'I do not look for any other means of converting men beyond the simple preaching of the gospel and the opening of men's ears to hear it. The moment the church of God shall despise preaching, God will despise her.' These are telling words and should challenge us as to what our confidence is in when it comes to evangelism.

Even the most unlikely people can be saved. A lady named Patricia was once walking through Nuneaton on market day. She approached one of the Mission evangelists who was standing by his board giving out leaflets. The one he happened to have in his hand was called *Time to Think about the Truth?* When Patricia saw this title she immediately said,

THERE IS STILL MUCH TO DO!

'I can't believe it! That is exactly what I am looking for, and I prayed before I left home that God would lead me to someone who could help me.' So began a conversation that would be continued for many weeks. Patricia had been a member of the Jehovah's Witnesses for a number of years, but was eventually put off by their tight control over people's lives. She had many questions about the Bible, which were answered for her very patiently. It took a while to expose the false teachings she had believed for decades. However, the Lord was working in her, and after a few months Patricia wrote to the Mission office to share that she had been saved and she wanted to express her appreciation. Concluding her letter, Patricia wrote, 'I am so glad that I met your evangelist that day. Praise God! Thirty years a *Watchtower* slave, but now I'm free!' It is so easy for us to think that certain people who are entrenched in their false beliefs will never come to the truth—but we are very wrong to think that.

All the words in the world can't hide the fact that going into the open air and preaching is a daunting prospect. It reminds me of an email from Jay in Australia. He saw an article about OAM in a Christian newspaper and wrote to ask for advice on going into the open air and preaching. We suggested various things, and a few weeks later the following reply came back from him:

I've just preached outdoors for the first time and, boy, I'm still shaking. I don't think I ever prayed so hard before. I went to one of the local markets. This one is located in a predominantly Eastern European community. I don't think I ever felt so self-conscious, but it soon left, as I watched with an aching heart the hardness on the faces of those passing by. Some jeered, some smiled benignly

THERE IS STILL MUCH TO DO!

and one couple stopped. Then I gave out about thirty tracts. When I returned home I had a wonderful sense of working for the Lord. This work is so exciting. As we would say here, it was ripper!

Back in 1883, the then General Secretary of OAM, who had the unusual name of Gawin Kirkham, was invited to the USA to promote open-air evangelism. The trip was very successful, and just before returning on the ship home Kirkham was interviewed by a newspaper reporter and asked what he would say to Christians in America. This was his reply, which is equally applicable to the UK in the twenty-first century:

If I could make my voice heard to my brethren throughout this vast continent, I would say: Preach in the open air; you have a population that needs it, a climate in which, for considerable periods, it can be done with ease. Be not deterred by difficulties. The work is of God, and the commission given by His Son, Jesus Christ, is as much in force now as when it was uttered. Go out quickly! Time presses. Souls are perishing. The need is urgent. Men will hear. God will bless, and soon there will be the 'Well done, thou good and faithful servant, enter thou into the joy of the Lord.

Notes'

1 *The Heart of Wesley's Journal* (Grand Rapids, MI: Kregal, 1989), p. 47.

2 John MacArthur, 'Foreword', in David Eby, *Power Preaching for Church Growth* (Tain: Mentor, 2009).

3 Norman P. Grubb, *C. T. Studd: Cricketer and Pioneer* (London: Lutterworth Press, 1941), p. 221.

THERE IS STILL MUCH TO DO!

14 Walking the walk

Do your best to present yourself to God
as one approved. (2 Tim. 2:15)

If we are those who are concerned to be evangelizing the people of our generation, it shouldn't be a surprise that God expects us to be people who are seeking to walk closely with Him. He wants us to be living examples of the message we preach. Charles Spurgeon said, 'How can you serve the Lord with your lips if you do not serve Him with your lives?' The Lord does indeed want us to talk the talk—He wants that very much—but He also wants us to be those who walk the walk. That's a bit of a cliché today, but it doesn't matter as it sums up well what is to be important to us.

Many Christians very diligently walk the walk, but they don't have much of a burden to share the gospel. In this chapter we are concerned to address those for whom it may be the other way round: those who are keen to share the gospel and who need to live it out as well. After all, in all that we have to say about evangelism, it would seem strange not to include the evangelists, the people who are going to do this God-appointed work—what they are to be like, what their qualities are, how they are to go about their ministry, what their profile should be. Second Timothy 2 is an appropriate place to go to in order to learn about these things. The great apostle Paul is writing his second letter to a young co-worker in the gospel called Timothy.

Some may want to challenge me at this juncture and

say, 'But Timothy was a pastor, and you are talking about evangelism.' This brings us to a very important point: part of the role of a pastor is to be an evangelist! How do I know that? Paul says so in this same letter. In the midst of other things he tells Timothy to do, he says, 'do the work of an evangelist' (4:5). An evangelist might not be a pastor, but a pastor is always to be an evangelist.

I was greatly impressed to hear some sermons of a well-known pastor and author from the USA. In virtually all his messages he mentioned conversations about the Lord that he had had with people on his travels. Here was a church leader who most definitely had the heart of an evangelist. If that heart is there, the pastor will want, and should make time, to be involved in the evangelistic work of the church. Not all of it—that would be impossible—but at least directly involved in some of it.

There are seven things in 2 Timothy 2 that Timothy is encouraged to be like. In some ways they are a mixed bag, but each has lessons for us to learn and apply. So let's look at each one in turn and seek to apply them to ourselves as evangelists and witnesses for the Lord:

1. A CHILD

'You then, my child ...' (2 Tim. 2:1). This is how Paul refers to Timothy. It shows us that there was real affection between them and that Paul was obviously deeply concerned for his young friend. You might say, 'But this is not anything to do with Timothy's character or conduct; this is merely an affectionate greeting.' No, there's more to it than that. In Paul's first letter he speaks of Timothy as 'my true child in the faith' (1 Tim. 1:2). There's an important principle here: there must be life before there can be work. This chapter of 2 Timothy begins with sonship and ends with service. There's something similar in Exodus 4:23, where the Lord instructs Moses to tell Pharaoh, 'Let my son go that he may serve me.'

How different things would be in many churches if only true believers were permitted to preach! There are so many around the land who are dead preachers, but who are expected to preach living truth. Likewise, there are dead choirs expected to sing praises to the living God. There are also dead Sunday school teachers expected to teach children the way of life. One OAM evangelist once met a man who said he was an atheist. Staggeringly, however, he was also a Sunday school teacher in church! I know, it's shocking! His explanation was that he felt it was important for children to learn good morals. What were the church leaders doing in allowing this?

We've previously mentioned John Berridge. Six years into the ministry he was unconverted. Then, one day, as he was reading the Bible, the following words darted into his mind: 'Cease from thine own works; only believe.' John commented, 'Before I heard these words, my mind was in a very unusual calm; but as soon as I heard them, my soul was in a tempest directly, and the tears flowed from my eyes like a torrent. The scales fell from my eyes immediately.' Of course his conversion transformed his sermons, but after three Sundays it seemed as if his new sermons were having as little effect on the congregation as his former preaching. Until, that is, a lady came to see him. He asked her, 'Well, Sarah?'

'Not so well, I fear,' she replied.

'Why, what is the matter, Sarah?'

THERE IS STILL MUCH TO DO!

'Matter!' she said; 'why, I don't know what is the matter! Those new sermons! I find we are all to be lost now. I can neither eat, drink, nor sleep! I don't know what is to become of me.'[1]

What became of her was that she was soon converted. This was the start of a tremendously fruitful ministry.

Getting back to Timothy, his sonship was not only positional, something that was true of him, but it was also progressive, something that his life gave evidence of and was developing. There had to be that evidence before he was ready to be a labourer in the harvest field. That was something Paul was very careful about. Timothy had come to Paul's attention during a visit to the church in the city of Lystra in modern-day Turkey. Acts 16:2 says something significant about Timothy: 'He was well spoken of by the brothers.' The church thought highly of him. He must have shown signs of spirituality in his Christian walk and signs of zeal in his Christian witness.

As an aside, it is true to say that the recognition of the church is a very important factor in the call to the Christian ministry. God primarily reveals His will through His Word, but He also does so through His church. Likewise, in our evangelism, we shouldn't just go off and do our own thing; we should be sent out from our home fellowship. The commendation of Timothy's church led to Paul taking him with him on his missionary journeys. Timothy became an apostolic delegate, visiting a number of churches and eventually becoming, it is thought, the pastor of the church in Ephesus.

2. A SOLDIER

'As a good soldier of Christ Jesus' (2:3). This seems to have

THERE IS STILL MUCH TO DO!

been a favourite picture of Paul's, as he used it frequently in his letters. The son is not at home playing with his toys; he is a man and he's been called up to serve in the army of the King of kings.

There are not many tougher jobs than being a soldier. That is brought home to us on a regular basis in the news. The key word in Paul's mind here is 'endurance'. There are at least three aspects of army life where that is an important quality:

(a) Training for the battle

To fight in the battle, something called 'discipline' is required, which most of us don't like very much. There are many aspects of our lives where we need to be disciplined. It may not be easy, but it is important. For the soldier, it can involve marching wherever and whenever told to do so. The recruit used to go wherever he or she liked, whenever he or she liked, but not any more. As believers, we're not doing our own thing any more either; we're doing His thing! We're following Him and obeying Him. It's not an easy ride; 'we're marching to Zion', not riding there.

There's learning for the recruit: the service manual, the code book and the history of the regiment. Knowing to what you belong, where the regiment has been and where it is likely to be going in the future are all important. That is all relevant for us as believers, too: 'This Book of the Law shall not depart from your mouth, but you shall meditate on it day and night' (Josh. 1:8).

There's cleaning: the uniform, the equipment, the rifle, and not forgetting the bed space. In the RAF they have what are called Bull Nights once a week. Everything has to be cleaned ready for an inspection. We need Bull Nights as well, but not weekly—we need them daily. Yes, we need to keep short accounts with God and with each other.

(b) Fighting in the battle

We have three very real enemies: the world, the flesh and the devil. As soldiers of the Lord Jesus we have battles to face; they may be different for each of us, but they are there. We have different flaws within us and we're susceptible to different temptations around us. So Paul gives a warning to the Christian soldier in verse 4a, warning us not to get 'entangled' or caught up in civilian pursuits. This word described the sword getting caught up in the soldier's outer cloak. If that happened on the battlefield, it could be disastrous. The lesson is that the battle must take precedence over civilian matters. It is so easy for us to get tangled up with other matters. We could apply this to so many areas of our lives. One small practical example: I'm very grateful to my wife for looking after our household accounts and paying the bills. It's a big help and it means I have more time to focus on other things.

(c) Enduring through the battle

The battles may be hard and long. We can sometimes feel that the devil is really having a go at us. When that happens, there can be the temptation to give up. We may face health problems, family problems or church problems that hinder us. Don't be surprised about that: the devil targets those in Christian work. He wants to prevent the spread of the gospel more than anything else in the world. Paul knew there were hard times ahead for Timothy. He would need divine help to see him through. In 2 Timothy 1:15 Paul mentioned those who had turned back; he doesn't want Timothy to fall by the wayside as well. Today there are many shipwrecks from the Christian ministry. We need the Lord's strength and help to ensure that we don't join them.

Paul reminds Timothy of a motivation that will surely help him endure even the toughest of battles. His aim should always be 'to please the one who enlisted him' (2:4). The word 'enlisted' was used of a general who called people into the army. Jesus Christ has come to us by His Spirit and called us to join His forces, to represent Him and to fight for Him. What an honour! So we are to show Him our allegiance, even in the darkest situations.

3. AN ATHLETE

'An athlete is not crowned unless he competes according to the rules' (2:5). Many soldiering qualities are needed by athletes. Paul focuses here on playing by the rules; he is urging upon Timothy the need for honesty and integrity. Every event in the Greek Games had its rules. Sometimes there were rules for the training as well. Every event carried a prize for the winner. These were usually evergreen wreaths, which the winners wore on their heads. Only those who took part according to the rules would qualify to win the prize, however talented they might be. It was a very serious thing to cheat. I used to tell my children, 'Cheating is as bad as lying.' To cheat in those Games would bring terrible shame, not only on the individual, but also on his family and home town.

As Christians we must seek to obey God's laws—and man's

THERE IS STILL MUCH TO DO!

laws too, of course. No, we don't have to keep those laws to be saved. That's what most religions teach. Rather, we keep them as evidence that we are saved. Now we're able do so in a way we couldn't before! In his book *The Holy Spirit*, nineteenth-century author Octavius Winslow said, 'The believer is released from the law as a ground of acceptance, but not as a standard of holiness.' The law for us is not an external enemy now, but an internal friend. God's law has been written on our hearts and we should delight to keep it. In 1 John 5:3 it says, 'For this is the love of God, that we keep his commandments. And his commandments are not burdensome.'

How strange it is that some Christians believe there is no place for God's law in the Christian life. Thomas Watson once responded to that by asking, 'Shall not a king appoint laws to His subjects?' Yes, He shall, but those laws are of a loving Saviour, not of a hate-filled tyrant. The athlete knows he *must* keep the rules, but, by contrast, because of our love for the Saviour, we *want* to keep them. We have a desire to keep them in a way we never had before we were saved. But if there is no law-keeping, there is no evidence that we are justified, and, as with the athlete, there will be no reward.

4. A FARMER

'It is the hard-working farmer who ought to have the first share of the crops' (2:6). Paul makes reference to the harvesting of a crop, and that requires hard work. All the various stages in farming involve hard work, whether it is ploughing, sowing, watering or harvesting. Sometimes we seem to have the attitude that evangelism should be relatively easy and therefore, if there are elements of it that are hard, we probably don't need to bother being involved in them. But biblically speaking, we have no reason to think that any form of gospel outreach is going to be easy. After all, all those whom we seek to reach are dead in their trespasses and their sins, so a miracle is going to be required to bring them to new life in Christ.

Take Debbie as a wonderful example. She tried cannabis at a party once. This led to her eventually becoming a heroin addict. Her life spiralled down and eventually, when she couldn't afford to feed her habit, she became a prostitute. Debbie became so depressed that she decided to end it all. She was walking through Bilston in the West Midlands on her way to commit suicide when she went past a preacher who saw her and, speaking directly to her, simply said, 'God loves you.' That spoke to her powerfully and began a journey that saved and changed her life. The miracle of salvation was worked within her heart. It is a reminder of why prayer is such an integral part of evangelism. God can take our words and use them to bless others. Bilston is as hard work as any other town as far as open-air work is concerned, but God can step in whenever He chooses to do so, in a wonderful way.

The toughest assignment I've ever had was not an open-air situation, but a mothers and toddlers group. A nearby church had a thriving weekly group and decided it would be good to try having a monthly speaker for the parents. I was the first of these. Oh boy! All I can say is, I am glad they never invited me back. I stood in front of a room full of ladies, but the trouble was that no one had thought to take the children to another room so the mums could concentrate on the message.

THERE IS STILL MUCH TO DO!

Because the children were noisy, it encouraged some of the mums to talk among themselves, which made it very hard. Worse still was that the church had no easel, so my dry-wipe board, upon which I put some visual aids, had to be propped up on a chair. The problem was that it was within easy reach of the children, and a few of the toddlers decided to come over and remove the visuals just as quickly as I placed them on the board. Give me a shopping precinct any day!

We must expect gospel work to be hard work and take to heart the words of a man like Thomas Watson, who wrote, 'If Christ spent His blood for souls, well may we spend our sweat.' We need to see it as long-term work as well. Everything today has to be done straight away. We live with instant news, instant communication and instant coffee, but evangelism usually runs contrary to that. We ran a monthly open-air witness in the centre of Dunstable for nine years before we saw the first person saved through the outreach. What a long time, but it was well worth it! Bob is one of the most delightful Christians you will ever meet.

There may be times when it is not possible to be out sharing the gospel as we have planned. Sometimes heavy rain can affect street outreach. When I started in the Mission twenty years ago, one of my senior colleagues asked me this question: what does the farmer do when he can't get into the fields? The answer is: he sharpens his tools! I learnt from that that there is always preparation and study we can be doing instead. Yes, there is always work we can be doing. At times there may be periods when we are unwell and so unable to work; these can be prolonged periods which we may find immensely frustrating, but we must never forget that the Lord knows what He is doing.

5. A WORKMAN

'Do your best to present yourself to God as one approved, a worker who has no need to be ashamed' (2:15). The key words here are *diligence*, or *reliability*, and *skill*. These are needed because the work of the gospel deserves nothing less, but also because they are necessary for our own spiritual well-being. 'Men, we are to work as we did as boys when we knew our Father was watching, because He is—always.'[2] That is a terrific quote as it is such a challenge. We're not to work as men-pleasers, trying to catch their eye, but we are to be God-pleasers, always conscious of His eye.

The value of Christian workers is seen in their ability to rightly handle and share the message of the Bible with others. Timothy is contrasted with two men who were most unreliable (2:16–18). The word 'swerved' (v. 18) that Paul uses here is very helpful. It is used of an archer who deliberately misses the target. Paul highlights the serious consequences for those who listen to men like this, whose teachings spread like deadly diseases (v. 17). False teaching spreads quickly and destructively. This is what gospel work has always faced. Wrong doctrines have found their way into the most unlikely places and brought about terrible damage.

Some professing believers have lost their faith over the years. There's the tragic story of Charles Templeton, who was a good friend of Billy Graham in the 1940s. He was reckoned to be a better preacher, and very large crowds would gather to hear him preach the gospel. Tragically, Templeton read the wrong books and then went to the wrong Bible college. The result? He ended up writing a book entitled, amazingly, *Farewell to God*, setting out his atheism.

Paul reassures Timothy that those who are truly the Lord's won't have their faith overthrown (v. 19a). Jesus Himself warned that false teachers would come, desiring to lead astray even the elect, if such a thing were possible. Thankfully, it is not possible! But that doesn't stop Paul feeling the need to warn his Christian brother to stay away from anything that could draw him away from the Lord, from anything that could harm his faith (v. 19b). We need to take care, too—even in things like the books we read. We are all weak, and we should never forget that.

So how was Timothy to handle the precious truth of God's Word so that he became that diligent workman the Lord wanted to see? The phrase translated 'rightly handling' (v. 15) means to cut it straight. I'm left-handed (and have felt myself to be part of a discriminated-against minority most of my life!). One of the effects of my left-handedness has been my inability to cut things out well with scissors. I sometimes try to help my wife wrap presents at Christmas time, but Ruth despairs when she sees my efforts to cut the paper nicely. Although I have an excuse for my poor handiwork, there are no excuses for doing the same with the Bible. We need always to remember that when we stand before other human beings with an open Bible, we are standing before immortal souls who need to hear the truth, and nothing but the truth!

Those who would teach God's Word to others have a very heavy responsibility. As James 3:1 says, 'You know that we who teach will be judged with greater strictness.' These are

THERE IS STILL MUCH TO DO!

very sobering words indeed for us! We must never be those who dare to twist the Bible to suit ourselves, not even just a little bit. Our role is plainly and openly to declare what God has to say. That is where our responsibility starts and finishes, and we can apply this not only to preachers of the Word, but to witnesses to the Word as well. As Oliver Cromwell said, 'It is better to give people what they need, than what they want.' That is not always easy, but it is our calling. In 1 Thessalonians 2:4 it says, 'We have been approved by God to be entrusted with the gospel.' What an awesome thing that is: that God should entrust us with His divine truth! Paul goes on, 'So we speak, not to please man, but to please God who tests our hearts.'

6. A VESSEL

This is what we find in 2 Timothy 2:20–22, which is a dramatic change of picture! Up to this point, various activities have been described as pictures of the gospel worker. Here we're pointed to an inanimate object: a vessel or container. This is the only passive picture; the others in this chapter of Paul's are active. The emphasis here is on what we are, rather than on anything we do. Paul is describing a mansion. He says there are two sorts of pots, pans and dishes to be found in this mansion. One is for ordinary, menial use, and the other is for 'best' (as we might say), which he calls 'honourable'. That could mean what we might bring out on special occasions, or, more likely, what is for the personal use of the master of the house. The metaphor in other places refers to servants of God, preachers of the gospel. For example, the Lord referred

THERE IS STILL MUCH TO DO!

to the newly converted Saul of Tarsus as 'a chosen vessel of mine'.

We have been chosen to serve as well. What the Master of the House, or the Head of the Church, or Lord of the Harvest, wants from us is that we will be clean vessels for Him, 'set apart as holy, useful ... ready for every good work' (v. 21). If we want to be useful to the Lord, we must be clean. Once again, this is not easy. It wasn't for Timothy. It isn't for us. Pollution of every kind is both within us and all around us. The old hymn says, 'I see the sights that dazzle, the tempting sounds I hear.' We must combat these by filling our minds with Scripture and our lips with prayer, day by day and moment by moment. I once saw the following words on the side of a bus in Norwich: 'If life is a journey, travel well.' I suppose it was referring to the quality of the bus. We should be concerned about the quality of us!

Our lives need to be as good as our preaching and our witnessing. How can we expect a change of life in those we share the gospel with, if there hasn't been a change of life in us? A man called Robert Sample wrote a paper in 1897 called 'Effective Preaching' in which he said these challenging words: 'The great want of today is a holier ministry. We do not need more mighty apologists, or preachers who compass a wider range of natural knowledge, important as these are; but men of God who bring the atmosphere of heaven with them into the pulpit and speak from the borders of another world.' That needs to apply to all of us, not just preachers. Oh, that we would seek the Lord for something of the atmosphere of heaven as we talk to others about the way of salvation!

THERE IS STILL MUCH TO DO!

In verse 22 Paul gives Timothy some practical things as advice, as a means to this sanctified end. Notice that these are not just negative, as we sometimes view holiness as being. They are not just things we should 'run from'; they are also positive, things we should 'run towards'. Notice as well the reminder given here that we are not to go it alone: 'with those who call on the Lord from a pure heart.' We're in this together. We're not meant to struggle through on our own. We're to go after the things of the Lord with the people of the Lord. What a difference that can make! Even just knowing that others are facing the same issues that we are can be such a comfort. How good to be able to encourage each other in our Christian walks and ministries!

7. A SERVANT

'The Lord's servant' (2:24). The final part of the profile of the Christian worker is that of a servant or slave of the Lord. The slave does not choose the Master; the Master chooses the slave. The slave does not select the place where he or she shall serve the Master; the Master chooses that. The slave does not choose the work, but carries out the work given by the Master. The slave does not carry out that work in his or her own way, but in the way the Master wishes.

The best servant is one who is willing to be most subject to the Master. An arguer is someone who is just out for him- or herself. We need to beware of having a contentious spirit. And if we are the type of people who are never willing to admit they are wrong, then it's time to admit we are wrong. People think more of those who are gracious and humble and willing to say when they have made a mistake. Some people just like to argue for argument's sake. In the context of dealing with unbelievers, great care is needed. When we engage with someone about the gospel, we know that what we are saying is right and true. However, we need to convey the gospel in the best way possible, and that best way is given to us in verses 24–25a: 'And the Lord's servant must not be quarrelsome but kind to everyone, able to teach, patiently enduring evil, correcting his opponents with gentleness.'

Sometimes we speak in a wrong way to people. Pride can come in, impatience can come in (I'm afraid it gets everywhere!), and so too can harshness. A man once went up to his pastor and said, 'I try to talk to people about the Lord, but sometimes people like to argue and I have a short fuse.' The pastor gave the man some wise advice: 'You need to ask the Lord to make your fuse longer.' Maybe we need to do the same.

How we need humility and patience to win people for the Lord! It's a reminder again that our arguments, be they watertight and foolproof, at the end of the day cannot win anyone. Paul describes the lovely fruit that may come from a humble approach: 'God may perhaps grant them repentance' (v. 25b). Yes, we believe that the Lord is the One who grants repentance. Like faith, repentance is a gift of God. And yet He calls us to use the right approach as we speak to people, that they might be brought to see their need of Him.

In my early days in OAM I could be found in Derby most Tuesdays. I remember having contact for about four months with a young woman named Almut. She was from Dresden in Germany and was working temporarily as a school teacher. The first time I saw her was in the March. She listened to me preach and then went away without speaking to me. Almut returned the following week. After I finished preaching I went over and asked her if she was a Christian. She burst into tears. That question doesn't normally produce a reaction like that! When she had composed herself, Almut told me her story. She was from a Moravian background and her father was the pastor of a church in Dresden. She knew that she wasn't a Christian, as she didn't want to lose her independence; however, she was clearly uncomfortable about holding this position. Almut continued to come, week after week. She asked lots of questions and I patiently sought to answer them. On one occasion I spoke with her for over an hour. I last saw her in the July a few days before she was due to fly home to Germany. By this time, she was very close to the kingdom. She said to me with tears in her eyes, 'I must give up and come to Christ.'

In all seven of the pictures that Paul gives profiling the godly evangelist, there are certain elements of hardness and toughness that will need to be faced. But what is equally true for each of these pictures is that there is also an emphasis on the tremendous privilege the gospel worker has: being a child of God, being in the Lord's army, living by the Lord's rules, farming for the Lord's harvest, handling the Lord's Word, being useful in the Lord's hand and being employed in the Lord's service.

And one final thing: some Christians say that we need to earn the right to speak to unbelievers about the Lord. In a sense I agree, and that is what this chapter has been about. However, there is another sense in which we don't have to earn the right to witness at all. An ambassador already has the right to speak for the one who sends him or her. Someone once said that the authority of Jesus and the blood of the martyrs have earned us the right to share the gospel. Perhaps the best answer is that we need to be guided by the context of the situation in which we find ourselves. For those who know us and to whom we try to speak about the Lord, yes, we need to show them a consistency of life, but for those we meet who don't know us, and whom we may not see again—well, they just need to hear the gospel.

Notes

1 Nigel Pibworth, *The Gospel Pedlar* (Welwyn: Evangelical Press, 1987), p. 34.

2 Kent Hughes, *Disciplines of a Godly Man* (Wheaton, IL: Crossway, 2001), p. 136.

THERE IS STILL MUCH TO DO!

15 Sowing the seed

A sower went out to sow. And as he sowed … (Matt. 13:3–4)

The Lord Jesus, in His very first parable, likened the sharing of the gospel message to a farmer sowing his seed in springtime. As the farmer went along with a basket over his shoulder or around his waist, he scattered the seed with his hand, and the seed landed in different types of soil. This was something very familiar to Jesus' hearers, as many of them would have been farm labourers. In the same way, as we sow the gospel seed it will affect different people in different ways. Perhaps we are guilty of not being very diligent in our sowing because, just as for the farmer, it involves work. However, if we truly want our churches to grow, we must be about the work of sowing. Let's give some thought to the kind of work that will be involved:

1. IT INVOLVES HARD WORK

If you know anything at all about farming, you'll know that it certainly is work. And evangelism is exactly that, too. The Lord Jesus Himself states that plainly in other places, such as Matthew 9:37, when talking about reaching people for his kingdom, He says that 'the labourers are few', and by 'labourers' he means workers, toilers, servants. Have you ever seen the hands of a farmer? They are big, hard and calloused—not smooth and manicured. Outdoor work is usually harder than indoor work! Farming is outdoor work,

THERE IS STILL MUCH TO DO!

manual work. 'A sower went out to sow.' He didn't stay indoors. He went out for what would have been long hours, and in all weathers.

Gospel work has always been hard work, but we can be guilty of looking back at church history with rose-tinted spectacles. For example, we can look back on the eighteenth century, when there was huge revival blessing. We can have a romantic view that it was all relatively easy. After all, the crowds were massive and the harvest was plentiful! It's true, the crowds often were massive, and the harvest was regularly plentiful, but it wasn't easy. Far from it! All sorts of missiles were thrown at the open-air preachers. It's quite rare to be at the receiving end of those these days. An OAM evangelist was preaching at Hull Fair some years ago when out of the corner of his eye he was aware of a missile coming his way. He instinctively put out his hand and, amazingly, he caught the missile. It was a pound of cheese, of all things. He called out instantly, 'Thanks very much for the cheese! We'll have that for our supper later this evening.'

Going back much further to the 1700s, on at least one occasion someone threw parts of dead cats at George Whitefield while he was preaching on Moorfields Common in London. Our children had a succession of pet rabbits and guinea pigs when they were younger. Those pets became very stiff when they died. I'm not sure if it's the same with cats! Anyway, in April 1742, Whitefield recorded in his diary, 'Stones, dirt, rotten eggs and pieces of dead cats thrown at me.' Can you imagine having the dead limbs of a cat thrown at you? Maybe even its head? Sowing seed easy? No! Not at all!

Gospel work is hard today for other reasons. Trying to

THERE IS STILL MUCH TO DO!

catch the ears of a passing crowd, when preaching in the open air, is much harder than speaking to those who have come prepared to hear you in church from beginning to end. Another reason for the hardness of the work, which is mentioned in the Lord's parable, is that many people have hard hearts. This reminds us of the four different types of soil that the Lord describes in the field. It isn't all good, dark soil. Some is baked hard, some is rocky and some is thorny. That's just how many people are. How we need to pray that the Lord would prepare the hearts of those we are going to have gospel opportunities with. He may even use us to soften those hearts.

One evening during a witness at Hereford Fair, a man named Richard was ambling past the evangelist who was preaching. He decided to stop and berate the preacher, saying he had no right to be in the city hammering on about the Bible. When he saw that this drew very little response, Richard changed tack and demanded to know why God, if He is there at all, had allowed his twenty-year-old cousin to die of cancer only a few months before. The preacher stopped his message and approached Richard, speaking very gently and sympathetically to him. Richard calmed right down and even apologized for the aggressive way he had spoken. A lovely conversation then ensued, and before going on his way Richard said, 'I know why you were here tonight: it was for me.'

Finally, the work is hard because we have a hard enemy. He wants to prevent there ever being a harvest. He wants to nip God's work in the bud. It's sobering to realize that he is present when the gospel is being proclaimed. He is busy sending various things into people's lives and into their minds

THERE IS STILL MUCH TO DO!

to distract and disturb them from thinking carefully about the big issues of life, death and eternity.

In September 2000 I spent a day with the OAM team preaching at Oxford Fair. We had a session of preaching through the afternoon and then again in the evening. When it was my turn to preach, two young women stopped to listen. Before long, one of them started to heckle me, and I tried to answer her questions as I kept on preaching. Afterwards I went over to have a chat. The more vocal of the two was called Nancy, and as I endeavoured to answer her further questions she seemed to focus particularly on the Fatherhood of God, which she strongly rejected.

Nancy then opened up and shared a very tragic story. She was a manic depressive, bisexual, and had a boyfriend who was a male witch; but worst of all, her father had raped her. It fell into place why Nancy struggled so much to think highly of God as a Father when she had had such a terrible earthly father. It was a good opportunity to sow further seed by explaining that God can be a Father like no other if we seek Him through His Son, the Lord Jesus. Nancy and her friend listened intently as these things were shared. I have prayed for Nancy every week ever since and have often wondered how things are with her now. So, yes, the devil is certainly working; how we need to be working as well!

Are we as Christians in danger of becoming a bit work-shy when it comes to church work and church outreach? Oh, we may happily give our all for our employer, for the one who pays our wages. We'll do over and above for him or her—but what about our attitude to the Lord's work? Do we say at times, 'Someone else can do it instead of me', or 'They should be glad to have any of my time at all'? Missionary to Africa David Livingstone was once told about men interested in joining him in the work. This was his reply: 'If you have men who will only come if they know there is a good road, I don't want them. I want men who will come if there is no road at all.' In other words, he wanted 'workers'—those willing and ready for hard work; those willing to be taken right out of their comfort zones at times so that needy people could receive the good seed.

It's like what happened while an OAM team were operating in Londonderry in Northern Ireland a few years ago. One of the team shared his story:

We were doing some door-to-door work in a predominantly Roman Catholic area of the city one evening. It started to rain so I sheltered under some trees. Suddenly a smart red BMW car drew up very near to me. A rather suspicious-looking character jumped out of the driver's seat and said to me rather menacingly, 'He wants to talk to you.' I looked into the car and saw a mountain of a man dressed in black sitting in the passenger seat.

Against my better judgement, and thinking that he looked the type who could cheerfully blow a man's kneecaps off, I hopped into the driver's seat next to him, while the other man got into the back. 'Are you born again?' he asked. 'Yes,' I replied. 'I'm a backslider,' he then informed me. His name was 'Big Al', and he was originally a Catholic from the Bogside area who had met some Christians a few years ago. He began attending their church and was born again. He and his mate both seemed to have had a genuine experience of the Lord and also a real fondness for the Scriptures. They knew they were regarded as traitors by the community, and this explained the rather secretive nature of their approach to me. Both men gladly received some booklets as well as details of a good local evangelical church, where I told

THERE IS STILL MUCH TO DO!

the men that they would be warmly welcomed. I left the scene renewing my vow never to get into a stranger's car again.

This story should challenge us as to whether we are ready for such times when the Lord might call upon us to step out in faith to bear witness for Him.

2. IT INVOLVES LONG-TERM WORK

Farmers don't sow one day and harvest the next. Most crops take many months to germinate and then grow. In James 5:7 we read, 'See how the farmer waits for the precious fruit of the earth.' In gospel work, we know that a harvest can come immediately if the Lord so chooses. But we must work to His timetable, not the other way around. Take Shaun as an example. A few years back, OAM had a team that was based for a week each summer in Eastbourne. On one of the days they would venture along the coast to evangelize in the centre of Brighton. It was during one of these occasions that a young man named Shaun was walking through the town and came past the team preaching. He had not planned to stop, as six months before he had come to Britain from South Africa with the purpose of getting right away from the Christian influence he had grown up with.

However, as Shaun was going by, a very aggressive character, who the team later found out was known as Spider, stepped out of the crowd and began to threaten the preacher. He stood face to face with him and was cursing and swearing. A young man from the local church which was supporting the witness, and who had been a Christian only for a couple of months, was so incensed to see a preacher of God's Word being treated like this that he ran over and

THERE IS STILL MUCH TO DO!

rugby-tackled Spider to the ground. Not something in any open-air evangelism handbook!

At that moment, two other men who were passing went over and started to kick Spider. As you can imagine, it was all becoming quite chaotic. The rest of the team helped Spider up and pulled the young Christian away. The preacher, wanting to take the steam out of the situation, invited Spider to go for coffee, an invitation which was accepted. (Just as an aside: that in itself proved to be a lovely opportunity. Spider calmed right down and shared that his life had fallen apart, with his wife recently having left him and taken their children away as well. He was by this time fairly open to thinking about the claims of Christ, and good seed was sown.)

The incident in the street had caused Shaun to stop and watch. Although a number of other people did the same, he particularly wanted to see how these Christians would cope when their backs were up against the wall. Shaun was so impressed by what he saw that he stayed to listen as the next preacher began his message. It was while listening that the Lord began to speak very powerfully to him, and he stayed to talk to the preacher. Shaun was told of his need to repent and turn to the Lord, and he said he would like to do that. He turned up a small alleyway nearby, bowed his head and sought the Lord. He then came back to say that he had found peace with God! A local team member arranged to meet up with Shaun for coffee a few days later, and afterwards he rang to share with me that he had no doubts that the Lord had dealt with Shaun. There was real evidence that he was truly saved. Shaun went back home to South Africa a few

THERE IS STILL MUCH TO DO!

weeks later. Having been reconciled to God, he wanted to be reconciled to his parents as well.

Sometimes a crop is described as outpacing the sowing of it, as recorded in Amos 9:13, which speaks of the treader of grapes overtaking the one who sows the seed. This is given as a picture of great gospel success. But this is most exceptional. It is not part of the ordinary experience of Christian workers any more than it is the ordinary experience of farmers; but how we should pray for much more gospel success in this generation!

Sometimes the seed can lie dormant for a very long time. For example, way back in 1939 a large crowd stood near Marble Arch in London listening to an OAM preacher. It was Good Friday and the theme of his message was, of course, the cross. When the preaching finished the other Christians on the team began to sing a hymn. Their choice was 'Nearer my God to Thee, Nearer to Thee'. At the sound of what was a beautiful melody, an Austrian gentleman standing among the audience showed signs of deep emotion. Approaching the one who had just preached, the Austrian shared in broken English the most extraordinary story: 'I was on the Titanic in 1912 and that was the hymn we sang on deck as the ship was sinking. I have never heard it sung from that day to this. I want to make it true in my own experience.' It was with great joy that the preacher explained further the way of salvation to this man who had been so touched by this old hymn. There seemed to be no mistaking the genuine desire of the man to know the Saviour. He went away overwhelmed and most grateful.

To us it may seem remarkable that the Lord can bring back to someone's mind words that he or she has heard many

THERE IS STILL MUCH TO DO!

years before, yet nothing is too difficult for Him. A couple in their late sixties made their way very deliberately down to the South Beach in Tenby, Pembrokeshire, one summer's morning. They asked to speak to the leader of the OAM beach mission team who were there, as they had something important to share. Their son, Liam, was in the army and at the time was stationed in Basra in Iraq. He and his unit had recently been traumatized after having to drag several dead bodies out of a helicopter that had just crashed. As Liam and his friends sat in the barracks dwelling upon what they had seen, they began to ask each other what life was all about. Some of the men began describing happy childhood memories, and Liam spoke about the times he had enjoyed as a boy on holiday in Tenby with his parents and especially the meetings run by the Mission. As he shared these experiences, something very surprising happened. Three of his colleagues said that they too had attended those meetings when they were boys on holiday in Tenby.

At this, the four of them began to recall some of the choruses they had sung, and Liam remembered the one he called 'the alphabet song' which began with the words 'A B C D E F G, Jesus died for you and me!' That time of reminiscing proved to be a big help to these men after all that they had seen, and Liam's parents had wanted to express their appreciation to OAM. We don't know if Liam was saved as a result, but there is no doubt that the Lord had brought back to his mind those simple truths from sixteen years before. This incident surely teaches us that we never know how the Lord may use seed that has been sown, even a very long time afterwards.

A part of the long-term nature of seed-sowing can be in terms of a friend or contact we have where there is an opportunity to keep sharing with him or her over a long period of time. We no doubt have family members who are in that bracket; perhaps we have prayed for them for years. In those cases we definitely have to learn patience. Perhaps we have reached a point where raising the subject of Christian things can cause a bit of tension. If that is the case, it is probably best to wait prayerfully for them to raise the issue, instead of us trying to do so. Then there will be a better opening to say something for the Lord. In the past, when a couple of my unsaved brothers have complained about where the conversation was going, I have said to them, 'Well, you brought the subject up'—and they have had to admit that they did.

3. IT IS VITAL WORK

It almost goes without saying that no farming equals no crops, and no crops equals no food. That's pretty serious! In Proverbs 24:30–34 there is a vivid illustration of a lazy farmer and the danger he faces at harvest time when his fields are empty. Again we can apply this to the spiritual farmer, the gospel worker, the preacher of the Word, the sower. If there is no sowing of gospel seed, there will be no harvest, there will be no fruit, there will be no souls won for the kingdom. This needs saying because at times we are guilty of doing very little sowing. Is the mantra used in our church, 'We tried that and it didn't work'? Yes, we do need to evaluate what we do in terms of our outreach, but I do wonder if, at times, the 'didn't work' more accurately reflects the mindset 'it didn't work straight away so we gave up'.

An evangelical Anglican pastor in Liverpool called Richard

THERE IS STILL MUCH TO DO!

Hobson, who was greatly used by the Lord in the neediest parts of that city, wrote in his journal in 1880, 'I do not see that faith in God and prayer to Him preclude the most strenuous efforts being made where the King's business is concerned.' I trust we are all utterly convinced of that. And if we are, we need to be living it out in the life of the church and in the ministry of the gospel. William Grimshaw (1708–1763), whose preaching ministry was used to the saving of several thousand souls in Yorkshire and beyond, once said, 'Oh, how good it is to work for God in the daytime, and at night lie down under his smiles.' He also said, 'Let me labour now: I shall have rest by and by. I cannot do enough for Christ, who has done so much for me.' There is a 'must' about this work, isn't there? Grimshaw felt it; we should feel it too. There are still so many souls perishing, and still among those perishing souls there are those that God intends to save! The Lord of the harvest clearly wants a harvest, and He has called His people, His church, to engage in this work so that the harvest may be reaped. The seed of His Word is the tool the Lord uses, but He wants labourers to put the tool to good use.

4. IT INVOLVES A TEAM EFFORT

At times we can struggle to be patient in our witnessing, and part of the reason for that is that we want to be a reaper and not just a sower. After the lovely incident of the conversion of the woman of Samaria, the Lord told His disciples that the 'sower and reaper may rejoice together' (John 4:36). As and when people come to know the Lord, we can give thanks for the privilege of having been sowers, just as much as reapers. Farming involves teamwork, and so does evangelizing. We

THERE IS STILL MUCH TO DO!

may be those who do a lot of sowing, but see very little fruit for our labours. Well, that is in the Lord's hands; what we need to do is prayerfully press on and trust the Lord to bring in a harvest at just the right time.

By and large the Lord uses more than one person to bring a person to Himself, so directly or indirectly there is a team effort in seed-sowing work. Take Clare as an example. She worked in Redhill town centre, and one day on her lunchbreak she stopped to listen to an open-air preacher. The next week she returned with questions that she had. This went on for several weeks, and eventually the preacher invited Clare to a Christianity Explored course run at his church. Clare attended those meetings and began to go to the church on Sundays as well. She came to know the Lord and was baptized a few months later. Clare began to take her sister to listen to the open-air preaching, as she wanted her to know about the Saviour too. The point is that an open-air evangelist initially sowed the seed, but others were involved in her spiritual journey as well.

Another example of the roles of sower and reaper being shared concerns a young man named James. A former OAM evangelist was in the open air in Aylesbury on a very quiet day. James was the only one who listened to the preaching, which focused on the subject 'The Unique Jesus'. As the preacher drew to a close, he offered James a Gospel of John, which James accepted. James explained that a week prior to this meeting he hadn't believed in God, but now he wasn't sure because he had been thinking about death since visiting his grandmother's grave a few days before. The preacher told James that God revealed himself through the Bible, so

THERE IS STILL MUCH TO DO!

if he wanted to know God, he should prayerfully read the Bible, asking God to reveal himself, and also go to a Bible-believing church. James said he knew of one in Chesham, as he had attended a youth club there in the past. About a year later that same evangelist went to preach in the church in Chesham, and who did he see but James, who was now a born-again believer! These stories are a reminder of 1 Corinthians 3:6 where Paul testifies, 'I planted, Apollos watered, but God gave the growth.' Teamwork is not only a biblical thing, it is also a beautiful thing when we see the Lord at work through it.

In 1 Corinthians 15:58 there is a wonderfully encouraging exhortation: 'Therefore, my beloved brothers, be steadfast, immovable, always abounding in the work of the Lord, knowing that in the Lord your labour is not in vain.' The word 'work' there means task or employment, but the word 'labour' translates a different word that means literally to strike or beat something. The thought is of physical work resulting in weariness. Yes, the Lord's work can be hard, it can be tough going, but we are encouraged to remember this fact: no work carried out in the Lord's name is ever wasted! There's a wonderful promise from the Lord in Isaiah 55:10–11:

For as the rain and the snow come down from heaven
   and do not return there but water the earth,
making it bring forth and sprout,
   giving seed to the sower and bread to the eater,
so shall my word be that goes out from my mouth;
   it shall not return to me empty,
but it shall accomplish that which I purpose,
   and shall succeed in the thing for which I sent it.

THERE IS STILL MUCH TO DO!

These words should help us to persevere for the long haul in our evangelistic efforts.

C. T. Studd wrote the following observation in his diary:

Last June at the mouth of the Congo there awaited a thousand prospectors, traders and merchants waiting to rush into these regions as soon as the government opened the door to them, for rumour declared that there is an abundance of gold. If such men hear so loudly the call of gold and obey it, can it be that the ears of Christ's soldiers are deaf to the call of God, and the cries of the dying souls of men? Are gamblers for gold so many and gamblers for God so few?[1]

We can take that picture a step further. Those prospectors would have worked enthusiastically and zealously to find and dig up that precious metal. Shouldn't we Christians be even more enthusiastic to scatter the precious seed of the Word of God that can so wonderfully transform hearts and lives?

We need to ask ourselves if we are always abounding in the work of the Lord. An evangelist in Ulster became quite ill with heart and lung problems. He used to be active in open-air preaching and door-to door work. When he became too unwell he began to think how he might still serve the Lord given his physical limitations. He hit upon the idea that on days when he felt a bit brighter he could catch the train from Belfast to Dublin and, as he sat next to different people, he would prayerfully seek to open up conversations about the Lord. He is quite masterful at doing this and has had many fruitful chats with a number of people. Perhaps many of us don't think that a ride on public transport could be a gospel opportunity, but there's a sense in which wherever the believer is there may well be the possibility of speaking to someone about the Lord.

So seed-sowing is work. It is hard work, so effort is needed. It is long-term work, so patience is needed. It is vital work, so zeal is needed! May the Lord give us an abundance of these, so that we may keep on being sowers in the 'work' of the kingdom!

Note

1   Norman P. Grubb, *C. T. Studd: Cricketer and Pioneer* (London: Lutterworth Press, 1941), p. 136.

16 Clinching the deal

For 'everyone who calls on the name of the
Lord will be saved'. (Rom. 10:13)

The title of this chapter may sound a very worldly way to describe someone becoming a Christian, but that is almost the level some are at in how they go about their evangelism. As I mentioned in an earlier chapter, for some the business model has replaced the biblical model. So it may be profitable to spend a bit of time looking at the final step in a person's coming to faith in the Lord, and to the part the evangelist is to play in that.

In a day when we mostly seem to be sowers rather than reapers, it is important to be equipped for any reaping which the Lord might ask us to be involved in. We never know when we may be called upon to be the last 'link in the chain' of a person's salvation. Sometimes we may be the very first link. And any number of responses may come from a person who hears something of the gospel for the first time.

For example, there was a man in Wolverhampton who was given the nickname 'Cowboy Dave'. He was known to be a little eccentric, as he was always seen in the town wearing a cowboy outfit (minus a gun, thankfully!). The first time he came across the gospel was through hearing a couple of evangelists from OAM preaching in the town centre. Dave's immediate response was to call them false prophets and then tell them that there were only two real Christians in the world: Mother Teresa and Billy Graham. Dave heard the gospel many times over the next few years, but he remained hardened against it. Eventually, however, Dave was persuaded to go to a local Pentecostal church, and through the witness of the pastor he came to know the Lord.

Perhaps more often than not we are a link somewhere in the middle of the chain, but we should be prepared for those occasions when the Lord would place us as the very last link in someone's being converted to Jesus Christ. As for every aspect of gospel communication, what we need more than anything else is God-given wisdom. The trouble is, the emphasis of some churches is that what we need above all else is a man-made technique. That is quite wrong and has actually had disastrous consequences for many people and many churches. That wisdom which comes 'from above' (James 3:17) will, in part, be given just at the moment we need it. In other words, if we are in a conversation with a person about his or her soul, and that person gives evidence of being near the kingdom, then, if we are 'prayerful' sowers, God will direct us to give just the right counsel which that individual needs.

But we might well wonder, what will that 'right counsel' be based on? There is only one correct answer: it must be based on the clear teaching of Scripture and nothing else. That means preparation is required on our part! So we need to know our Bibles—and I don't just mean ABC gospel texts to quote. Some like to use what is known as 'The Roman road'—Romans 3:23; 6:23; 10:9. Yes, we do need to know those verses, but we also need to know what the Bible says about how a person actually becomes a Christian and what our role is to be. We all know that what comes immediately before someone is saved, from a human perspective, is that that person asks for salvation. Romans 10:13 puts it like this: 'For "everyone who calls on the name of the Lord shall be saved".' Let's focus on our responsibility to the person seeking the Lord. There are three important things to notice about that call:

1. PEOPLE NEED TO BE CHALLENGED TO CALL TO THE SAVIOUR TO RESCUE THEM

This might seem pretty obvious, but we need ever to remember that this is the great work before the church today: graciously challenging people to realize that what they need most in life is to be saved from their sins through trusting in Christ. For that to happen, they need to call! In order to call, they need to hear that the greatest issue in their lives is their relationship with their Creator. It is sadly the case that a growing number of people in this generation are being persuaded that they have no Creator, other than their mum and dad. Paul goes on in Romans 10, 'And how are they to believe in him of whom they have never heard?' (v. 14). That being the case, our responsibility is to point people to the One who made them and to the fact that sin has separated them from Him. Not only that, but also that there is a Saviour who can take away their sin and reconcile them to the Almighty. Just like John the Baptist, our role is to tell people, 'Behold, the Lamb of God, who takes away the sin of the world!' (John 1:29). In other words, 'There He is! Go to Him, seek Him with all your heart. Call upon Him to save you.'

Sadly, at times, well-meaning Christians are guilty of presenting Jesus in attractive packaging, but not really explaining fully why people need Him, and need Him more than anything else in the whole world. A fairly typical

THERE IS STILL MUCH TO DO!

presentation is to tell people about their God-shaped hole: 'Our lives will be empty until Jesus comes in and fills that hole up.' Actually, the main problem is that people try to fill that hole up with a whole load of stuff, most of which is sinful. What they need first is to have their sin removed, and only then will the Lord Jesus come in and make them complete people. The greatest need for all is forgiveness, not satisfaction! Unless forgiveness comes first, a person cannot have real satisfaction! So the gospel needs to be explained to people fully. They need to realize that there are terrible, eternal consequences for rejecting this wonderful Saviour.

One of the great problems in our day is that people have a light view of sin. To many, sin is just a joke, just a game. But before a person will genuinely call to the Lord for salvation, that person needs to know how serious his or her sin is and feel something of the awfulness of that sin.

I was once preaching at Epsom Races when a group of five lads surrounded me. They were all larking about, except Steve. He began to ask serious questions. One of them was the following: 'I'm going to court next week because I stabbed someone. Do you think God could forgive someone like me?' It was obvious that even with the silliness of his friends around him, Steve was troubled by his sin. He felt something of the wrong he had done and knew it had a bearing on his relationship with God. Sadly, the other lads pushed our display board over and then dragged Steve away. Who knows where he is now?

We should desire to see conviction of sin as the first response to the gospel, followed by heartfelt repentance. One OAM evangelist in Dudley met a man called Ranjid, who after listening to the open-air preaching said in broken English, 'I feel my sin.' Isn't it just a huge problem, that people today do not feel their sin? It doesn't bother them. It isn't serious to them. Again, it comes back to the great need to preach the character of God in our evangelism. Most people compare themselves with those around them, and so they feel fine. They can always find someone worse than them, and this will make them feel better about themselves. It is when they hear about the One with infinitely higher standards, the holy God, and His Son, who is as a Lamb without spot and without blemish, that their consciences may begin to be stirred. Then a sense of moral dirtiness may begin to take hold. And it is a sense of sin, a feeling of sin, that is evidence that a person may well be near to being saved.

Some today are making a big mistake in allowing the experience of conversion to be downplayed in evangelism. It is, after all, the biggest event in a person's life! That's right: to pass from spiritual death to spiritual life is momentous! Yet people are sometimes being encouraged to just 'make a commitment', even though that is not to be found in Scripture. People are also urged to 'make a decision', but where is that in God's Word? Nowhere! In God's Word, people are commanded to repent and believe. Over and over again that is the emphasis; that is what is required. Acts 3:19 records Peter saying to a large crowd, 'Repent therefore, and turn again, that your sins may be blotted out.' If this gospel truth is not declared to people, they will never really see why they need to call.

2. PEOPLE SOMETIMES ARE COERCED TO CALL

It is common today to hear that what we should be leading up to in evangelism is getting a person to say the 'sinner's prayer',

THERE IS STILL MUCH TO DO!

as it is called. For some this has become almost a magic formula for bringing someone into the kingdom of God.

At a Bible exhibition some years ago I chatted with a teacher who was a Christian. She was absent one day as it was her father's funeral, but the next day she came with a class of children. I said how sorry I was to hear about her father. I asked if he was a believer, and this was her reply: 'No, he wasn't, but it's all right. We got him to say the sinner's prayer just before he died.' It's not for me to say where that man is now, but my impression was this: that lady was pinning her hopes on that prayer, on the power of that prayer, rather than on the power of the Lord to save her dad.

You may think this is rather surprising, but I would say that the sinner's prayer is not only unnecessary, but it can be dangerous too. I don't mean that sinners shouldn't pray for salvation. That's just it: *they should pray* for salvation, and not just read or repeat a prayer someone else has written. Leading them in prayer, with them just saying 'amen' at the end, may just be us putting words in people's mouths. Do we want to be guilty of that? It is, of course, true that some have been truly saved through praying the sinner's prayer. God is sovereign, after all. The Scottish theologian John Murray points out in his essay on co-operation in evangelism that 'God is sovereign and fulfils His holy purposes of grace through the medium of actions which are in direct contravention of His revealed will. The crucifixion of the Lord is the supreme example.'[1] God sometimes works despite us, rather than because of us. But if He has given clear directions in His Word, we must be guided by them, not by the practice of others, whether men or even churches, however successful they appear to be.

I feel the same way about what is known as 'the altar call', which in some evangelistic meetings is used to get people to the front so that they can then say the sinner's prayer. There are at least five reasons why we should steer clear of using both the altar call and the sinner's prayer:

(a) Neither is to be found anywhere in the whole Bible

They are not even found in the book of Acts. Read Acts through again and note all the incidents, all the places, all the preaching and all the witnessing; you won't find either of these things anywhere. Not even a hint of them!

(b) There was no trace of these things in the history of the church until the nineteenth century!

They were introduced and made popular by Charles Finney, mentioned previously. Finney used all kinds of gimmicks and techniques to get people to come forward in meetings, but so much of his work was very superficial. Very sadly indeed, most of his so-called converts were short-lived. Tragically, what were produced were mainly 'stony-ground' hearers. Interestingly, Finney summarized his own ministry like this: 'I was often instrumental in bringing people under great conviction, and into a temporary state of repentance and faith … but falling short of urging them to a point, where they would become so acquainted with Christ as to abide in Him.' In other words, he admitted that most of his wheat turned out to be chaff, and to cover his failings he developed a

THERE IS STILL MUCH TO DO!

doctrine of perfectionism, stating that this would be 'the real key to successful ministry'.

In Iain Murray's book *The Forgotten Spurgeon*, it is argued that ministries like Finney's helped to develop the Second Blessing teaching, because it was clear that the converts were so worldly and carnal. What they apparently needed was something else, a second experience—baptism in the Spirit. No; what they needed was real conversion. That's where the problem lay!

(c) These methods give the seeker the impression that he or she holds the ultimate power in salvation

Although the seeker comes 'asking, seeking, knocking', we must remember that the Lord is the One, and the only One, who can do the opening. Preachers love to quote Revelation 3:20, 'Behold, I stand at the door and knock.' But remember: the primary application of that was to the believers in Laodicea, not to unbelievers. Jonah declared these tremendous words from the fish's belly: 'Salvation belongs to the LORD!' (Jonah 2:9). Yes, it is of Him, not us! For the unbeliever, the handle is on the outside. Dr Luke did not say of that dear lady Lydia, 'The Lord opened her heart after she paid attention to what was said by Paul.' No, he said, 'The Lord opened her heart to pay attention to what was said by Paul' (Acts 16:14). Only when the Lord opens the heart, opens the deaf ear, opens the blind eyes, can the sinner call to the Lord for salvation.

(d) A willingness to come forward or to pray does not always mean that a person is ready to take the final step

I was once at a YWAM young people's meeting in Loughborough. The first thing of note was that throughout

THERE IS STILL MUCH TO DO!

the fifteen-minute gospel presentation, which had been preceded by lots of music, quite a few of the young people were being silly and, in some cases, quite disruptive, which to me was not evidence that the Lord was present in any significant way. When an altar call was made, there was no response. Then the speaker pointed to the door of a room behind him and said, 'Come with me through this door and meet Jesus.' The first teenager to get up from his seat was known locally as a joker. He was giggling as he stood at the front. He then beckoned his mates to join him. Before I knew it, around twenty of the sixty present were walking through that door thinking they were about to meet Jesus. It was little more than a sham.

When people express the desire to trust the Lord, we need to be very careful. One helpful thing to do is to ask questions to see if they really understand the gospel, really feel something of their sin, really grasp something of the cost for them to come to Christ, and really are sincere about wanting to call on the Lord. During His earthly ministry the Lord often asked questions. He did so to help people see where they were spiritually. Time after time He asked questions about what they wanted from Him. Blind Bartimaeus, for example, was asked, 'What do you want me to do for you?' (Mark 10:51). It was almost as though Jesus was trying to put them off, but actually He was just ensuring that they really were serious in their enquiry to Him.

Back in 1996 I was one of the leaders on a YP camp near Pwllheli in North Wales. A lad in my tent group called Philip came up to me out of the blue and said he wanted to become a Christian. We sat in a quiet spot on the campsite talking for two hours. There were a lot of tears, but Philip's tears seemed to be more about his family situation than his standing before God, which seemed secondary. There was little sense that it was Philip's sin that was troubling him. It occurred to me that I could get him to profess faith there and then, but I was convinced before the Lord that Philip wasn't ready, so I just urged him to seek the Lord. I went home from that camp feeling disappointed in some ways, but ten days later I heard that Philip had trusted the Lord and that there was real evidence it was genuine.

This seems a good point to say how important it is to be very careful how we counsel children. In my early days in the Mission I helped for a couple of years run a week of meetings at a church on the Isle of Anglesey. The first year, two nine-year-old girls showed some interest in becoming Christians and I mistakenly led them in a prayer of repentance. I really regret that now, as when we went back the following year there was sadly no sign of spiritual life in either of them. I tend to think that they had both just wanted to please me, something I was blind to at the time. Looking back, I think I just really wanted to see fruit—but we will only see real fruit when we exercise spiritual wisdom and use biblical practice. We all need to learn from our mistakes. How gracious the Lord is that He allows us to do that! In this work we have to remember that we are handling souls, a work which is of the utmost seriousness, and we should be sorrowful about those times when we let the Lord down.

(e) Praying a prayer can give someone false assurance

People are often told, 'Because you prayed, and if you really meant it, you are now a Christian, even if you don't feel anything.' The trouble is that a person may then go complacently on, thinking he or she is saved when perhaps that is not the case. Many such people will try church for a while, but are likely to drift away. It is fair to say that one of the toughest groups of people to reach with the gospel are those who think they have tried Christianity and it didn't work; they become hardened against it.

'But doesn't God use means to reach people?' you may ask. Yes, He does. There are even verses which indicate how closely involved we can be in the work of salvation, as it is the Lord's pleasure to do His work through human instrumentality. For example, Daniel 12:3 says, 'And those who are wise shall shine like the brightness of the sky above; and those who turn many to righteousness, like the stars for ever and ever'; and 1 Timothy 4:16 says, 'Keep a close watch on yourself and on the teaching. Persist in this, for by so doing you will save both yourself and your hearers.' What Daniel and Paul both mean is that by living holy lives and by being sound in the faith, our witness will help others to be saved. Maintaining these things will also help in our own spiritual progress, as well as in our being a blessing to others.

It is important to address texts which might appear to present a counter argument. Some would turn to John 1:41–42, where Andrew brought his brother to Jesus. We must be very clear and say that what Andrew did physically, we are not able to do spiritually. We can be signposts, but not deliverymen. Anyway, the scribes and Pharisees are said to have 'come to Jesus' many times, but it was never to trust Him as their Saviour. Physical bringing is not necessarily to be equated with spiritual bringing. There is also the well-known verse Proverbs

THERE IS STILL MUCH TO DO!

11:30: 'The fruit of the righteous is a tree of life, and whoever captures [or wins] souls is wise.' Again, these words are telling us that a godly life will have an influence for good on others. The word 'captures' literally means 'taking, bringing'. Perhaps the same thought was in the Lord's mind when He called the disciples to be fishers of men.

Where we must be careful—and this takes us back to the need for doctrinal soundness—is that we don't try to build our evangelistic methods on a few Bible verses that seem to say one thing, and ignore a huge number of others which indicate that God is the One, and the only One, who ultimately saves people. The Bible itself is always the best interpreter of the Bible! Think of the fishing picture for a moment (yes, it's here again!). Which of the following catches the fish: the bait on the hook, the hook on the line, the line on the rod or the rod itself? All of them are involved. But actually, they all need the fisherman to pull in the fish. Without the fisherman, nothing would be accomplished. Similarly, we have different parts to play in catching men and women, but ultimately it is the Holy Spirit who reels them in. Some like to talk about 'leading someone to the Lord'. But the Spirit is the one who leads people to Jesus! We don't—in fact, we can't—lead people to the Lord. That would be presuming to do the Spirit's work for Him. How dare we try to walk on His sacred territory! Even though we can be involved—and we should want to be involved— in His work, let's avoid the expression, if for no other reason than that it has the tendency to elevate us instead of elevating the Lord. Our constant prayer should be:

THERE IS STILL MUCH TO DO!

May His beauty rest upon me
As I seek the lost to win;
And may they forget the channel,
Seeing only Him!
                       (Kate B. Wilkinson)

Let's be honest: pointing someone to the Lord is as much as we can do. He graciously does the rest, and we should be content to trust Him to do the rest!

An OAM Associate evangelist in Northern Ireland got to know a contact called Molly. Molly was visited and the gospel was shared with her many times. On one particular day when he arrived at her home, Molly immediately announced, 'I need to get saved!' She was urged to call on the Lord Jesus, and Molly did so. The evangelist was simply the signpost directing Molly to the Saviour. That's what we have the great privilege of being as well. 'I pointed her to the Lord' were the evangelist's words. He knew he hadn't led her to the Lord.

3. PEOPLE MUST BE COMPELLED TO CALL

We can urge them, challenge them, persuade and invite them. We can emphasize the urgency of getting right with God as soon as possible, but, ultimately, it is the Spirit who compels a person to trust in Jesus. The Spirit's job is to convict the world of sin (John 16:8). A great illustration of this is on the Day of Pentecost: 'Now when they heard this they were cut to the heart' (Acts 2:37). A massive crowd of people were concerned about their sin. It was abundant evidence that God was working!

When I met Michael Jackson (no, not that one!) in Doncaster as mentioned previously, he told me that when we

THERE IS STILL MUCH TO DO!

make mistakes in life we just have to learn from them and move on. Nothing more is required. There is no need to feel any guilt or sorrow. 'Wait a minute,' I said. 'Would a judge accept that from a thief? Could he just say, "Sorry, your honour, I shouldn't have done it, and I realize I must think of others from now on"? No! The thief has to be punished. The law must "take its course", as we say.' The thief needs to feel something of how awful a thing it is to treat someone like that. A sinner needs to feel something of how awful it is to treat God as he or she does. The sinner must realize that every sin against a person is also a sin against God. King David prayed, 'Against you, you only, have I sinned' (Ps. 51:4). It is only when the Holy Spirit applies the message of the gospel to people that they begin to sense their sin. If that feeling is absent, it is a tell-tale sign that they are not near the kingdom.

We should be very concerned with someone who claims to want to become a Christian, but who doesn't feel anything. The tax collector in Luke 18 was a man who was being dealt with by the Lord. The evidence was all there: 'standing far off, [he] would not even lift up his eyes to heaven, but beat his breast, saying, "God, be merciful to me, a sinner!"' (18:13). His feet demonstrated what was going on in his heart: 'standing far off'. His eyes did the same: 'would not even lift up his eyes'; also his hands: 'but beat his breast'. Here was a man who was utterly ashamed of himself. He knew he had offended God and heaven. He knew how unworthy he was. He knew what a sinner he was. But he knew as well that the God of Israel was a God of mercy. So he dared to go into the temple courts and then he dared to call out to the Lord. His words so clearly express both the state and the desire of his heart: 'God, be merciful to me, a sinner.'

The Bible teaches something theologians call 'irresistible grace'. You see, God doesn't force anyone into His kingdom, but He makes it irresistible for those He is working in. It's as if He causes Jesus to appear to be so wonderful (which we now know He is!) that a person just can't say no. However, without that divine activity, it doesn't happen. Jesus once said, 'No one can come to me unless the Father who sent me draws him' (John 6:44). The word 'draw' here doesn't just mean beckon or invite. It describes a very powerful activity, and 'irresistible' is not too strong a word to describe it! Notice as well that the one who is drawn will benefit spiritually, physically and eternally: 'I will raise him up on the last day.' That's how great it is to be saved! Salvation is a miracle, then: nothing less than a miracle of God's grace! Naturally speaking, we have no desire for God: 'No one seeks for God' (Rom. 3:11). We are spiritually dead by nature, 'dead in … trespasses and sins' (Eph. 2:1). That's just where we all were and where we would have stayed if God hadn't powerfully drawn us to Himself!

A man named John once came into a church. He had very recently been released from prison. He listened to the gospel message and seemed very upset. Afterwards, the preacher went through the gospel again and urged the man to call on the Lord. What was John's reaction? 'I don't know what to say.' So the preacher prayed and asked John to say 'amen' if he agreed with it. He said 'amen' and was then assured, 'You are now a Christian.' Is there anything about that which troubles you? What troubles me is that John didn't know what to pray. That either tells me that John didn't

THERE IS STILL MUCH TO DO!

understand the gospel, or that he didn't feel real conviction after hearing the gospel. But someone may say, 'People need the opportunity to make a response!' Yes, that's right, they do—but wasn't John given that during the preaching? Dr Martyn Lloyd-Jones was once asked why he didn't have an appeal at the end of his messages. He replied, 'My whole sermon is an appeal.' If a person has heard the gospel, has been moved by the gospel, feels a sense of conviction for his or her sin and feels the need for the Saviour's forgiving power and love, will that person not simply call out? A drowning man knows his need and instinctively calls for help.

Think of Simon Peter sinking in the Sea of Galilee. He just cried out, 'Lord, save me.' The tax collector called, 'God, be merciful to me, a sinner.' The thief on the cross could cry, 'Lord, remember me.' Did any one of these men need someone to go through a form of words for them, so that they could just say 'Amen' at the end? Rather a ridiculous idea! Each one felt his need, each one saw the danger, so each did what he knew he had to do: he called! If the gospel has been correctly preached, with the free offer of salvation being made known, can anyone who is really ready to be saved say, 'I don't know what to pray'?

This transaction that needs to take place must be a personal one. It is not between the individual, the counsellor and the Lord. The counsellor is not some kind of priest, acting as a mediator. 'Clinching the deal' is simply between the individual seeker and the Lord Jesus! No one else! No one else can get that person into the kingdom. People must come as sinners to Jesus—on their own! They must come repenting and come believing!

THERE IS STILL MUCH TO DO!

What should be our part, then, as that final link in the chain? We must urge the person to seek the Lord. We must urge him or her to get alone with God. For one thing, that provides a little 'breathing space' between what we have said and what that person needs to say to the Lord. Someone might say, 'People might get run over by a bus before they do the calling!' No, they won't. Not if the Lord is working in their hearts. Not if the Lord is drawing them. Let's have confidence in Him!

But what if people say they want to call there and then? Again, we should be careful. It is better to urge seekers to find a spot where they can just call out to God. But if they then respond with something like this: 'But why can't I pray now? I need to call now', then, before the Lord, you can be pretty certain that they are ready, so just encourage them to pray. Or pray for them first, asking God to help them call to Him. Encourage them to repent. And while you're encouraging them, be praying for them in your heart, that the Holy Spirit will be working. So point people to Jesus Christ, and then point them to the church of Jesus Christ.

May the Lord give us many opportunities to do that in the coming days! And may many come to know His gracious and life-changing salvation!

Note

1 Prof John Murray, 'Co-operation in Evangelism: Can We Co-operate without Compromise?', https://www.the-highway.com/Coop_Evangelism_Murray.html.

THERE IS STILL MUCH TO DO!

17 Loving the lost

When he saw the crowds, he had
compassion for them. (Matt. 9:36)

One sunny summer afternoon, our three-year-old daughter Abigail was playing in the back garden. From time to time she would go up the side of the garden to where there was a metal-framed gate leading out onto the main road at the front of the house. Abi liked to put her feet on the bottom of the gate, hold on to the frame with her hands and rock the gate back and forth. This made quite a noise. My wife, Ruth, and I were never troubled by this as a chain kept the gate locked.

Ruth and I were in and out of the garden on this particular day and at one point were both in the lounge. After a few minutes the noise of the gate fell silent and we just assumed that Abi had tired of this game and moved on to pushing her dolls around the garden in their little pram. After a couple of minutes had passed I popped out to see exactly what she was up to. I looked down the side of the garden and, to my absolute horror, saw that the gate was wide open, the chain was on the ground and Abi was nowhere to be seen! My heart was definitely in my mouth! Our road is not very busy during the daytime, but it is on a bus route. I called out to Ruth and then rushed to the front and began calling Abi's name. I looked one way and then the other, but there was no sign of her. I threw up an arrow prayer as I tried to decide whether to run up the road to the left or to the right. My heart was pounding at the terrible realization that we had lost our precious little girl.

Just at that moment I became suddenly aware that I could hear someone singing. I listened closely and realized that it was Abi's voice. I tried to work out where the sound was coming from. It seemed to come from over the road, from the house opposite. I ran straight across the road, down our neighbours' path and into their back garden. To my amazement, there was Abi, skipping happily round their lawn and singing merrily! I picked her up with a huge sense of relief, hugged her as closely as I possibly could and ran back home to tell Ruth, tears rolling down my cheeks. What a sense of joy we had! Our little lost lamb had been found, and she was safe.

My love for my little daughter, who is now a married woman, is a very poor illustration, but perhaps in some small way it does show something of the Father's love for His own lost ones. Out of a tender heart of love He sent His only Son to go looking for each one, and when He finds them He carries them safely home. Didn't the Lord Jesus come as the Good Shepherd to seek and to save that which was lost? What amazing love He showed in doing so!

Are you motivated to share the gospel message with others? Do you have a desire to tell those around you about the Saviour, the Lord Jesus? Are you concerned about the spiritual well-being of people? Do you care about their souls? You may not think you have the ability, but do you have at least the longing to speak to others about Jesus? One of the OAM evangelists can frequently be heard to say in deputation meetings, 'It's not big brains that God wants, but willing

THERE IS STILL MUCH TO DO!

hearts.' He is absolutely right. To be quite honest, I find that my own motivation is something that ebbs and flows in my heart. Sometimes I feel greatly burdened for those the Bible calls 'the lost'. At other times, I have to confess that I feel no burden at all. What is it that is lacking in our hearts, which should be the chief motivator to get us witnessing to others? It is love. It is knowing the Lord's love for us and it's having the Lord's love for others.

Years ago, a certain missionary in Africa was asked by a visitor if he liked his work. His reply was very surprising: 'No, my wife and I do not like crawling into vile huts through goat's refuse; we do not like association with ignorant, filthy, brutish people. But we have orders to go and we go. You see, the love of Christ constrains us.' A nineteenth-century evangelist and temperance worker called Richard Booth once said, 'Oh for more Christians who are willing to do anything, be nothing, for Jesus.' That missionary couple were Christians like that, but are we? Instead, we can be so self-conscious at times, so concerned about our image. Yes, even as believers we can crave acceptance, even by the world, and we can long to be popular. We want to have a certain reputation. Let us never forget that we serve the One who made Himself of no reputation—for our sakes!

Those words of the apostle Paul in 2 Corinthians 5:14, 'For the love of Christ controls [or 'constrains'] us', are speaking not so much of our love for Christ, but of His love for us. The Lord's love that was displayed in His substitutionary atonement on our behalf was a big part of what motivated Paul to go on preaching the gospel. We must always bear in mind that any love we have for God is a mere reflection of

THERE IS STILL MUCH TO DO!

His love for us. The word 'constrain' means to be hemmed in between two walls. Paul couldn't *but* preach the gospel because he was so confined by the divine love of Jesus. He couldn't escape it. So does the love of Christ constrain *us* to be willing to go anywhere and do anything for our great God and Saviour Jesus Christ? Because He first loved us, we now love Him back. It is surely the only right way to respond; and if we do love Him back, we should quite naturally love those whom He loves.

The apostle Paul was very much an international missionary. He travelled to many different countries preaching the gospel. However, it is noteworthy that he always had a special place in his heart for his kinsmen, the Jews. In Romans 10:1 he writes, 'Brothers, my heart's desire and prayer to God for them is that they may be saved.' What a burden he had for his fellow Jews! He really longed for them to be saved. That longing was exemplified in his practice of always, when visiting a new city, going to the synagogue first; it was from that initial opportunity that he would venture out to preach to the Gentiles. Do we love our own people? However cosmopolitan our town, city or even village may be, there are so many of our own nationality who are all around us and who need the gospel.

Yes, it is true that the average Brit is very hardened towards the gospel, but that shouldn't keep us from being very concerned for them. Perhaps it should make us even more concerned. Anyway, we never know if the next person we come across is actually going to be very interested or at least is going to have his or her interest sparked by something we say.

THERE IS STILL MUCH TO DO!

While we were preaching on the promenade in Sandown one evening during the beach mission OAM used to hold there, two brothers, Danny and Alex, were standing on a pub veranda some way away. Despite the distance they heard something of the message and it prompted them to want to find out more. They left the pub and came down to the prom. An interesting conversation developed. Danny proved to be far more open than his younger brother, even arguing against some of the questions Alex was posing. After a while, the mother of the boys, named Kay, came and joined in. Amazingly, she had been given a copy of the evangelistic booklet *Journey into Life* by Norman Warren only three days before. These things are no coincidence, are they? I offered Danny a John's Gospel and Kay urged him to accept it, even offering to read it with him. We all parted very amicably, and they made their way back to their hotel. You just never know …

In the Gospels we find plenty of examples of the Lord's love for others, something that we need prayerfully to cultivate more and more. The well-known passage at the end of Matthew 9 is a good example. Here is fresh motivation, which we all need at times. There are three 'M's here to motivate each one of us to share the gospel message with others more diligently and more consistently:

1. THE MULTITUDES

'When he saw the crowds …' (Matt. 9:36). It must have been a huge number of people. The word for 'crowds' that Matthew uses here can be translated 'populace' or 'multitude'. It doesn't have reference to a specific number, but it certainly does have reference to a large number. What comes into your mind when you think of multitudes? To me, it's at least thousands!

Once a year, my two sons and I go to Villa Park to see our beloved Aston Villa. As we walk away from the stadium at the end of a match (more often than not feeling thoroughly miserable!), we are part of a great throng of people, literally thousands, walking down Witton Lane. I often imagine people in these numbers on their way to hear the preaching of the Lord Jesus. Oh for days like that again!

The 1909 OAM Annual Report had on its front cover the words 'Great Britain's Christless multitudes'. There are many, many more now than in 1909. Perhaps we have the mindset that, OK, all these people need reaching, but it's best if we leave it to the professionals. Actually, that is a most unbiblical way of thinking. In Ephesians 4 the apostle Paul writes that the reason why the Head of the church, the Lord Jesus, gave some to be pastors and teachers was for the following reason: 'to equip the saints for the work of ministry' (4:12). The word 'saints' in the Scriptures always refers to *all* Christians. It certainly does not refer to any elite dead ones, but to all those believers who are alive and who are kept alive for the supreme work of serving the Saviour.

Those multitudes were made up of individuals. In South Wales there was a preacher and church-planter called John Pugh (1846–1907), who became a gospel preacher. It was later said of him, 'A new love was born within him from the day of his conversion—a love not so much for humanity in the mass, as for men, women and children.' He loved to sing later, 'If Jesus has found you, tell others the story.' He came to be concerned for individuals, just as the Lord Jesus

THERE IS STILL MUCH TO DO!

was. Sometimes He went out of His way to find them, like the woman at the well in Samaria. One person, one despised person at that, but the Lord was going to radically transform her life.

The ministry of OAM is to go among the multitudes, but we always seek to be conscious that crowds are made up of individuals. During our outreach events we start a week with a blank sheet of paper—or these days, a blank page on a laptop. As a week of outreach goes on, names are recorded. These are people who have been contacted on the streets. A few details of the conversation that took place with them are included as well. It is such an encouragement, especially at the end of the week, to see the list of all those we've met! The Mission had two weeks of evangelism in central London during the Olympic Games in 2012. I was sent a report afterwards by the team leader of the first week. It was twelve pages long and contained almost two hundred names. I didn't bother to count those on week 2 when I saw it was seventeen pages long.

There are certain things that all those in a crowd have in common: 'they were harassed and helpless' (Matt. 9:36). The religious leaders, the Pharisees, burdened the people with hundreds of regulations and ceremonies, but all any of it amounted to was dead works. The real soul-needs of the sheep were neglected. We've previously mentioned the eighteenth-century curate in the village of Stapleford near Cambridge, John Berridge. He looked back at six years of fruitless ministry and felt 'wounded that he could not heal'. He realized that he was just like the Pharisees and that his ministry had been totally useless. It was this realization that

THERE IS STILL MUCH TO DO!

was part of the means the Lord used to save him. What a transformation in his ministry followed his conversion! He moved to Everton in Bedfordshire and saw many hundreds come to know the Lord through his preaching ministry, both in that village and in many other places. As a little aside, are we praying that our local unconverted clergy would come to know the Lord? It would mean there would be instant labourers available to share the gospel.

Something else crowds have in common is that they are 'like sheep without a shepherd' (9:36). Isn't that an awful thought to us now: to be without the Shepherd and to remember the consequences of not having that Shepherd! Yes, without the Shepherd they are lost. They are perishing and on their way to an eternity without Him in hell. How can that realization *not* stir us up to tell people about the Saviour of sinners, especially since we were once among them? We were part of that number, that multitude. We were wretched, lost and blind. We were helpless and hopeless! We can sometimes be tempted to look down on the unsaved, but we really have no right to do that whatsoever. We were saved by grace and we are kept by grace. And praise God that He sent someone to us with the gospel! Someone pointed us to the Saviour, and because of that we are part of another number, 'a great multitude that no one could number' (Rev. 7:9)—the redeemed of God, and not thousands now, but millions!

2. THE MASTER

'When he saw the crowds ...' (Matt. 9:36). Have you ever played bingo? If you have, you'll know that when a game is about to begin the person at the front who calls out the numbers will shout, 'Eyes down.' That is just how most people in the world are living their entire lives. People are increasingly persuaded that our ancestors were monkeys, so there is no cause for them to set their eyes on things above! But you know, that can be true of Christians as well: not looking up, and not looking out, either. We can be so busy focusing our attention on *ourselves*, and upon what we want for *our* church, that we don't see those around us, so absorbed are we by our own little worlds. As a consequence, we can be guilty of just not noticing the lost, let alone caring for them.

The Lord did see the lost and He saw them as they really were. Jesus knew that the spiritual needs of people were more desperate even than their need for physical healing. What a mistake many churches have made when they try to offer people physical healing, instead of focusing on the much bigger issues of the soul and the need for salvation!

Not only did the Lord see these issues in people, but He felt for them: 'He had compassion for them' (v. 36). We know we are called to be like Jesus, don't we? Well then, we need to have something of His compassion for the lost. We need to love the people around us, and if we're called to preach, we need to love the people before us! It was said of the famous hymn-writer and minister John Newton (1725–1807), 'His love to people was the signature of his life'. Dear friend, may I ask you: what is the signature of your life?

The word 'compassion', which Matthew used to describe how the Lord felt, is a strong one. It means that the Lord was moved in His inmost parts. His heart went out to them. And not only was this true on this one particular occasion, but the Lord felt for people consistently. In several other places we're

THERE IS STILL MUCH TO DO!

told that Jesus felt exactly the same, for groups of people and for individuals: a great crowd on the seashore (Matt. 14:14), a crowd with Him on a mountain (Matt. 15:32), two blind men (Matt. 20:34), a leper (Mark 1:41), the crowd of five thousand fed on the fish and loaves (Mark 6:34) and the widow of Nain (Luke 7:13). There was also that very moving occasion when the Lord wept over Jerusalem (Luke 19:41). This is how the Lord was! He felt so deeply for lost men and women.

In Hudson Taylor's book *A Retrospect* he describes one particular occasion while he was living in London doing his medical training when he was able to witness to an eminent doctor. Taylor said afterwards that he was so thankful 'That I had had the opportunity and had embraced it'. Oh, that everywhere we go we would be so full of compassion for those around us that we would let nothing stop us from embracing every opportunity the Lord gives! The following was said of William Grimshaw: 'He thought his tongue should never lie still in guilty silence, whilst he could speak to the honour of that God who had done so much for his soul. And whilst he saw sinners perishing for lack of knowledge and no one breaking to them the bread of life, he was transported by love to pity them.' What a tremendous summary of his life and ministry!

This compassion of the Lord Jesus was such that it prompted not just a deep feeling within, but decisive action without. The same word is used to describe the response of the father to the reappearance of his prodigal son in the famous parable: 'While he was still a long way off, his father saw him and felt compassion, and ran and embraced him and kissed him' (Luke 15:20). Just as the father took the

THERE IS STILL MUCH TO DO!

initiative and went to the son, so we see the Lord Jesus doing throughout His earthly ministry. His incarnation itself was such a wonderful act of compassion, and His death upon the cross was compassion that doesn't have words to describe it.

His work was not confined to the synagogues. He was out among the people. Our problem today is that so few people are coming in to us; so few ever darken the door of a church. We sometimes joke that the only time a minister sees people come to a church service is to 'hatch them, match them and dispatch them'. It is only too true! So if the people won't come to us, we must go to them with the news of the Good Shepherd who loves lost sheep.

3. THE MISSION

In Matthew 9:37 we are reminded that there are many, many people to be reached with the gospel: 'The harvest is plentiful'—for us individually, for our churches and for our mission societies! And this surely means that there should be much urgency to share the gospel. The people around us are a 'harvest'. I don't know very much about farming, but I do know that a harvest requires immediate attention. It cannot wait. The work must be done now. So our mission is urgent. Do we behave as though that is the case? If we're preachers, is it reflected in our preaching? Are we urging people to be reconciled to God while they can be?

If what is recorded in 2 Corinthians 6:2 is true—'Behold, now is the favourable time; behold, now is the day of salvation', Paul quoting from Isaiah 49:8 to reinforce the urgency to tell sinners about the Saviour—we should be greatly encouraged to share the gospel. We also know, and

THERE IS STILL MUCH TO DO!

should be moved by the fact, that this day of grace will one day come to an end. Jesus said to His disciples, 'We must work the works of him who sent me while it is day; night is coming, when no one can work' (John 9:4). So why are we not busier, doing all we can to rescue the perishing?

In Matthew 9:37 the Lord goes on to say that there are few workers to share the gospel. This is a perennial problem. Paul Bassett, in his helpful book *Reaching a Lost World God's Way*, wrote, 'Christ did not say that the Christians are few, but the labourers are few.'[1] Why are there few labourers? Is it simply because we Christians don't care as we ought? Because we don't love as we ought? Someone once said that if we have no compassion for the lost, it is doubtful the Lord is calling us into Christian ministry. These are challenging words if you are among that number. But we need that challenge, don't we?

There are so many churches around the UK that are low in numbers. And how many towns in the UK have no gospel witness at all? How many towns have no open-air witness, where unchurched people can hear something of the gospel message being preached, or receive a little gospel leaflet or have a gospel conversation? Another problem we face today is that so few men are attending theological college to prepare for Christian ministry. As a result, there are many evangelical churches that have no pastor to shepherd the flock and lead them in evangelism. How many churches, even with pastors, have little appetite for direct evangelism! So many more of all these is required!

There should be much prayer for more workers: 'therefore pray earnestly to the Lord of the harvest to send out labourers into his harvest' (v. 38). We know that there are many encouragements to pray in Scripture, but this is not one of them. Here we have far more than an *encouragement* to pray: we have a *command* to pray. Charles Spurgeon describes it like this: 'There are some prayers you must not pray. There are others you may pray, but there are a few you must pray. This is a petition which Christ has commanded us to offer, and yet we very seldom hear it.' He was right in his day, and, sadly, it is still the same in our day. Rarely in our church prayer meetings are we calling upon the Lord to raise up more workers to go and serve Him, either in the local church or further afield, with the gospel message. If the Lord of the harvest has identified that more gospel labourers are needed, we must be praying for Him to raise them up; beseeching the One who is the supreme ruler of the harvest to add to the number, to send out more workers into the harvest field.

Of course, the need to be among the pray-ers should not lesson our desire to be among the go-ers. Sometimes, the Lord would have us be the answer to our own prayers. We need to realize that! Have you ever thought about that? Are you willing to be that? If we're not willing, maybe it would be better not to pray for more workers at all. But, again, He commands us to pray, and if we love the Lord we will do so. What He commands is so important for us and our churches— which links us back to the need for more labourers.

We must appreciate that there is nothing so important in the world as sharing the gospel, whether from the pulpit or from the pavement, whether in an email or in a text message. Thomas Watson once wrote, 'Love never thinks it can do enough for Christ.' Is that what we think?

THERE IS STILL MUCH TO DO!

It's important to remember that a good measure of our love is our obedience. We don't always feel like going, do we? We need to be quite honest about that. Many years ago I was involved each Wednesday afternoon in an open-air meeting in Leicester. Usually there were four or five of us, but from time to time, when the others couldn't make it, I went on my own. It isn't easy at the best of times to be on your own, but this particular day I had to face what proved to be a huge battle. I have to say, to my shame, that I had to force myself to leave the multi-storey car park. Twice I started to get my display board out of the boot of the car, and twice I put it back in the boot again, got back into the car, then prayed really hard for the strength to go! I'm so glad that I did eventually go, as a man stopped to listen to the preaching. His name was Gary and he turned out to be a backslider. We had a really good talk together and he seemed helped by the conversation. When he left, I felt greatly encouraged—though I have to admit that I also felt greatly rebuked.

To close, here's a true story to challenge us again as we think about loving the lost. There was once a crippled orphan boy called Tom. He lived during the nineteenth century in the East End of London. It was a very poor area. When his parents died, Tom was taken in by his grandmother. She was very harsh and kept him in a room on the top floor of her home, where he could cause the least amount of trouble and be out of the way.

Just before Tom's mum died they had visited a Gospel Hall, and this put a desire within him to find out more. He wanted to get hold of a Bible, but his grandmother was no help. However, one day, a friend visited and gave Tom a shilling

THERE IS STILL MUCH TO DO!

as a present (five pence in today's money). Tom asked the friend to go and buy a Bible and bring it back to him, which the friend did. After reading it for many days, Tom came to know the Lord as his Saviour.

As the days went by, a longing rose up within Tom to do something for his new Lord. 'It won't do to keep all this blessed news to myself,' he said to himself. After much thought, as his bed was near the window at the front of the house, Tom got a pencil and paper and wrote out Bible texts, folded them up, prayed over them, and then dropped them one by one into the busy street below. Tom wrote on the outside of the paper the words 'To passer-by—please read'.

Tom's grandmother began complaining about all the paper that was being used. So Tom offered to give up his daily glass of milk to pay for the paper. The weeks went by and Tom continued to do the same each day. He wrote the texts out, prayed over them and dropped them into the street below. One particular day, a well-dressed gentleman unexpectedly visited Tom. He had been a backslider, but was now restored, thanks to reading one of the texts which had fallen at his feet. He also knew of others who had been blessed, and he had come to thank Tom for the way the Lord had used him. The man asked Tom if he was happy doing this work for Christ. Tom replied, 'I couldn't be happier. Are people happy who have lots more that they are able to do for the Lord?' The man replied, 'Lad, you are a great deal happier in this wretched room, making sacrifices for Jesus, than thousands who profess to belong to Him and who have time, talents and money, and yet yield little or nothing to Him.'

Are you fit and able? Even if you are not, the Lord has

THERE IS STILL MUCH TO DO!

given us all gifts and talents to use for Him. May the story of young Tom move us, perhaps quite literally, to love and to go—with this great message of salvation to the lost who are all around us!

Note

1 Paul Bassett, *Reaching a Lost World God's Way* (Welwyn: Evangelical Press, 1988), p. 134.

THERE IS STILL MUCH TO DO!

18 Redeeming the time

*... making the best use of the time, because
the days are evil. (Eph. 5:16)*

As we draw to a conclusion, it is good to be reminded that none of us knows how long we have left in this life. We may have many decades before us, but we may, on the other hand, be living our very last day on earth. The word 'time' in the above verse of Scripture refers to a fixed or allocated period. Appreciating the brevity of life ought to wake us up to the need to be making the most of every opportunity to serve the Lord.

In 1805 William Carey and his fellow missionaries in southern India drew up what they called 'The Form of Agreement', which set down the principles by which they would work. The fourth one stated the following:

To carry on conversations with the natives almost every hour in the day, to go from village to village, from market to market, from one assembly to another, to talk to servants, labourers, etc., as often as opportunity offers, and to be instant in season and out of season—this is the life to which we are called in this country. We are apt to relax in these active exertions, especially in a warm climate; but we shall do well always to fix in our minds, that life is short, that all around us are perishing, and that we incur a dreadful woe if we proclaim not the glad tidings of salvation.[1]

For Carey and his team, time was of the essence. They couldn't afford to waste it. What urgency there was to share the gospel

THERE IS STILL MUCH TO DO!

with others! How we need to see and feel something of that urgency ourselves! How we need to seize the day before it comes to an end! John Newton once remarked,

I am well satisfied it will not be a burden to me at the hour of death, nor be laid to my charge at the day of judgment, that I have thought too highly of the Lord Jesus Christ or laboured too much in commending and setting Him forth to others, as the Alpha and Omega, the Lord our righteousness, the sufficient atonement for sin, the only Mediator between God and men, the true God and eternal life. On the contrary, alas! My guilt and grief are that my thoughts of Him are so faint, so infrequent, and my commendations of Him so lamentably cold and disproportionate to what they ought to be.[2]

I'm sure we all feel as Newton did many times over. Thomas Watson felt the same burden: 'Methinks we should sometimes go aside into our closets and weep to consider how little work we have done for God.' Still, with the Lord's help we can go forward, 'forgetting what lies behind and straining forward to what lies ahead' (Phil. 3:13). That is what counts now: what is ahead of us. William Grimshaw, who never wanted to miss an opportunity, told of a meeting he had with one of his parishioners he met on the moors as he rode along on one occasion. He knew he had never seen her in church, so he asked whether she had ever heard a gospel sermon preached. 'No,' replied the woman; she had not. 'If you have never heard one before, you shall hear one now,' was his prompt reply. He was straight in there with the gospel. What compulsion! What boldness!

During an open-air meeting in Luton once I remember meeting a lady who had recently come to know the Lord. As

THERE IS STILL MUCH TO DO!

she shared her testimony with me she became quite angry. She said something like this: 'Why did it take until I was fifty years of age before anyone told me about Jesus?' On the one hand, we have to answer that by saying that it was the providence of God, but on the other hand, I could see what she was saying. She had lived in the UK all those years, but no one had ever shared the gospel with her until she was half a century old. I would think there are many, many people of a similar age who have never heard about the Saviour either.

As Christians, our future is bright, and that is because it is secure in Christ Jesus. However, so many around us have no such security. William Grimshaw, again, once wrote, 'If Christians really believed what the Word of God declares concerning the reality of hell, surely we could not hold our tongue, nor look them [our unbelieving friends and family] in the face without tears. Rather than cowardly restraint, let us wear sinners out with loving and earnest entreaties.' Don't we need more of that attitude of heart towards others?

Sometimes a writer uses a turn of phrase to describe something that to him or her is very much the norm but which we would find it difficult to say is true of us. For example, in his book *All Things for Good*, Thomas Watson writes, 'Love is never weary. He that loves God is never weary of telling it.' Perhaps we would need to alter that slightly to say, 'He that loves God should never be weary of telling it.' How much better, though, if we could say, mean and know the truth, by personal experience, of the phrase as Watson puts it. Oh, that witnessing was just as prayer is described in that famous hymn of James Montgomery (1771–1854): 'Prayer is the Christian's vital breath, the Christian's native air.'

THERE IS STILL MUCH TO DO!

There will be a sense of urgency about our witness for the Lord if concern for others is upon our hearts. Thomas Watson, again, wrote, 'Love is like fire; where it burns in the heart, it will break forth at the lips.' If we are unwilling to share the good news with others, is it because of a problem in our hearts? There is no fire there; they are cold and damp. If that is the case, we need to get alone with the Lord, fall to our knees in His presence, and cry out to Him to warm our hearts, to set them aflame with His love for sinners. If the problem is a church one, we must get together before the Lord and unitedly seek the help of the Holy Spirit to come among us and grant us that divine love. D. L. Moody once said, 'If the church is sound in love, I think it will be sound in everything else.' If that is true, the opposite must sadly be true as well: if the church is not sound in love, it will not be sound in anything else. We can apply that to love for God, to love for one another, but, especially in this context, to love for the lost.

Someone once described Seth Joshua as follows: 'His creed was wrapped up in the name of Jesus Christ, and his consciousness of God's condescending love for the world overflowed from him.' That's just it: if the heart is overflowing with something, that something will spill out. If our hearts are overflowing with love for God and for the unsaved, speaking to others about Jesus will just happen and will keep happening.

In our churches we can spend a great deal of time formulating correct theology, but how often are we then quite satisfied that all is now well with us? Pastor and author Ian Hamilton gives us this challenge in his book *The Faith Shaped*

Life: 'Compare the hours and energy we expend in getting our doctrine right and the hours and energy we expend in seeking the lost.'[3] How would we fare if we made that comparison, either as churches or as individual believers?

During the Second World War people used to talk about 'doing their bit' for the war effort. In the grand scheme of things, a particular job might have seemed quite insignificant, but every role counted. Everyone was part of the national team serving king and country. Are we not in a war? Are we not under orders? Then have we earnestly sought God's will as to where we will serve Him and what we will do for Him? Up to this point in our Christian lives, we may feel that we have done very little for our Lord and Saviour.

The hymn-writer Frances Ridley Havergal was a terrific evangelist for the Lord. It was said of her that 'she wanted to bring a blessing to everyone she met'. We need something of that, don't we! So often we talk to people and don't even think that it might be an opportunity to speak a word for our Lord. Frances was always on the lookout to share the gospel with others. She died at the age of just forty-two in June 1879. In her last hours, Frances said to friends and family, 'Oh, how splendid to be so near the gates of heaven!' 'Oh, I want all of you to speak bright, bright words about Jesus! Oh, do, do … It is perfect peace.' May the Lord give us that confidence!

Let us end where we started—there is still much to do, so much to do for the Lord. George Whitefield, such an amazingly used evangelist, wrote on his fifty-second birthday, 'O loving, ever-loving, altogether lovely Jesus, how little, yea how very little have I done and suffered for Thee! I am ashamed of myself; I blush and am confounded. Tomorrow,

THERE IS STILL MUCH TO DO!

God willing, I intend to begin, to begin to be a Christian.'
May the Lord help us today to go and do likewise!

O Father, who sustained them,
O Spirit, who inspired,
Saviour, whose love constrained them
To toil with zeal untired,
From cowardice defend us,
From lethargy awake!
Forth on Your errands send us
To labour for Your sake.

(Frank Houghton)

Notes

1   John Appleby, *I Can Plod* (London: Grace Publications, 2007), pp. 214–215.

2   *The Works of John Newton*, Vol. 1 (New Haven: Nathan Whiting, 1824), p. 442.

3   Ian Hamilton, *The Faith Shaped Life* (Edinburgh: Banner of Truth, 2013), p. 127.